The Greek World

Edited by Hugh Lloyd-Jones

Penguin Books

Penguin Books Ltd, Harmondsworth, Middlesex,
England
Penguin Books Inc., 3300 Clipper Mill Road,
Baltimore 11, Md, U.S.A.
Penguin Books Pty Ltd, Ringwood, Victoria,
Australia

Most of the essays in this book originated as talks in
the B.B.C. series 'The Greeks', broadcast in Network
Three, 11 January to 15 March 1961

First published as *The Greeks* by A. C. Watts 1962
Published in Penguin Books 1965
Copyright © A. C. Watts & Co. Ltd, 1962

Made and printed in Great Britain by Cox & Wyman
Ltd, London, Fakenham, and Reading

Set in Monotype Bembo

Contents

List of Plates

*Plates whose source is not
acknowledged were supplied by the B.B.C.*

Introduction

All the chapters of this book except those of Professor Andrewes and Mr Huxley originate from talks forming part of a series called 'The Greeks' broadcast on Network Three of the British Broadcasting Corporation and published in the *Listener* between 19 January and 16 March 1961. The talk on 'The Growth of the Polis' in that series was given by Mr M. I. Finley; but since Mr Finley is planning a book on an allied theme, his talk was not available for inclusion in this book. Accordingly Professor Andrewes has supplied a new chapter on this subject, which is about twice as long as Mr Finley's broadcast talk. Mr Huxley's chapter on 'Greek Mathematics and Astronomy' has been specially written for this book, and several of the other contributors have revised and increased their contributions, including Professor Robertson, whose talk has been very much enlarged and developed.

All the contributors to this book are professional scholars actively engaged in trying to extend our knowledge of their subjects. For that reason, few of them have hitherto had the time to present the results of their researches to the general reader. So great is the mass of material which the active researcher must master nowadays that a comparatively small proportion of the large number of translations and interpretative writings dealing with the classics which are now appearing is the work of professional scholars. This is surely a matter for regret.

Classical studies in this country in modern times have suffered much from the undue persistence of their interpreters in attitudes and prejudices which have become antiquated, and from their determination to go on asking old questions when it is time to ask new ones. This state of affairs is now beginning to be remedied. It is true that certain obvious scandals persist;

for example, I feel that the whole conception of Greek tragedy put forward in the most popular handbooks of that subject continues to be bedevilled by the unconscious interpolation of Christian and other modern notions. But now a new school of translators and interpreters has come forward, and is doing much to reanimate general interest in antiquity by re-examining it from a modern point of view.

Modern interpreters of the classics, no less than old-fashioned ones, run the risk of importing into their picture of antiquity too much of their own contemporary world. Let us consider first the type of translation now being offered to the public. The new school has sharply reacted against the bogus archaism of its predecessors. It renders the Greek poets into a lively, fast-moving, but somewhat flat prose, well calculated to appeal to those who enjoy popular historical novels and detective stories. It is now possible for immense commercial success to be enjoyed by a dexterous rendering of Homer in this manner, a rendering from which few readers, who had not been warned, would guess that the original had been a poem, and a poem whose style and diction are nothing if not poetic. Even when a distinguished English *poet* translates Homer, he produces a version of this sort, one that contrasts most unfavourably with the excellent poetical translations now being written in America. Professor Richmond Lattimore and his followers have realized that modern poetic idiom offers rare opportunities to the translator of the classics. In the past the dominance of English verse by rhyme has severely restricted the opportunities of those who have tried to give a notion of the real nature of quantitative poetry in verse translation; now that that dominance has been broken, the way is clear for a new type of rendering. That has been seen much more clearly in the United States than in this country.

Most modern English translations of classical literature try to make it more acceptable to the modern reader by toning down its heroic and poetic aspects and presenting it simply as a collection of good stories, or of political and moral tracts. In the same way, many modern attempts to interpret that literature go wrong by making out the Greeks as more like our contemporaries than they really were. It is possible for a shoddy and pretentious book about an ancient poet, full of errors both of fact and taste, to win favourable reviews in some of the literary weeklies, partly through the impression of up-to-dateness given by its invocation of various fashionable names, but partly because the modern-seeming travesty of its subject that it offers is more acceptable to some readers than a serious attempt at understanding would have been.

It cannot, unfortunately, be claimed that active researchers are immune from this kind of error; and as critics of the type I have described will be ready to remind us, professional scholars can easily become dry and prosy. But this much may be said for them, that on the whole they are more on guard against reading the present into the past than are interpreters of other kinds. They devote, or ought to be devoting, their lives to the attempt to see antiquity not as they would like it to have been, but as it was.

Looking through the chapters of this book, I have asked myself what common characteristic seems to emerge most clearly in comparison with works of the same nature available when I first became interested in the subject. William James divided philosophers into the tough- and tender-minded. The classical scholars of the first quarter of the twentieth century were, like the contemporary philosophers, for the most part tender-minded. So are some of their successors even now; but the contributors to this volume seem to me, with the possible exception of Professor Armstrong, tough-minded. Let me take a few examples. Our predecessors were accustomed to hold up their hands in horror over the Athenian Empire, which in their view degenerated into a brutal tyranny which thoroughly deserved to be suppressed. No one could accuse Professor Jones of sympathy with tyranny; yet how much more tolerant towards Athens is he, both here and in his important account of Athenian democracy! Writers of the last generation, including even so eminent an authority as the late Sir William Tarn, took a view of Alexander the Great that is coloured by a romantic tinge. No wonder that the more realistic assessment of Dr Badian shocked several respectable people into writing protesting letters to the *Listener*. It is good that this book should contain a chapter (that of Professor Armstrong) which presents with sympathy what are nowadays the most unfashionable characteristics of Greek philosophy: but Mr Kirk's sharp criticism of Plato's attitude towards science and technology is more symptomatic of the general trend.

Our predecessors were certainly too much inclined to idealize the Greeks; we have moved in the opposite direction. Perhaps we sometimes go too far; but our tendency is less dangerous than its opposite. Toughness, rather than tender-mindedness, was the character of the Greeks themselves, especially during the period when they were at their best; and tough-minded people are on the whole likelier to understand them. But the reader of this volume will not fail to notice that the more ruthlessly realistic the point of view from which we approach the Greeks, the more clearly we realize both how much they achieved and how much we can still profit from the study of their achievement.

HUGH LLOYD-JONES

I   The Homeric World

Denys Page
Regius Professor of Greek, Cambridge University

According to the Statutes of Oxford University Greek history begins in 776 B.C. What this means is that we know a great deal about what happened from then onwards, and until quite recently we knew very little about the preceding thousand or twelve hundred years. In the time of our grandfathers you would have been told that we knew next to nothing about that very long space of time, say from 2000 to 800 B.C., except what you found in the poems of Homer; and that, you would have been warned, was not history. All that our grandfathers knew, in fact, was what the Greeks themselves knew (or thought they knew) and handed down to us in written tradition.

All this has been completely changed by the discoveries of modern archaeology, and for us today the difficulty is not to find anything at all to say about Greek history before Homer, but rather to decide how much to leave out. If one had to summarize the bare outlines in a few words, one might say this: sometime about 2000 or 1900 B.C. Greece was invaded and permanently occupied by a new people, the first speakers of the Greek language. After some hundreds of years of living and no doubt to some extent blending with the native population, these Greek invaders came under the spell of Minoan Crete, and the fusion of the two cultures resulted in one of the most brilliant periods of civilization in the whole history of Greece – the period of Mycenaean art and architecture, commercial expansion, and political organization. The Mycenaeans disappeared from the scene in a rather sudden and mysterious way during the twelfth century B.C., and from then onwards all is darkness or dimness for about four hundred years, until the founding of the Olympic games in 776 B.C. At that time, the Greeks themselves knew nothing whatever about their past, except that a large body of epic poems had somehow survived – and this was almost the only record they had of their own history.

It is easy, looking back, to trace the milestones on the road by which we have learned so much in so short a period of time. The first step was the discovery of the nine cities of Troy by Schliemann from 1870 onwards, and the further discovery by Blegen in the 1930s that one of the cities, the seventh, was destroyed after a siege about the date of Homer's Trojan War. Then came the excavations at the great palaces of Mycenae and Tiryns, on the Greek mainland, also by Schliemann, in the 1870s; that was our first picture of any period of prehistoric Greeks – a picture of the artistic and wealthy and adventurous people whom we call the Mycenaeans, the ruling class in Greece from 1600 to 1200 B.C. The next landmark took us even farther back. It was the resurrection of the Minoan world by Sir Arthur Evans in Crete, revealing a most brilliant civilization, one of the great cultures of the ancient world, a culture which both materially and spiritually played a leading part in moulding the character of the Mycenaean Greeks. These great discoveries wrote a new chapter, indeed a whole book, in Greek history: but for some time it was all archaeological, a matter of inference – perfectly good inference, in the broad outlines – from the vast number of objects of all kinds turned up by the excavators. There was still nothing in writing: nothing in writing had been found at Troy or in Greece, and what had been found in Crete could not be read. The gap was to some extent filled by the next two major events; from 1906 onwards some ten thousand written tablets, contemporary with the Mycenaean period in Greece, were excavated at the capital of the Hittite Empire in the centre of Asia Minor: their decipherment filled a huge gap in the history of the civilized world at this period. Very few of the documents – less than two dozen – refer to the Greeks; but by a lucky chance they do just what we wanted most – they throw some light on the state of affairs in Western Asia Minor, including the neighbourhood of Troy, at the time of the legendary siege, which Blegen's excavations have now shown to be a real siege of Troy. Finally, in 1939 some six hundred clay tablets, inscribed in what we had thought of as a Minoan–Cretan script – the so-called 'Linear B' – were found on the Greek mainland at the palace of Pylos. In 1952 Michael Ventris succeeded in proving that the language of these was Greek, and it is now possible to read a good deal of what is written on them. These are the headlines: I need hardly say that a great many other important discoveries have been made all over the Greek world. Today, in fact, we know a great deal more about the Greeks' past than, for example, Pericles or Plato did; and we can judge much better than they could how to distinguish fact from fiction in the Homeric poems. There are those who will say that this is a most pedantic professorial way to look at the *Iliad* and *Odyssey*: they are poetry, not history, anyway. But the truth is that to the Greeks themselves the *Iliad* owed a great deal of its interest and authority to the fact that it was thought to embody their own history; and it is still impossible either to read it intelligently or to appreciate it artistically without coming to terms with this question.

The *Iliad* and *Odyssey* have been read by very large numbers of people in every generation for over 2,500 years; and they still are. There has never been a time when they have not been regarded among the highest creations of the artistic imagination of man. And here I am in great difficulty, because this is the moment when I am presumably expected to say *why* – how it is done; what exactly are the qualities that make Homer great as few writers have ever been great. And I cannot do it; and I have never seen it done by anyone else. The appreciation of art, in this as in other fields, is possible only through personal experience. All comment is futile unless you know the poems; much of it remains unimportant even if you do. One might say, and truly, that Homeric Greek, like Elizabethan English, is in itself a beautiful language. You can add that Homer, although his characters are in many ways remote from us, and his way of thinking and material background totally different from ours, nevertheless has the gift of talking across the barriers of time and place – a peculiar gift of imagination and expression which has, as a matter of fact, made the same immediate impact on everyone everywhere. It is largely a matter of the power of description: few if any writers have ever surpassed Homer in this quality. No matter what he is describing, events or things or emotions, it is simple and natural and highly picturesque; it rings true; it is as recognizable by you in your surroundings as it was by Agamemnon in his. I quite despair of communicating anything of this in translation; but here is an attempt, an example of Homer's descriptive art on a small – you may think even a trivial – subject. The situation here is that when Odysseus returned home after twenty years his favourite dog, named Argus, saw his master and fell dead. Odysseus is talking to one of his former servants, Eumaeus, who has not yet recognized him. This is how it runs in a perfectly literal translation:

While they were talking to each other, a dog lying there pricked up its ears and raised its head. This was Argus, whom Odysseus himself had bred, but then went away to Troy before it could be any good to him. There had been a time when the younger men would set him on wild goats and deer and hares, but now he lay there, and nobody cared for him, his master being so far away. There he was in front of the gate, on the dung-heap, full of vermin: yet the moment Odysseus approached he knew him, and thumped his tail and dropped his ears and tried to get near his master, but could not walk so far. And Odysseus looked aside and brushed away a tear so that Eumaeus should not notice, and hastily said to him, 'How can they let such a dog lie on the dung-heap, a fine dog like this, though of course I don't know whether he has speed to match his looks, or whether he is one of those pets that people keep at home for show.' Eumaeus replied, 'Ah, that dog had a master once, but he died in a far-off land. I wish you could see him as he was, and the things he could do, at the time when Odysseus left him and went to Troy; you would be astonished to see how fast and strong he was. There was never a wild beast could escape his pursuit, not even in the thickest bush, so good was he on the trail. But now he has fallen on evil days, and his master has died far from home, and the women neglect the helpless thing. When the master is no longer there to give orders, servants will not trouble to do their proper work.' . . . Saying this, Eumaeus went indoors and made his way straight along the hall among the suitors; but the darkness of death came over Argus the dog, the moment he saw Odysseus again after twenty years.

In Homer, the poetry is the thing, and the question whether his stories are fact or fiction makes no difference to their life-like quality. The one-eyed giant Polyphemus and the nymph Calypso are just as lifelike as heroes and heroines like Achilles or Andromache. But there is one big difference between the *Odyssey* and the *Iliad*. The story of the *Odyssey*, the ten years' wanderings of Odysseus on his way home to Ithaca from the siege of Troy, is pure fiction from start to finish: but what the *Iliad* claims to describe are episodes from the siege itself, and no one can read it without feeling that this is fundamentally an historical poem – the detail may be largely fictitious, but the background and the people, at least the leading characters, are real.

The Greeks themselves took this for granted. They had no doubt that there was a Trojan War, and there really were such people as Priam and Hector, Achilles and Ajax, who did, in broad outline, what Homer says they did. The material civilization, the political and social background, though not like anything known or remembered in historical times, were thought by the Greeks to be a true picture of Mycenaean Greece about 1200 B.C., when the siege of Troy occurred. It is on this point that we are so much better informed than the Greeks were, since the decipherment of the Hittite and Linear B documents and Blegen's excavation of Troy. We now know for certain that there was a siege and sack of Troy near the end of the Mycenaean period; and we know that at that very time, and in the area concerned, Greek military and commercial forces were at work on a large scale. We have good reason to believe that the names of the principal Homeric heroes, Priam and Hector and Achilles and Patroclus and Ajax, are the actual names of men who took leading parts in the fighting in Asia Minor at that time.

When we turn to the political and social background of Homer, the difficulty has always been that it seems to be a composite picture, with elements from different civilizations all mixed up – Early Mycenaean and Late Mycenaean, Bronze Age and Iron Age, Dark Ages and later. It has always seemed likely that there are not many of the very old elements – the elements peculiar to the Mycenaean age, descriptions of things and techniques and political and social factors which existed in the time of Agamemnon and then disappeared from the world for ever. It is remarkable enough that any such elements should have been preserved at all: but it was the Linear B documents which first taught us how very little the Homeric poems do preserve of the true picture of the Mycenaean past. The lesson of the documents was, though perhaps it ought not to have been, a considerable surprise. They give us no help with the main political structure of Greece as a whole. For that, we still depend on Homer and the archaeologist. According to Homer, Mycenaean Greece was a network of more or less independent kingdoms, large and small, each centred on a great palace – Pylos, Athens, Mycenae, Sparta, Thebes, and others – all in some ill-defined way owing allegiance to one kingdom, that of Agamemnon at Mycenae. This is almost certainly a true picture, and the Linear B documents say nothing either for or against it. What the documents do is tell us a great deal about the internal economy of one of these kingdoms, that of Pylos; and the tale they tell, in very great detail, is of an autocratic, bureaucratic government, operating through an army of officials, measuring and counting, collecting and distributing, ordering and recording. Slavery was widespread and highly organized; labour was specialized; land-tenure was organized in a most complicated way. There is no trace whatsoever of this picture in Homer. He has no notion that his heroic world was in fact a model bureaucracy, a society divided and subdivided and labelled and rationed and in general controlled in all its doings by an army of busybodies, whose least report, even to the counting of a single goat, was entered on a form by a secretary in the palace. Of course the Linear B documents are very one-sided. They say not a word, or hardly a word, about aspects of Mycenaean life known to us from other sources. The Homeric poems portray the great kings and their retainers much as a Spanish poet might represent the great nobles of the fifteenth and sixteenth centuries in Castile – as a small and highly privileged class, created by pedigree and fostered by hereditary wealth, bound only by loose allegiance to a supreme overlord and a strong but very elastic code of honour, in which personal courage was the first requisite.

The simple philosophy, *noblesse oblige*, is most clearly stated in the twelfth book of the *Iliad*, where one great hero speaks to another in these terms, quite literally translated:

Why is it that we are privileged above others in Lycia, with the front seat, and food, and full cups of wine, and all men look upon us as if we were gods, and we have a large cut of land beside the river banks, good land, of orchards and cornfields? This makes it our duty now, to stand in the front ranks of the Lycians, face to face with scorching battle, so that some tight-corseleted countryman of ours may say 'Truly these are great and glorious men who rule in Lycia, these kings of ours who feed upon our fattest sheep and drink the choicest of our honeysweet wines: there is indeed good strength in them, for they fight in our front ranks.'

My friend, supposing you and I, escaping from this war, were destined to be for ever ageless and immortal, then neither would I fight in the front lines, nor would I urge you into the battle where men win glory; but now, since the Spirits of Death stand close about us, innumerable – no mortal can escape or slip from under them – let us go forward, whether we yield glory to other men, or they to us.

The archaeologist has taught us a lot about a quite different class, the merchants. From 1400 to 1200 B.C. the Mycenaean traders carried their products as far west as Sicily, as far east as Egypt and Palestine. They settled in Crete and on the island of Rhodes, in Cyprus and on the coast of Syria. Putting the evidence all together, and confining ourselves to a quite summary statement of the result, we can now not only say that Mycenaean Greece was dominated by a group of independent kingdoms, owing some kind of allegiance or at least war-service to an overlord at Mycenae; we also know that they lived in considerable comfort, or even luxury, created by the enterprise of a large commercial class; and they kept very close control of their subjects through a civil service of a quite exceptionally intrusive and pervasive kind. Of all this, both in outline and in detail, Homer knows nothing except the purely political aspect.

And now we come to a difficult question, to which again the correct answer was not given till quite recently. Everybody agrees – even the Greeks agreed, more or less – that Homer lived hundreds of years after the events he describes, and that he had no written documents from the past. The question, therefore, is not 'Why is he unaware of so much about Mycenaean Greece?' but 'How can he possibly have known what he does know?' The answer is that the Greek epic is poetry of a very peculiar kind – it is oral, and it is traditional. By oral, I mean that it was composed in the mind without the help of writing. And by traditional, I mean that it was preserved by memory, and handed down by word of mouth from generation to generation. It was never static. It was continually growing and changing. The *Iliad* is the last stage in a process of growth and development which began at or very soon after the siege of Troy itself. This kind of poetry (and this is true of epic poetry in many languages besides Greek) can only be composed, and can only be preserved, if the poet has at his disposal a ready-made stock of traditional phrases – half-lines and whole lines and groups of lines, ready-made for almost every conceivable purpose. He composes while he recites; he cannot stop to think how he is to go on; he must have the whole of his story in his mind before he begins, and he must have in his memory the whole – or almost the whole – of the phrases which he will need to tell that story. The Homeric poems are in fact composed like this – not in words, but in sequences of ready-made phrases; in 28,000 lines there are 25,000 repeated phrases, large or small. Take for example the opening lines of the Odyssey:

ἄνδρα μοι ἔννεπε Μοῦσα πολύτροπον, ὃς μάλα πολλά
πλάγχθη, ἐπεὶ Τροίης ἱερὸν πτολίεθρον ἔπερσε.

This is a chain of half a dozen formular phrases, almost all of which recur quite often elsewhere in Homer. The great point is that whatever you want to say in a given part of the verse, there is one ready-made phrase, and only one, supplied by the storehouse of formulas. In these lines, the poet had no alternative – he *had* to say ἄνδρα μοι ἔννεπε Μοῦσα, and πολύτροπον, and ὃς μάλα πολλά, and Τροίης ἱερὸν πτολίεθρον.

But we have still to face the most difficult question of all, a question to which there is no certain answer. The *Iliad* is specially connected with the name of Homer: but if it is, as most people agree, not a new poem like *Paradise Lost* but the last stage in a very long continuous process of development, what room is left for Homer? What is the relation of his *Iliad* to the stage immediately before it? We do not know the date at which the *Iliad* reached the form in which we have it: but whatever the date, what was its form fifty years before? Are we to think of numerous relatively short lays transformed by the genius of Homer into a long unified epic, much or most of it of his own composition? Or is there no single master hand, only a kind of gradual evolution, a poem enlarged and improved by many composers over a long period of time? Or is the truth half-way between these extremes – that Homer made the *Iliad* out of earlier poetry in which a quarter or half or three-quarters of his work had been already done for him? This is, essentially, the Homeric question; and it is no more answerable today than it was two hundred years ago. There are no hard facts to go on, only private opinions and sometimes public emotions. The nearest thing to a fact is the name of Homer: the Greeks remembered that somewhere in the remote past there had been a great name connected with their famous poems. They did not know when he lived or where he lived; they knew no other facts about him at all, and they could no more have answered our question than we can. They did not know, any more than we do, what the poetry about Troy was like fifty years before Homer; and if you do not know that, it is idle to pretend that you can say in what way Homer differed from it. This is, in short, a question which is not only unanswerable now; it never will be answered.

The rise of the Greek epic is a miracle and a mystery. It is one of the very few things which survived what we call the Dark Ages of Greece. Sometime soon after 1200 B.C. the Mycenaean civilization was wiped off the face of the earth. The great palaces – Mycenae, Tiryns, Thebes, Pylos – were destroyed, the great kings and their peoples were killed or driven out or enslaved. For the next three or four hundred years Greece was isolated, impoverished, parochial. The art of writing was lost; contact with the outside world was reduced to little or nothing; the arts and crafts of Mycenaean Greece were disused or greatly debased. The contrast is about as extreme as it could be: no period in all Greek history surpasses the Mycenaean in unity, in wealth and strength, in political stability and commercial enterprise, combined with a very high level of art and technical skill. The world would have to wait some hundreds of years before it saw again such delicacy of carving in ivory, such ornaments of gold and precious stones, and architecture using blocks of masonry so huge that later Greeks could only suppose it was the work of giants – the lintel across the door-posts of the so-called Treasury of Atreus at Mycenae is a single block weighing about one hundred and twenty tons.

Then everything either stops or is greatly reduced quite suddenly. There are some who try nowadays to minimize the extent of the change: it is up to them to show us a great building or a great work of art or a specimen of writing or something of quality in politics or commerce or society for two or three hundred years after the fall of Mycenae. Nobody has done it yet; and it is not for want of trying. We do not know exactly what it was that destroyed the Mycenaeans and started this long period of darkness and degeneracy. Traditionally we speak of the Dorian invasion; and there must be some truth in this, for the one thing certain is that when the Dark Ages are over the greater part of Greece is seen to be occupied by a non-Mycenaean tribe of Greeks, the Dorians. The obvious conclusion is that the Dorians pushed the Mycenaeans out: but it is probably not as simple as that. The collapse of Mycenae ought to be looked at in a wider context – it was not the only great power which came to a sudden and violent end about that time. For all we know, the Mycenaeans collapsed in the same great movement of peoples as that which overthrew the Hittite Empire in Asia Minor, and many great cities of Syria and Palestine – the peoples who penetrated as far as Egypt in the reign of Rameses III, about 1170 B.C. But whether the Dorians invaded Mycenaean Greece or merely occupied a vacuum created by others, the result is the same: several hundred years of darkness or dimness, slowly climbing

23

back to the respectable level of civilization attained at the beginning of the historical period. All through this period of darkness one thing had been growing up: the epic poetry of the Mycenaeans, enlarged and adapted by generation after generation, without the help of writing. We have some reason to believe that this process of development went on for some time during the historical period; we cannot be sure that the *Iliad* and *Odyssey* had reached anything much like their present form earlier than the sixth century B.C. For the next thousand years they exercised an unparalleled influence over the Greeks, not only over their literature but also over the education of the young and the political and moral thinking of the adult. Homer was the only thing in Greek history that can properly be called international – the common property of Greeks everywhere, the one uniform civilizing factor. There has never been anything quite like this in the history of civilization except the Bible. It is a curious reflection that the earliest extant work of European literature should still be thought, by so many of those who can judge it, to be the best; and that this should have been the creation of one of the darkest ages in recorded history.

European civilization is continuous from its beginnings in Greece to the present day. It has always seemed to emerge rather suddenly, and on a surprisingly large scale, everything more or less reaching its peak at the same time. We have always been able to follow the trail back till it was lost in the Dark Ages of Greece: and the only real difference now is the fact that we know a great deal about what happened before the Dark Ages. Of course there must have been some degree of continuity from the Mycenaeans through the Dark Ages into classical Greece: but I see no indication that any of the most significant and valuable parts of the legacy of Greece jump the gap of the Dark Ages back to Mycenaean Greece. The Mycenaean political and economic organization may well have been the best that Greece has ever had: but the foundation of modern politics and philosophy, law and literature, mathematics and medicine, astronomy and architecture, are all to be found in the period *after* the Dark Ages, from the eighth century B.C. onwards. In all that we know about the Mycenaeans, and we know a lot, there is no indication that any of the really important aspects of classical Greek civilization was an inheritance from its Mycenaean past. The historian of European culture must begin with his eyes on the end of the Dark Ages and the following centuries, not earlier; after the Homeric poems, not before them or even including them. And this is the last of our curious reflections about Homer – that the poems which Europe has most admired and felt most at home in were completed before the foundations of European civilization were laid.

Bibliography

DUNBABIN, T. J., *The Greeks and their Eastern Neighbours*, Society for the Promotion of Hellenic Studies, London, 1957

DOW, STERLING, *The Greeks and the Bronze Age*, Extrait des Rapports du XI Congrès International des Sciences Historiques, Stockholm, 1960

KIRK, G. S., *The Songs of Homer*, Cambridge University Press, 1962

NILSSON, M. P., *Homer and Mycenae*, Methuen, 1933

PAGE, D. L., *History and the Homeric Iliad*, University of California Press, 1959

WEBSTER, T. B. L., *From Mycenae to Homer*, Methuen, 1958

2   The Growth of the City State

A. Andrewes
Wykeham Professor of Ancient History,
Oxford University

The Dark Ages of Greek history are genuinely difficult to penetrate. The darkness of the early feudal age of western Europe is only relative: the Church at least remained literate, chronicles of a kind were kept, charters and other documents light up even the dimmer corners. Early Greece was illiterate without qualification, and, therefore, for several centuries it has no history at all in any real sense of the word. The Homeric poems, and the material remains studied by the archaeologists, do something to fill the gap, but the result is not quite history, and more than one could write a history of early medieval France from the epics and the architecture, with no other aid. The best that the historian can do with the Greek Dark Ages is to observe, as exactly as he can, the nature of the society which prevailed in Greece when writing began again, and make his guess at the conditions which shaped that society.

The characters of the *Iliad* and *Odyssey* are grouped round a relatively small number of kings and princes. Their whole world consisted of great princely houses with their dependants. Telemachus, seeking news of his long-lost father Odysseus, travelled from Nestor's palace at Pylos to Menelaus' palace at Sparta, and nothing is said of what he may have passed on the way. The poet's eye takes in only the great princes, and that is part of the explanation, but there is presumably a real implication that all Greece was in fact dependent on great houses something like these palaces, though many of them will have belonged to lesser lords who were themselves dependent on rich kings like those whom the poets delight to tell us of.

This is not a true picture of the Mycenaean world (see Chapter 1). To the extent that the poems give us a coherent picture of any age, they describe rather one of the stages that Greece had passed through since the fall of the great Mycenaean kingdoms; a monarchical stage, but of a simpler and bolder style, not at all like the elaborate bureaucratic organizations which the newly deciphered Linear B documents have revealed to us. When the curtain lifts again, the kings have largely vanished, and we find instead an aristocratic society, itself already moving towards its dissolution.

One major change since Mycenaean times is a great increase in the number of independent political units. Instead of the comparatively few great kingdoms, perhaps all of them subject to the overriding rule of the king of Mycenae, we find in almost every separate valley a city claiming to be a sovereign power on its own, owing no allegiance to anyone outside – in fact, the 'city state' characteristic of classical Greece. This was a natural development in a period of insecurity, when men were concerned with immediate protection, and no central power had the resources to intervene effectively or continuously at a distance: comparable insecurity caused a comparable fragmentation of authority at the beginning of the feudal age of western Europe, when the local count or other magnate became practically an independent power. Greek geography certainly helped this development, with its tall barren mountains separating one cultivable valley from the next. But geography did not impose permanent division – the Greek mountains are not as high as all that, and even militarily there are few passes that cannot be quite easily turned: nor has Greece ever again broken up into these small splinters since her conquest by Rome in the second century B.C. Somehow, this political fragmentation became a permanent and irremovable feature in the mind of these ancient Greeks, so that their small states never coalesced like the numerous small kingdoms of Anglo-Saxon England. It is significant that the

Greek transported his city-state system with him when he emigrated to lands with less abrupt geographical divisions.

Monarchy and aristocracy

Some vestiges of the original monarchy remained in most of the classical Greek states. There was often an official with the title of 'king' – sometimes several of them – though this would now be a magistrate elected annually. Such a magistrate might, as at Athens, be entrusted with traditional sacrifices and other priestly duties of considerable antiquity, and the fact that he was called 'king' evidently satisfied some feeling for continuity which was important to the Greeks. But though it was a familiar idea to them that religious functions should be hereditary in a particular family, they seem to have shed quite easily the notion that the inherited qualities or the traditional expertise of such a family might entitle it to retain in its hands the entire political power of the state. A hereditary title to rule, with strong religious associations, was claimed by Greek aristocrats, and the claim was to a significant extent recognized by public opinion, but no special divinity hedged their kings for any political purpose.

We shall never know in detail how the transition from monarchy to aristocracy was effected, but there are symptoms to suggest that the process was not in general violent. At Athens the functions of the king seem to have passed piecemeal and by stages to aristocratic magistrates. At Sparta, where the hereditary kings survived with attenuated powers down to the end of the third century B.C., annual magistrates called ephors were set up at an early date as a second executive beside the kings, and wielded great authority. The transition was probably not very different elsewhere, though no doubt some kings were overthrown by force. The aristocracies, on the other hand, often met a violent end at the hands of one of those dictators whom the Greeks called tyrants.

It is at this stage that we begin to have enough contemporary information to speak, though still in a sketchy way, of history. Much of this evidence is from the poets: the Boeotian Hesiod, using the epic form to give his fellow farmers practical advice; Archilochus of Paros, a misfit in the society of his time and a robust complainer; and many others, known to us in more or less coherent fragments, down to the Athenian reformer Solon at the beginning of the sixth century, who used verse as a vehicle for immediate political argument. There begins now also to be an oral tradition of a more solid and credible kind: especially, something was remembered of many of the founders of the Greek colonies which from the middle of the eighth century spread round the coasts of the Mediterranean. This same century saw the oracular shrine at Delphi rise to become an institution of widespread importance, and some of the verse oracles attributed to these early years are genuine.

Most important of all, the Greeks now began to write again, adapting a Phoenician alphabet to their own language in a script much more manageable than the Linear B syllabary. The earliest surviving inscriptions are mostly verse, and the poets now become writers, not oral composers in the epic tradition. In the seventh century law began to be fixed in writing too, a momentous change.

We have to try to seize the character of the aristocratic age which passed away in the course of these developments. We can see something, and can infer more from later vestiges, of its relatively simple politics. It is harder to reconstruct its social or economic system – and considering the convulsions that Greece had been through it is unlikely that this system was simple or uniform – but certain features stand out as relatively certain.

The Greek World

Aristocratic politics

It must be emphasized again that the aristocratic age was already an age of numerous small states, each claiming for itself a passionate loyalty whose natural expression was war against other similar states, over disputed territory or other grievances, or for dominion over a weaker neighbour. Here and there this process produced slightly larger units. Athens united under her control an area which might as easily, in Greek conditions, have become three or more separate states; but even Attica was small enough, its most distant parts not more than two long days' walk apart. Sparta conquered her neighbour Messenia and reduced the inhabitants to slavery, and the need to hold this conquest down absorbed a large share of Sparta's energy and did much to determine the unusual form of her institutions. But most states were much smaller than this, a single small city at the centre and some outlying villages. The island of Ceos, no more than fifteen miles long and eight miles broad, was divided for much of its history into three independent sovereign states. And independence, on this small scale, was as rampant and assertive in this early period as ever it was later.

Such a state would at this time be controlled, in every sphere of life, by a larger or smaller group of families claiming descent from a local hero or an early king. The mechanism of politics was in general simple. Magistrates were chosen for a term from among the nobles, sometimes (Aristotle says) a single magistrate with wide powers and a long term of office, sometimes a college, and often for a single year. Policy was deliberated in a council of some sort, the descendant of the council which had once advised the king. There might also be some form of larger public meeting, at which the people would be present to accept and applaud, but only the nobles would be likely to speak – such a meeting as the assembly of the army described in the second book of the *Iliad*, where the commoner Thersites spoke out of turn and was whipped for his pains. Alcaeus, an embittered aristocratic poet of Mytilene in Lesbos, writing about 600 B.C., complains that during his exile, among other deprivations, he can no longer attend the council of his city: direct participation in politics was an essential part of Greek life, for those who were currently entitled to participate. But politics meant internal faction as well as external war, and this same Alcaeus is an eloquent witness to the extent and virulence of the internal quarrels between aristocratic parties within the same city.

Tribes and kinship

Greek ways and Greek institutions are often comprehensible enough and their basic problems recognizably similar to those of later ages, however much historians may wrangle about the details. It is less easy for the modern world to grasp the nature and function of the system of tribes with their subdivisions which classical Greece inherited from the Dark Ages and preserved long enough to give us some idea of its structure, based at least nominally on pure kinship. Some light has been cast on this by anthropologists working on comparable kinship structures, among the North American Indians and in Africa and Australia and elsewhere: but the societies they study are usually in important respects at a somewhat different level of development, and the survival of these in some sense primitive elements can prove a hindrance to our study of Greek society, which in many other respects seems so surprisingly modern. But social anthropology makes one thing at least very clear, that institutions of this kind, for all their primitive look, are enormously adaptable and are very readily changed to fit changing conditions.

In almost all Greek states the population was divided up into several tribes: their armies were composed of tribal regiments, and the tribes also played an important part in civil administration. There is no great problem here. Some sort of internal division was necessary for these purposes, and the uses to which tribes were put are plain enough. That the divisions were based on kinship, membership of a tribe depending in theory on direct descent in the male line from the original tribal hero, might have its inconveniences in practice, and it is noticeable that in many states, though at very different dates, it was thought necessary to change the basis of the tribes from kinship to locality, bringing together into the same tribe those who lived in a particular area, either to improve the structure of the army or to simplify peace-time administration. But even after such a regrouping membership of the new sort of tribe might still be hereditary, as it was at Athens, where a man did not change his tribe when he changed his residence – a tribute to the continuing importance of the notion of kinship.

It is less easy to understand the meaning of the smaller divisions: phratries (from a Greek word meaning originally 'brotherhood', which has been adopted into the vocabulary of modern anthropology), clans, and the like. Every citizen of classical Athens belonged to a phratry, a body smaller than the tribe but still of considerable size, which met for common worship, above all at the great family festival of the Apatouria in the autumn, the occasion when the sons of old members were usually admitted to the group. The phratry was interested in marriages, births, and adoptions, and its evidence was often produced in court to establish the status of one of the litigants, especially in property cases. It is in these ways that we mainly hear of the phratries, though they doubtless had other social functions besides. At Athens they gradually died out after the fourth century.

The groups I have called 'clans' differ in one important respect from the clans of Scotland, in that in classical Athens at least they did not include the whole people but were exclusive aristocratic bodies, tracing their descent from some primeval Attic hero, and their consequent social prestige enabled them to survive into Roman times. Every such clan maintained its own religious cults, and indeed the priesthoods of several important state cults were reserved to members of a particular clan. But the clans also controlled local cults in the countryside, where the noble family had had its original seat. Membership of clan and phratry was hereditary in the male line, and in classical times their members might be scattered all over Attica. But it is noticeable that the phratry as well as the clan seems generally to have a strong connexion with a particular locality where a proportion of its members actually lived, and thus, though the basis of both was kinship, they had a local character too, which is likely to have been more pronounced in earlier times.

The original character of these institutions has been very much debated, especially the question whether the clans were always strictly aristocratic bodies, or whether they had in early times included all the free inhabitants of Attica. The problem is not to be solved by reference to any theory about the original character of kinship institutions among primitive and migratory peoples, for the Greeks had had ample time since their first settlement in the country to modify out of all recognition any system which they brought with them from the days of their early migrations. There is indeed much to be said for the view that Greek clans and phratries, as we know them, were created or at least remodelled as part of the aristocratic structure of the various states of the Dark Ages. In later democratic Athens these kinship groups stand out as a sort of enclave in which aristocratic influence was still of serious importance; their local and religious character tells the same way; but they seem to be unknown to the epic tradition which Homer used and the two references to phratries in the *Iliad* are not well fitted to their background. If this is right, we may conjecture that the purpose of the Dark-Age phratry was to organize in a single group the dependants or retainers of a particular aristocratic clan, while these clans themselves served as a framework for the rivalries of contending groups of nobles. In any case, whatever explanation is adopted, it is clear that this form of organization played a larger and more effective part in the archaic period than it did in later times, when it appears as a survival of decreasing importance.

The preceding argument is based mainly on what we know of Athens, where the later evidence is most plentiful. But there are signs enough that similar institutions existed in most Greek states, with whatever differences of detail and nomenclature; and though the rate of change in historic times was not uniform, the direction of change was everywhere the same, even in conservative Sparta.

It may be well to emphasize, before we leave this subject, the importance of the relatively obscure cults of the Greek countryside. The more spectacular manifestations of Greek religion – the great temples of the Athenian Acropolis, the shrines at Delphi and Olympia, the great cult statues known to us from literary sources and from late copies – relate to cults of the city, or of the whole Greek nation, and tell only half the story. The innumerable local shrines have left less record and make less impression, but they may often have meant more to the individual worshipper: dedicated to one of the major gods with the addition of a special local title, or to a local hero with an obscure name (sometimes with no name at all), they were a focus for local loyalties and helped to preserve the influence of the families who had them in their care.

Law

The law is another sphere in which the nobles might claim an inherited expertise which set them apart from ordinary men. In a period of illiteracy the law can only be determined by oral tradition and is very much in the hands of those who claim to state and interpret it, over the area where they are strong enough to make their claim good. Thus first the kings, then the nobility, were the real source of law through the Dark Ages, claiming of course divine sanction for their judgements: but no doubt Hesiod was not the first to complain that they tended to give judgement in their own favour.

The first serious breach in this system came when law codes were set down in writing. The earliest surviving city ordinance inscribed on stone belongs to the seventh century and was set up at Dreros in Crete. We do not know where this new fashion began, but we may take it as certain that both single ordinances and more comprehensive codes were thus published in writing during this century. A famous example is the code of the Athenian Dracon, which had the reputation of being extremely harsh and was replaced in the next generation by the legislation of Solon, except for its provisions about murder. But whether harsh or mild (and not enough of it survives for us to form our own judgement), it was a great advance that the law should be fixed and ascertainable at all. The administration of justice, however, remained in the hands of aristocratic magistrates or councils till the time when the aristocracies themselves were overthrown.

Violence, inevitably, was one of the main problems of these states as they emerged into civilization. Greek states, like others at a comparable stage, gradually restricted blood feud and private vengeance and brought the violence of individuals under some degree of public control. In this sphere there is one very noticeable change since Homer, the emergence of ideas of pollution and purification which were unknown to the epic tradition but of great importance to later generations. Here the nobles were again in demand as religious experts. In classical times their inherited knowledge of ritual had no very wide sphere of action – when the state wanted religious guidance it turned rather to the great national oracles like Delphi, or to a class of professional 'seers' whose standing was very different – but we still hear of men turning to them for this matter of purification, and no doubt in early times their range was wider. Otherwise Greek codes consist mainly of piecemeal instructions to magistrates about the rules which should govern their decisions in cases of kinds which had forced themselves on the notice of the community. Greek law indeed remained a somewhat piecemeal affair even in days when society had grown more complex: there was never any Greek science of law, and nothing comparable to the great achievements of the Roman lawyers, in spite of the deference which was paid to the idea of law by Greek thinkers, and the continual professions of politicians of every colour that their states were under the rule of law and not subject to the whims of individuals or even of public assemblies.

Trade and colonization

One of the most impressive achievements of this aristocratic period is the settlement of so many new Greek communities all round the Mediterranean from the Levant to Spain, and round the Black Sea. We call these new cities colonies, but they were not conceived along the lines of the nineteenth-century partition of Africa. Instead, each 'colony' was a separate new state, which normally retained religious and sentimental ties with the founding city, and was often, no doubt more often than we can directly prove it, of economic benefit to it. But the link was not normally one of direct political dependence, and in unfavourable circumstances it might snap altogether, as in the case of the Corinthian colony of Corcyra (Corfu), which quarrelled early with the mother city and maintained the quarrel obstinately.

For a long time after the fall of the Mycenaean kingdoms there was little contact between Greece and the outside world, nor is it easy to say exactly when the world became open again to a significant extent. But the reopening was well under way when the main wave of colonization started in the last third of the eighth century, and it is to be noted that the Greek trading settlement at the mouth of the Syrian river Orontes, the site called Al Mina excavated by Sir Leonard Woolley just before the war, goes back at least to the early years of the century: this was the easiest route from Greece to Mesopotamia, and when Greek traders settled there their home cities began to receive again the products of the older civilizations of the East. In this direction the Greeks might trade, but they could not settle in large numbers on the territory of populous and long-established states like these. The main directions of their colonization were north and north-east, to Thrace and the Black Sea; west to Italy, Sicily, and beyond; to a lesser extent, south to the African coast. Here it was easier to make room for colonies by elbowing the native inhabitants out of the way, but trade must have been largely in corn and primary materials, and in slaves.

It has long been disputed how much trade influenced colonization, what share the Greek nobles had in trade, how much the policy of Greek cities was affected by trade and the possibilities of its expansion. It is certain, indeed, that the primary motive of the colonists, in the vast majority of cases, was not trade but the acquisition of new agricultural land: this is evident from the sites they chose for their new cities, especially in the fertile corn plains of north-east Sicily and south Italy, and there can be no reasonable doubt that the population of the Greek peninsula, having declined heavily after the collapse of Mycenaean civilization, had increased again by the eighth century to a point where the bare land of Greece could no longer feed it.

But this does not settle the whole question. The oldest Greek settlement in the west, Cumae in the Bay of Naples, is oddly placed for a purely agricultural colony: its founders passed by many more fertile sites, and we must presume that at least a large part of their aim was to send back from Etruria the metals in which Greece has always been poor. The settlement at Al Mina must always have had commercial, not agricultural aims; and the sites of some colonies, notably the Chalcidian colonies on either side of the Straits of Messina, suggest the desire of their founders to control or safeguard a through route.

Further, it seems eminently possible that the nobles of this distant age were more concerned with trade than their successors were. In classical times the Athenian or Spartan gentleman looked down on trade (which was mostly carried on by the resident foreigners called metics), and the state, though it was concerned about the import of corn and other necessities, showed no interest in securing export markets for the city's products. But these early centuries cannot have possessed anything like the developed metic system of the fifth century, and it is to be noted that at the beginning of the sixth the well-born Solon himself engaged directly in trade, and other cases are known. If the attitude of the early aristocracies to trade was less fastidious than the attitude expressed by Plato, then state policy under their control may well have been more affected by questions of commerce and colonization. In particular, the great war called the Lelantine War between the cities of Euboea, which split Greece into two contending alliances late in the eighth century, certainly involved the distant colonies of the participants, and quite possibly arose out of differences in the colonial area.

In any case, whether the nobles themselves took part in trade or not, this vigorous expansion affected their lives tremendously. The opening of the East, especially, introduced the Greek upper classes to new forms of expense, new comforts, and new luxuries, and it had a profound effect on the arts and manufactures of Greece itself. Such a change was bound to have varied and far-reaching effects. To put it shortly and perhaps too simply, the rich man's wealth was more valuable to him now and could be put to uses that were unknown to his fathers; surviving complaints of the greed and rapacity of the aristocrats point to the fact that they had a new incentive now for greed. For Hesiod in the eighth century (probably: his date is not easy to fix exactly, but he lived at a time when Greek horizons were already beginning to expand) the wealthy man is one whose barns are filled with corn and whose flocks bring forth abundantly. Solon, not long after 600 B.C., puts silver and gold on a level with land, or before it, and complains that men never think they have enough of them.

Land

But land was never unimportant, and the matter of land tenure provides some of the knottiest problems of the Greek Dark Ages. Here again we must turn in the first instance to Athens, where the fragments of Solon's poems and laws give us evidence, lacking elsewhere, of an agrarian situation which by this time needed drastic remedy.

In default of evidence, modern inquiry has tended to assume too simple and uniform an origin for the problem: that the troubles of the peasant in Solon's time were the troubles of an independent smallholder, whose land was in some sense his property but who had fallen into debt. (The notion that the land belonged rather to the family, and that the current cultivator had the use of it but could not sell it, has also been influential: but Hesiod speaks unequivocally of selling land, and treats it generally as individual property; and as there is really no firm evidence at any later date of group ownership of Greek land, the notion is best left out of account.) But medieval analogy suggests that the position would not have been simple, and that we are not likely to be dealing only, or even predominantly, with independent small farmers.

The universal later tradition about the reforms of Solon leaves us no doubt that debt was one of the most pressing problems of his time, and that his remedy was the cancellation of existing debts and the abolition of all debt slavery for the future. We hear also of a class of peasants who were compelled to pay one sixth of the produce of the land they cultivated, on pain of falling into outright slavery if they failed in their payments – not, on the face of it, an oppressive proportion to pay, but a formidable penalty. It is usually assumed that these are the peasants whom Solon rescued from debt: but some of our sources distinguish them from the debtors, and the burden on these peasants may rather have been an obligation inherited from the insecurity of the Dark Ages, when the weaker members of society chose, or were driven, to purchase protection at a price which came in time to press hardly on their descendants living in a very different world. Whatever the position was, and it is impossible for anyone now to be very precise about it, Solon liberated these people from their burden, and in writing about his achievement claimed that he had 'set free the land from slavery', an elastic metaphor which might cover a variety of situations. It must certainly cover also liberation from the burden of debt, though there is no unequivocal reference to this in the poems; and the debtors were no doubt mainly free men, owning their own land and being within limits their own masters, the class for which Hesiod in neighbouring Boeotia wrote his *Farmers' Calendar*.

It is clear at all events that many Attic peasants in the late seventh century had fallen into a condition something like serfdom, with little hope of rescue on their own resources and with the prospect before them of becoming chattel slaves to be sold abroad or at home. If, as seems likely enough, situations of this kind were repeated elsewhere in the Greek world, then no doubt agrarian trouble was an important cause of the series of revolutions which in the seventh and sixth centuries overthrew the aristocracies in so many Greek cities.

If we ask why the problem had become so acute at this particular time, no single firm answer can be given, but it is of course overwhelmingly probable that the political upheaval is directly connected with the economic change, which had already gathered momentum before the opening of the revolutionary period. Partly, no doubt, the nobles' monopoly of power was increasingly resented by those non-nobles who were rich enough to have leisure for politics. Partly, and Solon's complaints about the rich point this way, the rich were now squeezing their inferiors more ferociously than they had done in a simpler past. Partly also a change in tactics and armour had widened the basis of the states' armies and this in its turn encouraged political change; and there were other factors.

Arms and war

The characteristic style of Greek warfare was the close hand-to-hand struggle of tight formations of heavy infantry in depth. It was these heavily armed fighters, known as hoplites, who either in the armies of their own cities or as mercenaries in foreign service proved so formidable a force for several centuries of Mediterranean and Near Eastern history. It is at first sight surprising that the steep mountains of Greece should have produced warriors who were only fully effective in formation on relatively level ground, but the level corn plain was vital to the city's existence, and the purpose of these armies was to dominate that, and either protect or devastate it. From the evidence of Greek art it is clear that this style of fighting was adopted early in the seventh century, or, in some places, late in the eighth.

Before that, it seems that a looser and more individual style had prevailed, more like the single combats of the heroes in the *Iliad* – though they of course are stylized and romanticized. The basic difference is that the hoplite was armed in such a way that he could only fight effectively in formation, with his shield firmly fixed on his left forearm to protect his own left side and his neighbour's right. All this required adequate training, less limelight on individual prowess, and larger numbers. Accordingly the hoplite army included all who could afford to fit themselves out with the appropriate armour and weapons. It was, so far as the term is applicable, an army of the middle class: the aristocratic arm, in the classical period, was the cavalry, which was confined to those who were rich enough to maintain horses, and had considerable social prestige but no great role in fighting in the Greek homeland, where it could never by itself decide the issue of a battle.

Training together in such an army, the hoplite class acquired a feeling of solidarity, and the nobles' grasp of power was weakened when they were no longer the primary defenders of the city's freedom: it was less easy to exclude from public life the class which now provided the dominant force on the battle-field.

Aristocracy and tyranny

The nobles had gained their power in a time of insecurity and violence, isolation and poverty, in which their special virtues were needed; and in this inarticulate prehistory they had no doubt protected their dependants as well as exploited them. Vigorous and proud, delighting in war, athletics, and hunting, with an uninhibited pleasure in wine and love, music and poetry, they lent some life and spirit to a period when life was generally hard and poor. We catch something of their spirit in their poetry – clear, outspoken, highly individualistic, and quite immoderate in its expression of love and hate: but by the time that poets began to write and their verses began to be preserved, the world which needed such leaders had begun to vanish, and much of their surviving verse is occupied with complaint about the encroachment of the base born. The circle of those who felt that they could look after themselves was wider now: worse still, in the quarrelsome days of their decline the nobles began to oppress their inferiors more recklessly, and it was easier now for the oppressed to find a champion.

This, basically, is the origin of Greek tyranny. The Greek word *tyrannos*, borrowed from some other language early in the seventh century, seems originally to have meant no more than 'king', and to have carried no unpleasant overtone: indeed, the tyrants themselves were often addressed as 'kings', and it was only gradually and unevenly that a distinction between the two terms made itself felt. The seventh century saw the rise to power of autocrats who had no hereditary claim to rule and recognized no constitutional limits to their power. This was a new phenomenon, and it was felt in time that the new word 'tyrant' was the appropriate word to describe it. And as tyrants in the end proved no less oppressive than the aristocracies which they had displaced, the word 'tyrant' acquired an ugly note, whereas 'king' remained innocuous and called to mind rather the old kings of the heroic tradition.

Tyrants were needed as leaders for an unorganized opposition. Thersites in the *Iliad* had complained about royal privilege, and Hesiod was not silent about the corrupt and unjust judgements of the Boeotian nobles, but in a world dominated by these same nobles there was no alternative authority that a man could appeal to, and no easy way to reform or replace a system which was ceasing to work. So the change came all too often by violent means, as with the Bacchiadae of Corinth, an exclusive group who claimed descent from one of the early Corinthian kings. They had been extremely powerful in their day; they founded the great Corinthian colonies of Syracuse and Corcyra, and Corinth had prospered greatly under their rule. But in their latter days they got a bad name for cruelty and misrule, and after their fall they were not regretted. The agent of their overthrow, in the middle of the seventh century, was a certain Cypselus, about whom we know little in detail, but in spite of the real violence with which his revolution was conducted he is said to have been a mild and popular ruler, and it seems that he had the respectable support of the Delphic oracle. He was succeeded by his energetic and more ruthless son Periander, who in the course of his long reign alienated the supporters of the tyranny, which collapsed very shortly after his death. It was succeeded by an oligarchy of unusual stability, and Corinth suffered no further internal change for very nearly two centuries.

Cypselus had many imitators, and with variations of detail the course of tyranny was much the same wherever it arose: a transitional régime, which might last two generations but seldom three.

The tyrants' contribution

The negative side of the achievement of these tyrants is clear enough. Their function was to liberate their city from a system which was no longer adequate to the conditions of the time, and here and there we can see something of the way they went to work in detail. Pisistratus of Athens, for instance, who seized power comparatively late, in the middle of the sixth century, notably encouraged the state cults of Athena and Dionysus, and in other ways fostered the growth of a city patriotism to override the local patriotism of the country districts: the state cults grew at the expense of the local cults presided over by the local nobles.

Further, they provided peaceful conditions for the expansion of their cities' material prosperity. Some of them owed their successful seizure of power to a general weariness with the internecine quarrels of the aristocracy and fulfilled an important function merely by providing a period of internal peace. And for the most part they kept peace with their neighbours too – notably, again, Pisistratus and his sons at Athens. There were no great wars between contending alliances, like the Lelantine War which divided all Greece at the end of the eighth century. On the positive side, Cypselus and Periander founded many new Corinthian colonies in north-western Greece; Pisistratus, by his own action and indirectly, acquired for Athens a foothold in the neighbourhood of the Hellespont, that important highway to the Black Sea and the corn of south Russia. The tyrants in general were great builders and patrons of the arts, constructing magnificent temples and taking thought for the water supply of their cities. These building programmes stimulated economic growth, and in other ways too the tyrants contributed something directly to the increasing prosperity of their subjects.

It is less easy to assess the difference they made to political and social institutions. Our Greek sources, preoccupied in the main with the more obvious evils of autocracy, make no attempt to tell us in detail how these autocrats governed, and we can only guess at the internal developments which made it possible to set up stable governments when the tyrants were overthrown. No doubt in the main they governed through existing institutions, revivified by the admission of many who had hitherto been excluded altogether from any concern with public business. Once more, we have the most precise information from Athens. But here Athens is exceptional, in that her first great reformer Solon refused to have a tyranny thrust on him: his reforms did not indeed prevent the later seizure of power by Pisistratus, but they meant that the Athenian tyranny came at an unusually late date, and when it came the tyrant could build on the foundations which the reformer had laid.

Solon of Athens

It is clear from Solon's poems that Athens in 594 B.C. was faced with a revolutionary situation of the type which had elsewhere produced a tyranny, and he tells us repeatedly that he could have been tyrant if he had wished. In this case the internal trouble was primarily agrarian, but Solon speaks also in general terms of the oppression of the poor by the rich and powerful, and it is clear that he himself stood, to begin with, very much on the side of the poor: the upper classes, it would seem, accepted his mediation only for fear of the violent revolution which might otherwise sweep them away.

Something has been said already of the immediate measures which Solon took to remedy the grievances of the Attic peasant, and much more has been conjectured about the encouragement he gave in other ways to the development of the Attic economy. Here we are concerned with the arrangements he made for the better government of Athens. Control had lain in the hands of nine annual magistrates called archons, with the famous council of the Areopagus. It is not certain that office was ever formally confined to members of the aristocracy called Eupatridae, but there is no doubt that in practice they controlled the whole machinery of state: and Solon broke their monopoly. Disregarding the claims of birth, he established four classes graduated in terms of their income in kind from the land. These classes formed the qualification for office, the higher posts being confined to the higher classes, while the lowest and poorest class had only the right to attend the general assembly and to sit in the appeal court which he instituted to review the judicial decisions of the magistrates where they did not give satisfaction.

Whatever the precise position before Solon, there can be no doubt that he altered it radically by his formal establishment of wealth as the criterion of privilege. Henceforward, though at Athens as elsewhere any amount of informal respect was accorded to the claims of high birth, Attic society became in principle mobile: any citizen who made enough money and invested it in land could hope to rise to the highest class and take his part in the government of the city. Solon did not indeed, as later democrats claimed, institute democracy at

Athens – that was a long process, not completed till well into the fifth century – but his institutions provided a framework, never wholly abandoned while Athens remained free, in which these later developments were possible.

But for the time being his reforms provoked as much strife as satisfaction. The upper classes resented the loss of their privileges, the lower classes felt that a cleaner sweep should have been made and would have preferred the bloody revolution that Solon was at such pains to avoid: hence his later poems are full of rebuke to the people and of protest that he had in fact fulfilled the programme of reform which he had promised. In particular, strife over the archonship troubled the next fifteen years, and it looks as if the struggles of various local factions among the upper classes were the main reason for the eventual establishment of the tyranny of Pisistratus in the middle of the sixth century. But Pisistratus is said to have maintained the laws of Solon as they stood, except that he and his sons took care to see that the offices of state fell to their friends; and thus the Solonian framework survived. During the internal peace imposed by the tyranny, Solon's machinery of government continued to be worked by a variety of hands under the tyrants' supervision, and when the tyranny was overthrown in 510 B.C. the Athenian people had somehow grown up politically and took the government into their own hands, refusing to return to the anarchic strife which had obtained before Pisistratus' seizure of power.

We do not usually know in any detail what happened at the overthrow of other tyrannies, mostly at an earlier date, but in one way or another some effective form of government was evolved, mostly of a kind which later theory would classify as oligarchic, and most cities found in the course of the sixth century some system which was at least for the time being workable.

The Greek World

Sparta

Meanwhile, in the southern Peloponnese, Sparta had developed her own individual system, which was recognized (and indeed admired) as something strange and unique in the Greek world, a military aristocracy under the strictest discipline, whose army was to dominate Greece for some two centuries.

Greek theorists liked to emphasize and exaggerate the eccentricity of Spartan institutions, which could be used to point the moral that it was the business of the state to train its citizens with the utmost rigour in the practice of virtue. Looked at more closely, the government of Sparta seems less resolutely abnormal, more like an archaic and conservative model of oligarchy: but it was given a special twist early in its history when it conquered the neighbouring state of Messenia and reduced its inhabitants to a form of slavery.

The city of Sparta, at the northern end of a fertile plain and for a Greek city remote from the sea, was founded during the period of migrations by a band of Dorian Greeks, one of those invading bands from the north (see p. 23) whose entry into southern Greece followed, if it did not cause, the collapse of the Mycenaean kingdoms there. The countryside was occupied by a class of free men, who may have been predominantly Dorian too, who developed into the class called *perioikoi*, living in their own communities under Spartan supervision, serving in the Spartan army, in the main quite content with their lot, but having no share at all in the government of the state. The original inhabitants of the land were reduced to a sort of slavery, under the title of helots: they worked the estates of the aristocracy (called Spartiates), rendering them a fixed proportion or a fixed amount of the produce, but to some extent under the control of the state rather than of an individual master; for instance, helots could not be privately sold.

With the conquest of Messenia, which was completed late

in the eighth century, the Spartans extended this system over an area nearly as large as their own original territory, sharing out the fertile land among themselves and reducing the Messenians to the status of helots. From this time on the Spartiates formed a small and highly trained aristocratic garrison holding down, with the cooperation of their *perioikoi*, a subject population many times their own number. The conservation of this system was an enormous strain, and was only possible under the strictest military discipline: on the other hand, the garrison was liberated from the grinding effort of wringing a living from the soil and could devote itself to hunting and military exercises in a way which was impossible for even the upper classes of the average Greek city. And archaic Sparta at least could relax into a civilized gaiety, though as time went on the strain of their dedicated lives made for increasing grimness.

Spartan education was a fierce training in endurance and obedience, the boys being ranged in age groups with curious archaic names under the supervision of their elders, and much of their adult lives was still spent in public in a kind of barracks. The whole of this system, with the political constitution to be described in the next chapter (p. 68), was believed in antiquity to be the work of a single lawgiver, Lycurgus, at a single early date, usually calculated to the ninth century. The Greeks liked to ascribe institutions to the personal will of a lawgiver, and indeed to discuss his moral intentions as if they had been exactly realized in subsequent practice: and the tradition which ascribed all Spartan institutions to a shadowy early lawgiver may be in part a product of this kind of schematic thinking. The question is one of the standard controversies of early Greek history: the ninth-century Lycurgus has his fervent defenders, but to me it seems more probable that the institutions were not all of the same date, but that some later changes, particularly some important political reforms that took place in the seventh century, were all ascribed to Lycurgus to give them greater authority.

The Spartan system was kept going, no doubt, mainly by its success: the army, more fully and effectively trained than any in Greece, was universally feared, and it was gratifying to the individual to be a member of this formidable force. Their sense of solidarity was heightened by the pretence that all members of the Spartiate aristocracy were equal, and that in their austere barrack life no one fared better or worse than his neighbour: such equality could not of course be literally maintained, and some families were evidently richer or more influential than others, but while some effort was made to obliterate these distinctions in public social life, the pretence had its uses. And no doubt also the strict training had some of the effects that Greek theorists claimed for it, in keeping the mind of the Spartan turned towards the military virtue of discipline and submission to the existing system.

The Peloponnesian League

In the course of the sixth century the military predominance of Sparta in the Peloponnese bore fruit in the establishment of a widespread alliance under Spartan leadership. For a period, it seems that Sparta contemplated subjugating parts of Arcadia in the manner in which Messenia had been subjected but after a heavy defeat – her last for many years – she turned instead to organizing an alliance and by the end of the century this league began to be extended beyond the Isthmus of Corinth.

To a large extent this alliance was based on simple fear of the Spartan army, coupled with the expectation that Sparta with her allies could resist any attempt by any outside power to make conquests in the Peloponnese. But Sparta also posed as the enemy of Greek tyranny – though not many tyrants were actually expelled from Greek cities by Sparta – and as the champion of constitutional government. In this field and at this stage, Sparta was perhaps something of a pioneer. The characteristic system by which so many Greek cities were governed, the important decisions being taken by a citizen assembly subject to the restraint of a council which prepared the business, is found at an early date and in an archaic form at Sparta, and may actually have been invented there. True, the Spartan 'people' was a small aristocratic minority, and their small council of elders holding office for life was very unlike the council of more modern states: but the Spartan system has the central feature that the assembly was only allowed to consider business on which the council had already deliberated; and the Athenian Solon may have been imitating this feature of the Spartan constitution when he set up a special separate council to prepare business for the much wider Athenian assembly.

In this sense, in the days before the Athenian type of democracy had developed as a specific and distinguishable form of government, Sparta might pose as a model of progressive constitutional government as opposed to the irresponsible autocracy of a tyrant, even though the Spartan institutions were not in detail such that any other Greek state could exactly copy them.

Certainly, Spartan propaganda made much of the theme that she was the tyrants' enemy, and this will have helped to solidify her alliance.

Cleisthenes of Athens

The conspicuous instance in which Sparta did take action against a Greek tyrant was in 510 B.C., when a Spartan army under King Cleomenes helped to expel the sons of Pisistratus from Athens. The natural consequence of this would have been the incorporation of Athens in the Spartan alliance, the Solonian constitution conforming quite closely enough to the ideal which Sparta was supposed to uphold. But in fact political strife broke out at once between rival Athenian leaders in something of the old aristocratic style, and when the party favoured by King Cleomenes had got the upper hand, the rival leader Cleisthenes, in Herodotus' words, 'took the people into partnership', with momentous results for Athens, and so defeated his adversaries and embarked on new constitutional reforms.

The technical details of his reform are not all of them easy to interpret, but the general tendency of it was to diminish still further the area in which aristocratic influence might still be effective: the most conspicuous item was the substitution of ten tribes based on locality for the four old Attic tribes based on kinship, for both military and civil purposes, while the phratries ceased to play any part in the formal organization of the state and became purely private corporations. In effect, aristocratic patronage ceased to be the main principle of social and political organization, however much weight was still attached to the ancient prestige of old-established houses, and the people became, so to speak, their own patron.

There was still much to be done before the Athenian democracy reached its full development, but if we are to date its inception to one year rather than another, then 507 B.C., the year of Cleisthenes' legislation, is the most appropriate one to choose.

Sparta, Athens, and Persia

The rise of the aggressive empire of Persia and its rapid conquest of the old familiar kingdoms of the Near East posed a new problem for the leaders of Greece. Shortly after the middle of the sixth century Cyrus the Great defeated King Croesus of Lydia and annexed his kingdom, and with it the Greek cities of Asia Minor which Croesus had ruled. For many years to come Greece was faced with the prospect that Persia would pursue her career of conquest into European Greece, where the fierce strife within the cities offered many opportunities for intervention. Sparta at this time was clearly the most powerful single state in Greece and the head of the largest and most coherent alliance. We cannot prove in detail how constantly the leaders of Sparta kept the Persian menace in mind, but it is conspicuous that throughout the period which leads up to the decisive battles of 480 and 479 B.C. any state which was threatened by Persia appealed at once for Spartan help – however seldom it was forthcoming – and conversely anyone who had quarrelled with Sparta was likely to seek Persian help.

Cleisthenes' reform and the defeat of Sparta's friends in Athens thrust this dilemma at once on the infant democracy, which certainly tried to obtain Persian help, though not to much effect. The democracy survived two Spartan attempts to install a more complaisant government at Athens, mainly because Sparta's allies, and especially Corinth, saw no reason to overturn the form of government established by Cleisthenes, and regarded it as conforming sufficiently to the ideal officially championed by the League: it was left to the next century to show how subversive democracy of the Athenian type could be to the older ideal.

The fifth century opened with the six years' revolt of the East Greeks from Persia. Athens, still moving very uncertainly, sent help to the rebels but withdrew after the first year's campaign, thus providing the Persians with a formal excuse for their first expedition to Greece in 490 B.C. The Athenians beat off this attack at Marathon before the arrival of Spartan help. Their confidence was restored by the victory, and in 483 B.C. on Themistocles' advice they expanded their navy and thus laid the foundation of their future greatness. There was no further suggestion that they might come to terms with Persia, and when Xerxes' vast army invaded Greece in 480 B.C. they stood firm on the side of Sparta and resistance. For Sparta was inevitably the leader, and the Peloponnesian League the nucleus, of Greek resistance. The glory of the heroic defeat at Thermopylae and of the final victory at Plataea belonged to Sparta: but the naval battle at Salamis, though fought under Spartan command, was the special glory of Athens and fore-shadowed the coming of her empire. Thus, when the external enemy had been repulsed, these two Greek powers, so different in character and tradition, were left face to face, only to destroy one another in their struggle for dominion over Greece.

Outer Greece and federalism

The Greece whose history we mainly study is the southern half of the peninsula, the Peloponnese and the area immediately north and east of the Corinthian isthmus, with its off-shoots overseas – the Greece of the city state.

But not all those who spoke dialects of the Greek language and were at one time or another reckoned to be part of the Greek people organized their lives in the way we have come to think characteristic of Greece. There were also those whom ancient theory classified as 'races' rather than 'cities', areas which might indeed contain cities or villages but had never coalesced or been brought under the control of a single centre in the way Attica had been unified under Athens. The Arcadians, pent up in the central mountains of the Peloponnese by the Dorian invasion, had something of this character; but their cities developed an independent and highly quarrelsome character which prevented their union in a single Arcadian state, though the attempt was made. Across the Corinthian Gulf, to the north and north-west, lay other 'races', not always quite recognizably Greek, who were much less touched by the ideals of city life, such as the Aetolians or the people of Epirus, who had always some loose political unity, but made no serious appearance in history till the Greece of the cities, weakened by their struggles against one another, had ceased to count in a world dominated by the great Macedonian monarchies of the successors of Alexander.

Further east lived two racial groups much nearer to the main current of Greek civilization, the people of Thessaly and Boeotia, who deserve a word to themselves. The Thessalians were conquerors who had invaded the great inland plain of Thessaly during the Dark Ages and had reduced the earlier inhabitants to a state of slavery not unlike that of the Spartan helots. In the archaic period the landowners with their great estates counted for more than the cities. A Thessalian union in some sense existed, with a curious constitution which provided for the unitary control of the whole area under a single leader, but only intermittently and in cases of emergency, though such a leader once in power was likely to hold on to his office as long as he lived. But the country relapsed easily into anarchy, and in spite of its considerable resources the Thessalian union never held together long enough to become an effective power in Greece. In the course of the fifth century the cities grew in importance, and early in the fourth century the tyrants of Pherae developed a power comparable to that of the great tyrants of an earlier age in the south: the greatest of them, Jason, succeeded in getting control of all Thessaly and was credited with great designs, but was murdered in 370 B.C. before he could put them into effect. Thessaly fell under the control of Philip of Macedon not very long afterwards, and played no independent part thereafter.

Boeotia was much more a land of cities, each with their own independent pride, but the Boeotians were always conscious of their racial unity and made interesting experiments towards federal government, complicated by the continual ambition of Thebes, the largest city, to bring the whole area under its control. Some signs of a Boeotian League can be seen before the end of the sixth century, but this was broken up after the Persian Wars when Thebes could be charged with having betrayed the national cause, and it was some time before the Boeotians fully recovered their self-confidence. In the middle of the fifth century a new League was created, which provided for a uniform system of oligarchic government in each of the constituent cities, and divided the country as a whole into eleven roughly equal districts, each contributing its quota to the federal army, sixty councillors to the federal council, and one to the board of eleven federal magistrates called Boeotarchs.

This was an interesting attempt to maintain the local autonomy of the cities, large and small, while introducing something like a modern system of representation into the federal government. (In the leagues headed by Sparta and Athens, the disproportionate power of the leading cities gave them effective executive control, while in council each of the constituent cities, great or small, had an equal vote, with results that can easily be imagined.) The system was undermined as time went on by the growth of Theban power within the League: the League was dissolved again in 386 B.C., only to be formed again in a more democratic and centralized form; by this time the experiment in representative federalism may be reckoned to have ended. When the Boeotians defeated Sparta at Leuctra in 371 B.C., and entered on a brief period of hegemony, their domination proved no more acceptable to the Greek cities than that of Athens or Sparta, and the attempt to maintain it quickly exhausted Boeotia's resources.

The idea that voting power might be proportioned to the size of the member city was incorporated in the constitution of the League of Corinth, the league of Greek cities organized by Philip of Macedon after his victory at Chaeronea in 338 B.C.: but this League, created as an instrument of Macedonian domination, was never a live political organism. There was more life in the Aetolian and Achaean Leagues, both of which in the third and second centuries broke their original racial bounds and included alien states from quite far afield. The Aetolians had already made themselves felt as a military power outside their mountainous home in central Greece: the Achaeans, a group of cities in a narrow coastal strip along the north shore of the Peloponnese, were of no account till Aratus of Sicyon, a Dorian city lying between Corinth and Achaea, brought his city into their League about 250 B.C. These two Leagues, with the remarkable personality of Aratus and the impressive series of the contemporary kings of Macedon, between them dominated the Greek scene for a century before the final Roman conquest in 146 B.C. Both Leagues had councils in which the constituent states were represented according to size: the Aetolians, following the old democratic principle, reserved important decisions for a primary assembly – held in their own land, so that they naturally dominated it: the character of the Achaean assembly is much disputed, but it is clear that its politics also were mainly guided by considerations local to the League's original area. Neither League could quite transcend the particularism of the cities to unite a coherent block of Greek territory large enough to stand on its own feet as an independent state: indeed, it was too late by then for any form of unity but that which was imposed by foreign conquest.

Thus the principle of city autonomy affected in various ways even those Greeks who lived outside the area in which the city state first and mainly flourished, and prevented any different form of development.

*

These, in rough outline, were the circumstances in which the Greek city state developed and reached its full growth, so far as they can now be recovered. The big questions remain: how did Greece come to take this particular turning, why did city autonomy mean so much to them, what did they gain from it, what contribution did it make to European civilization as a whole?

Greek national consciousness

Though there was never a political unit called Hellas in antiquity, the Hellenes, as the Greeks called themselves, used that name freely and were acutely conscious of the difference between themselves and other peoples.

It is not easy to define Hellas geographically. There were always marginal areas in the northern part of the peninsula whose title to inclusion was at least doubtful: in southern Asia Minor there were half-Greek cities among whom no easy boundary could be drawn: distant and perhaps isolated colonies might be much more obviously members of the Greek community than peoples within a few days' march of Athens. Nor can we apply any convincing racial test: it is always difficult to find an objective criterion of race, and in this case it is evident from the start that the Greeks were a mixture, invaders from the north or east having imposed themselves in different proportions at various places and times upon an earlier population whose composition is not itself easy to ascertain. In the last resort, those men were Greeks who felt themselves to be so, and whose claim was widely enough accepted by others who felt the same.

The Greeks themselves recognized mainly the ties of language and religion; and what they called 'customs' and we may loosely call 'culture'. The language, with a considerable admixture of foreign forms, belongs to the general Indo-European family but is not very close to any other large member of that group. It had diverged into a number of dialects, some of which look bizarre enough to us who are brought up to treat Attic Greek as the norm, but in ancient times the speakers of the various dialects were readily intelligible to one another. Some cities on the fringe were criticized for their bad Greek, but in general the language was an effective criterion to distinguish Greek from foreigner.

About Greek religion it is never easy to generalize, and the subject must be discussed at slightly greater length. Their gods had many aspects. The great Olympian family of Zeus, as Homer treats them, are persons with very human passions, but distinguished from mankind by their immortality and their wider power: and so they remained for most poets and artists and for the ordinary man, despite some protest from puritans like Xenophanes and Plato. But they were also the great powers of nature, Zeus in the sky and Poseidon in the sea; Artemis the 'mistress of beasts' and others are linked with older worships dating back before the arrival of the Greeks; Demeter and Persephone are familiar figures of those rituals concerned with the fertility of the earth which appear wherever man has taken to agriculture; and others were the patrons of various human activities, as Athena and Hephaestus of the arts and crafts of civilization. All these were national gods, however much the particular city might appropriate one of them as its own patron – Athens might claim Athena's favour almost as a right, but this did not discourage Sparta from worshipping her own 'Athena of the Brazen House'. Beside them there were innumerable local divinities of less widespread fame, some assimilated to one of the Olympian family, some obstinately anonymous: any spring or tree might harbour its own minor divinity, and receive due reverence from passing strangers as well as from the peasants of the neighbourhood.

This hospitable riot of polytheism defies close analysis and discourages systematic theology. Impiety could indeed be recognized and punished – the disrespect of an individual towards some powerful god might endanger the whole community, and even minor gods might avenge disrespect on a surprising scale – but there was no body of dogma expounded by a unitary Church. Religion permeated every department of human life, and almost any kind of association had its common cult and appointed a priest to preside over it: but priesthood in such terms was not a specialized profession, though it might in some cases require specialized knowledge of traditional rituals. Individuals for the most part conducted their own sacrifices to the gods of their special choice. This god might of course be an importation from abroad – indeed, as with Greek nationality itself, a god became Greek if enough Greeks felt him to be so – but among all this loose chaos there was a nucleus of uniformity: a group of recognizably Greek gods presided over by Zeus, a similarity of ritual, a common attitude to the divine.

This community of feeling found its clearest expression in great national gatherings, like that which took place every fourth year in the late summer at Olympia in the western Peloponnese, where the Greeks characteristically honoured Zeus, the patron of the festival, with elaborate athletic and musical contests, under the shelter of one of those sacred truces which intermittently interrupted their warfare. This festival, traditionally founded in 776 B.C., was at first local to the west Peloponnese, but before the end of the eighth century it had spread more widely, and in the classical period it was genuinely panhellenic. Admission to the games was to some extent a test of acceptance as a Greek, as when Alexander I of Macedon (an early fifth-century ancestor of the great Alexander) made good his claim to compete, on the basis of his alleged descent from the Dorian kings of Argos; and the heralds who went round to announce the sacred truce went only to accepted Greek communities. Second in importance were the games at Apollo's sanctuary at Delphi, the Pythia, founded on a regular basis early in the sixth century: and there were many similar festivals of more or less widespread fame.

The great festivals gave regular material expression to the Greek feeling of unity, but they thought primarily of their temples and altars at home when they spoke of defending the shrines of their 'ancestral gods' – a varied group but in the mass distinguishable from the gods of foreigners, worshipped with a Greek and not a foreign ritual.

When they spoke of *nomima*, 'customs', they included much that we should classify as religious practice, as well as a clutter of social habits, in detail quite indifferent, but in the mass a criterion by which again Greek could be distinguished from foreigner. This is worth mention, if only because the Greeks themselves were much interested in the matter, and their writers made large collections of the 'customs' of various states and of 'barbarian customs', showing again their belief that they formed a separate nation. Something nearer our concept of culture is meant when the fourth-century publicist Isocrates, involved in this question of who should count as Greek, solved it by saying that anyone who had partaken of Greek education was a Greek: but this is perhaps a sophisticated and uncharacteristic view.

But for all their consciousness of belonging to the same nation they still shrank from political union and clung to their local independence, resisting the attempt of any one city to impose unity on them.

The political microcosm

The origins of Greek particularism go back into the inarticulate Dark Ages, and we can do nothing but note the fact that the political conditions of the period of migration and the geographical features of the country make the original fragmentation entirely natural. The question is rather, why the process was never reversed: and when scholars argue, as they sometimes do, about the date when the *polis* emerged (the word is simply the Greek for 'city', and it is entirely characteristic of the whole situation that it should have given rise to the modern word 'politics'), the question is rather at what date this form of organization had developed so far and so fruitfully that it came to be inconceivable that Greeks should ever live under any other. It may be that the answer to this, too, is in a sense lost in prehistory, and that this fierce city patriotism was already an ingrained feature of the mind of those aristocracies from whose decline Greek history begins. But we need to know why the later Greeks clung so steadfastly to the same system, and even if the reasons were not always the same

– the *polis* will have meant one thing to Alcaeus or Solon at the beginning of the sixth century and another to Demosthenes or Aristotle in the middle of the fourth – we can only try to take the phenomenon as a whole and try to see what made it so attractive for so long.

The Greeks had plenty of opportunities to observe what large territorial states were like, and they were certain that their own institutions provided a better life. They tended to express this by saying that Greeks were governed by law, whereas these large states were all absolute monarchies, and the barbarians must be slaves by nature to submit themselves as they did to the whims of a single autocrat. The fact that many Greek states had been subjected for long periods to a tyrant was dismissed as an aberration: the tyrant had temporarily shelved the law. So, for instance, Aristotle distinguished three types of constitution, each according to law but each having its lawless counterpart: the rule of the just king accords with law because he is just, but tyranny is lawless monarchy; aristocracy is the rule of the virtuous few, but oligarchy is the perversion of this, corrupted by the power of money; there is a constitution in which the many rule according to law, but in its degenerate counterpart democracy the people have carried freedom to excess.

This analysis gives too neat a scheme. The just king and the virtuous aristocrats are theoretical possibilities not to be found in real Greek life, and the virtuous alternative to democracy is another abstraction, though examples were pointed out and attempts were made to realize it. The real tests were willingness to accept government by free discussion and to submit to the rotation of office: and these were things that could only be tried out in a small community whose members were all more or less familiar to one another. Government by primary assembly, as opposed to government by elected representatives, is indeed a feature of Greek life which our large nations cannot imitate, a luxury only possible to units the size of a moderate English county or less. The attraction is obvious. Not everyone wants to take an active part in politics all the time – even the Athenians, with their passion for political activity and discussion, attended the ordinary meetings of their assembly somewhat thinly – but it must be gratifying to feel that one can if one wishes go and vote on all the public questions of the day, and that the people's fate is genuinely in their own hands. The simple preference for managing one's own affairs goes far to account for the persistence of the city ideal, whether the managers were the whole people or an upper-class oligarchy: and that in spite of the evident inconvenience of having a separate state with its own foreign policy every few miles, or the fact, which history eventually made plain, that autonomous cities might in the end prove literally too small to survive when serious force was brought to bear on them. The Greeks beat back the assault of Persia with an effort which they could not repeat against Macedon.

But their political experiments were not simply a luxury for the Greeks to enjoy for themselves. To an extent which it is hard to realize now, many of the ordinary mechanisms of what we call constitutional government were new when the Greeks began to use them. For instance, among other races early attempts to create republican government have been paralysed by the fact that they would only accept decisions which were unanimous. It requires considerable restraint for the minority to submit to a majority vote: the Greeks themselves often failed to exercise this restraint, but they tried, and majority rule was found tolerable to all but a few extremists in the long career of the Athenian democracy. And these are alternatives which could only be tried out at all on a small scale: the practical difficulty even of merely taking a vote of the whole Persian Empire would have been insuperable, if anyone had thought of trying it. In such ways the Greeks tried out many experiments in practical politics, and often the results are with us yet, transmitted to posterity in Aristotle's analysis, the influence of which was not sensibly diminished by the fact that its medieval and modern readers live in states of entirely different structure.

In a wider sense too the rule of law is not easy to enforce over a large area. It is only in the last century or so that this country has been, so to speak, tamed; and that is almost entirely due to the enormous improvement in communications. Where transport, or even a message of any complication, could go no faster than a horse, the difficulty of maintaining any kind of order over a whole kingdom was insuperable, as English medieval history abundantly shows. There was, of course, disorder and violence enough in Greece, but that was partly due just to the multiplicity of their states and their wars, and more developed cities like Athens achieved a stability which for its time was admirable. It would have been much more difficult to uphold the rule of law in a united Greece, quite apart from the difficulty of providing such a state with an agreed form of government.

Lastly, it is difficult to believe that the freedom and vigour of Greek thought and art are wholly unconnected with the political and social freedom which the best Greek states achieved, hazardous as it always is to attempt such correlations. These are matters which must be discussed in later chapters: and this one may appropriately end with the bold but plausible assertion that the Greek spirit, and those manifestations of it which we most admire, could not have come into being in any atmosphere but that of the cities which they loved and defended.

Bibliography

ANDREWES, A., *The Greek Tyrants*, Hutchinson, 1956
BURY, J. B., *History of Greece*, 3rd ed., revised by R. Meiggs, Macmillan, 1951

Cambridge Ancient History, vol. II–IV, Cambridge University Press, 1924–6

FINLEY, M. I., *The World of Odysseus*, Chatto & Windus, 1956

GUTHRIE, W. K. C., *The Greeks and Their Gods*, Methuen, 1954

HIGNETT, C., *A History of the Athenian Constitution*, Clarendon Press, 1952

SINCLAIR, T. A., *A History of Greek Political Thought*, Routledge, 1952

URE, P. N., *The Origin of Tyranny*, Cambridge University Press, 1922

ZIMMERN, SIR ALFRED, *The Greek Commonwealth*, 5th ed., Clarendon Press, 1931; paperback edition, 1961

3   Athens and Sparta

A. H. M. Jones
Laurence Professor of Ancient History,
Cambridge University

For more than a century after the Persian war, Athens and Sparta were rivals for the leadership of Greece. Two cities could scarcely have been more unalike. Athens lay at the crossroads of Greece and was a busy centre of trade and industry: its chief agricultural product, olive oil, was grown mainly for export; its harbour town, Piraeus, was one of the greatest ports of the Mediterranean. Sparta, secluded in the remote valley of the Eurotas, was a self-sufficient agricultural state; its only currency was iron bars. Athens was thronged with strangers, both visitors and permanent residents; at Sparta foreigners were unwelcome and were periodically expelled. Athens was a great naval power; Sparta's strength lay in her army. The Athenians beautified their city with splendid temples and superb statues; Sparta looked like an overgrown village. Athens produced great drama, the tragedies of Aeschylus, Sophocles, and Euripides, and the comedies of Aristophanes, and was the home of historians like Thucydides and philosophers like Plato. Sparta produced no art and no literature, and played no part in the intellectual life of Greece. Above all Athens was progressive, burgeoning with new ideas; Sparta was intensely conservative; Athens was the inventor of democracy, while Sparta clung stubbornly to an archaic constitution. It is understandable that Sparta should have appealed to many old-fashioned Greeks as the embodiment and champion of traditional ideas. What is odd is that quite a number of intelligent Athenians admired her way of life and compared her favourably with their own city.

Sparta's cultural sterility was the inevitable result of her social and political structure. Her citizens were rigorously trained from infancy for one thing only – to be good soldiers; and these citizens, the Spartiates, were a tiny *élite*, supported by the labour of many times as many serfs, the helots. Many of the helots no doubt acquiesced in their situation, particularly those of the original Spartan territory, Laconia. But those of Messenia, which had been conquered later, bitterly resented their subjection, and always nourished hopes of recovering their independence – which they ultimately did in 369 B.C. Of one thing there can be no doubt – the Spartiates maintained their supremacy by terror. Every year the ephors, the chief magistrates of Sparta, declared war on the helots: the object of this curious ceremony was to enable any Spartan to kill a helot without incurring the guilt of murder. Every year the ephors sent out picked young Spartiates to spy out the land and kill any helot they thought dangerous. Such routine measures were not always sufficient. In 424 B.C. the Spartans, nervous at rising helot unrest, invited them to enlist, offering them freedom as a reward. Two thousand volunteers were enrolled; they were never heard of again.

What did Athenians find to admire in this? There are various possible explanations. Like most people the Greeks were impressed by power, and Sparta remained for centuries the great military power of Greece. Her army was trained and disciplined as no other Greek army was, for most Greek armies were only levies of amateurs. The Spartans moreover had a deserved reputation for courage, steadiness, and devotion to duty. As a result they were never beaten in a straight fight until the battle of Leuctra in 371 B.C. In the second place Sparta's political stability was something very exceptional in the Greek world. It was her proud boast that since the time of the semi-mythical Lycurgus her constitution had remained unchanged, and that never had there been either civil strife or tyranny. Almost alone among Greek cities Sparta preserved the monarchy; there were two hereditary kings from two royal families, possessing equal powers. The kings had lost most of their power at home, but they remained the commanders-in-chief of the Spartan army, and in the field their authority was absolute. There was a council of elders, numbering thirty including the two kings: its members were very literally elders, having to be over sixty when they were elected and sitting for life. There was also an assembly of all Spartiates, which voted on important issues, such as peace and war, but had no powers of initiative or debate. Finally there was the annual board of five ephors, the real government of Sparta. They were chosen by a method which Aristotle describes as 'exceedingly childish', but which enabled even the lowliest citizens to hold office. The constitution was thus, within the Spartiate body, roughly democratic, and since the Spartiates were a very homogeneous group – they called themselves 'the peers' – and, moreover, had a strong bond of common interest, unity was not difficult to achieve. The contrast with the rest of the Greek world was striking. In many cities there was a continuous class struggle, and revolutions and counter-revolutions followed one another with dreary monotony. In such a world, stability was something precious, however achieved. And admirers of Sparta conveniently ignored the struggle of the helots against the Spartiates, which was normally below the surface and rarely broke into an open revolt.

The major attraction of Sparta, however, was that it was a perfect aristocracy. The Athenian admirers of Sparta were almost exclusively upper-class citizens, men of birth, wealth, and education, who resented the fact that at Athens they had to accept peasants and workmen as their equals. As one of them says:

At Athens slaves and aliens enjoy the utmost licence; you are not allowed to beat them and a slave will not make way for you. I will tell you why. If it were the law that a slave or an alien or a freedman might be beaten by a citizen, one would often strike an Athenian thinking that he was a slave; for the common people and the aliens are no better dressed than slaves.

To a man of this type Sparta naturally seemed an ideal state. There, not only political power but the most elementary rights of citizenship were reserved for gentlemen.

There was a more respectable reason for Athenian intellectuals admiring Sparta. All Greeks agreed that the state existed in order to improve the life of its citizens. To some this meant the state ought to train and discipline its citizens to lead good lives. To such thinkers – Plato is an outstanding example – Sparta seemed an approximation, if an imperfect one, to their ideal. The Spartan conception of the good life was a limited one: the only virtues which it recognized were patriotism, courage, and discipline. But at least Sparta did attempt to mould its citizens to this pattern, and with some success. This was a step in the right direction; could not other and higher virtues be instilled by rigorous indoctrination from childhood?

On this issue there was a fundamental cleavage between the school of thought represented by Plato and the ideals of Athenian democrats. One of the leading slogans of democracy was freedom, freedom of speech, and freedom of action, and by this they meant what we mean, the right of the individual to think, say, and do what he likes – naturally within the limits of the law. Plato does not dispute that this was the Athenian ideal of practice –

The city is full of liberty and free speech and everyone in it is allowed to do what he likes. This being allowed it obviously follows that each man can plan his own life as he pleases.

But he regards this state of affairs as deplorable: the citizens are as a result all different, instead of conforming to one ideal type laid down by a wise government. Pericles, in the Funeral Speech, the great panegyric on Athens which he delivered in the opening year of the Peloponnesian War, glories in this individual liberty:

We live as free citizens not only in our public life but in our attitude to one another in the affairs of daily life: we are not angry at our neighbour if he behaves as he pleases: we do not cast sour looks at him, which if they do no harm, cause pain.

The boast was true. Aristophanes could not only produce comedies which ridiculed the basic institutions of the democracy, but was awarded prizes for them. Philosophers and political theorists like Plato, Isocrates, and Aristotle could publish their radical attacks on the whole democratic ideal, and live unmolested. Very different from Sparta, where, says Demosthenes

> You are not allowed to praise the laws of Athens or of any other state; far from it, you have to praise what conforms with their institutions.

Democrats had another radical quarrel with Plato. He maintained that government was a skilled art which should be restricted to experts, and he devised a constitution in which a self-chosen *élite* of wise men should hold irresponsible power. But the second great slogan of democracy was equality. All citizens had not only equal rights before the law, but an equal voice in deciding public issues, and an equal share in the actual government of the state. This is what democracy meant to the Greeks. They distrusted representative institutions and would have regarded our parliamentary system as a kind of elective aristocracy. True democracy required in their eyes that each citizen should personally hear every issue debated – and if he liked contribute his own opinion – and vote direct upon it: even in administration all the citizens should govern and be governed in turn. In a Greek city this was literally possible. Athens was an exceptionally large city, but its territory, Attica, was about the size of Bedfordshire, and its citizens numbered only twenty to forty thousand. On an average only about five or six thousand citizens seem to have attended most meetings of the assembly, but on important occasions many more came, and all could take part if they wanted.

Modern critics often reproach the Athenians for limiting

their principles of freedom and equality to citizens only, but it is hardly reasonable to blame them for this. In antiquity a political community was conceived of as an enlarged family group, and citizenship therefore depended on descent. Foreigners who settled in another city did not become its citizens except by special act, even if they lived there for generations, any more than by living in Scotland you can become the member of a clan. At Athens there came to be a considerable population of foreigners, for it was an attractive place to settle, with its many-sided culture and thriving commercial life. According to the standards of the time, these foreigners were very well treated. They enjoyed the full protection of the law and shared the burdens of taxation and military service on an equal basis with the citizens. Their main disability was that they could not own land or houses – they could only rent them. But they certainly felt no grievance at not being admitted to the family group of Athenian citizens, and many of them were deeply attached to their adopted city, and assisted it generously in times of stress.

A second excluded class was women. But we can hardly be censorious on this as we only gave women the vote ourselves less than fifty years ago. The third and last excluded class was the slaves, and here again it would be unfair to condemn the Athenians for accepting an institution which the whole contemporary world took as a matter of course. The Athenians naturally owned slaves, and probably, being richer than most Greeks, they owned more slaves than the average community. There is no clear evidence how many slaves there were at Athens at any time – and the number undoubtedly varied. My own estimate is that in the fourth century there were about twenty thousand slaves, male and female. In the fifth century the number of slaves was certainly greater, but so was that of the citizen body. However, I must admit that many scholars would put the figure considerably higher.

Some critics have claimed that, because they owned slaves,

Athenian citizens were a privileged *élite* supported by the labour of a disfranchised majority. However high the real number of slaves may have been, this charge would still be untrue. Some rich Athenians – and resident aliens, for they, too, owned slaves – possessed large number of slaves who worked in factories and in particular in the silver mines, and lived on the profits which they drew from their labour. But the great majority of Athenians owned no slaves at all, or at most a domestic servant, or perhaps an assistant or two in the workshop or on the farm. The mass of Athenians were peasants cultivating little family holdings, or craftsmen working independently; the poorest were hired labourers. The Athenian assembly was composed, in Socrates' words, of 'laundrymen, shoemakers, carpenters, smiths, peasants, merchants, and shopkeepers', and it was precisely this fact that excited the ridicule of aristocratic critics. The Athenian democracy was not a sham. It was, it is true, limited to Athenians by descent, but the citizen body comprised all classes from the richest to the poorest, and it was the poor, the peasants and manual workers, who formed the majority.

The principle of equality was applied with remarkable thoroughness and consistency. In the first place all citizens – unless disfranchised for some offence, such as an unpaid debt to the treasury – were entitled to attend the assembly and vote, and if they wished, to make speeches and move amendments. The assembly's meeting place was in the open air, on the hill of the Pnyx, opposite the Acropolis: and as it met frequently – at least forty times a year – and decided both major questions of policy and the most minute administrative details, the ordinary citizen had ample opportunity of making his opinions felt, and a serious responsibility for the conduct of public affairs. The Greeks certainly had their doubts about the wisdom of entrusting vital decisions to the majority vote of a mass meeting, but democrats thought that the merits of the system outweighed its defects. In the first place they had a certain faith, not altogether unjustified by the results, in the collective wisdom of the masses. As Aristotle puts it:

A large number of men who are not individually good can nevertheless be better than the few best when they combine – not individually but as a whole, just as subscription dinners can be better than those provided at the expense of one person. For each of the number has a bit of virtue and judgement; and, by combining, the mass as it were becomes one man with many hands and feet and senses.

Secondly, they argued that in most political questions the ordinary citizen was the best judge of issues which affected his own welfare. Let us quote Aristotle again:

About some things it is not the maker who is the best or only judge: . . . for instance it is not a builder who can judge a house, the occupant will be better, and similarly a steersman is a better judge of a rudder than is a carpenter, and the guest a better critic of a meal than the cook.

Finally they held that while on technical questions the expert knows best, most political issues depended on moral considerations, and on these everyone was equally qualified to judge – for Zeus had implanted in all men a sense of decency and fair play. The assembly did listen to expert advice on technical questions, and indeed booed and shouted down speakers, however eloquent, who did not know their facts. But on general issues they listened to any speaker, noble or simple, rich or poor, thinking that they were all qualified and entitled to state their views. The Athenian assembly was occasionally swayed by mass emotion, and was capable of unjust and brutal decisions. Once it voted for the execution of the whole male population of the rebel city of Mytilene, but it was ashamed of its cruelty the next day and countermanded the order in time. And such ruthless acts were not peculiar to the assembly of Athens.

The great mass of business which came before the assembly could not be presented to it undigested. To prepare the agenda there was a steering committee, the council of Five Hundred. No question could be discussed or voted upon unless the council had, with due publicity, put it on the agenda, and snap votes of the assembly were thus precluded. The council also saved the assembly's time by preparing draft resolutions on uncontentious or technical issues. With such powers the council might have become an influential body, controlling policy and reducing the assembly to a rubber stamp: but its structure was so devised that this could not happen. The councillors were chosen annually by lot from all the wards of Athens and the villages of Attica, roughly in proportion to their population; and no citizen could serve more than twice in his life. Such a chance collection of citizens, which changed every year, could hardly develop any corporate sense: the council was in fact a fair sample of the whole citizen body. The system was useful in another way, since a very high proportion of the citizens must have served their turn on the council and thus gained useful experience of government.

Another important element in the constitution was the Law Courts, for they not only decided private cases, but conducted the routine examination of magistrates on the termination of their office, tried impeachments of generals and politicians, and were the ultimate arbiters of constitutional issues. Here too any citizen could take his part.

Finally the three hundred and fifty-odd magistrates who carried on the administration were nearly all chosen each year by lot, and no citizen might serve in the same office twice. Here most of us would be inclined to agree with Socrates:

It is absurd that the rulers of the city should be appointed by lot, when no one would be willing to employ a pilot or a carpenter or a flute-player selected by lot, though their mistakes cause far less harm than mistakes in public policy.

This system was not quite so absurd as it sounds. The ballot was drawn only among citizens who put in their names, and the Athenian people expected and exacted a high standard from its magistrates. Every magistrate – and for that matter every member of the council – was subjected after his year of office to a scrutiny, in which any citizen could charge him with misconduct. On the whole, therefore, only those citizens would put their names in for the ballot who were, in their own opinion at any rate, capable of coping with the duties involved. And these were of a fairly routine character, such that a man of average competence could fulfil them. For the Athenians were not so doctrinaire as to leave to chance the choice of the really responsible magistrates. The ten generals and a few other military officers were not appointed by lot but elected by the assembly, and for these posts there was no bar to re-election.

The Athenians regarded the lot system as one of the cornerstones of democracy. Election they considered to be an aristocratic rather than a democratic procedure, for, they argued, in an election the man who has a name, wealth, position, or a ready tongue will usually get in, and the ordinary man will stand little chance.

The lot was thus a key institution in maintaining equality. The other key institution was pay for political services. The jurors, the councillors, and the magistrates were all paid a daily wage, and so, in the fourth century, were citizens who attended the assembly. Thus no one was excluded by poverty from taking part in the government. In fact the pay was very meagre, about the wage of an unskilled labourer for magistrates and councillors, and half that sum for jurors. Since no citizen could serve on the council more than two years in his life, or any office more than once, and assemblies were only held forty or fifty days in the year, no Athenian could make a livelihood from state pay. He could only hope to get continuous employment as a juror, and here the pay was so meagre that it would attract only the destitute, or elderly men past active work.

The strangest thing about the Athenian constitution to our eyes was that there was nothing corresponding to a government in the modern sense of the word. There can be no doubt that the assembly controlled policy, and that the magistrates, even the generals, were its servants, who received strict and detailed orders and had to obey them. This is not to say that there were no political leaders; there were. Thucydides speaks of Athens in Pericles' day as 'nominally a democracy but really the rule of its leading man'. This is true in the sense that Pericles did guide Athenian policy during the last fifteen years of his life. But he did not do so in virtue of any constitutional powers. He governed by persuading the assembly to take each step that he advocated, and his ascendancy depended, as Thucydides says, on his moral authority.

The Athenians admitted that there was a place in their constitution for political leadership, and claimed that in this respect their constitution was an aristocracy in the literal sense of the word – the rule of the best men. As Pericles puts it in the Funeral Speech, all citizens have equal rights,

> But, when a man is distinguished in any way, he is more highly honoured in public life, not as a matter of privilege, but in recognition of merit: on the other hand anyone who can benefit the city is not debarred by poverty or by the obscurity of his position.

This last claim is perhaps exaggerated. Any aspirant to political power had a full-time job to keep himself informed on foreign affairs, public finance, and all the complex business of state, and without an unearned income he could hardly find the necessary time. In fact most leading Athenian statesmen were drawn from the old wealthy families. But it remained possible for a poor man to become a political leader, and we know of several who did, including Demosthenes, and his two great rivals, Aeschines and Demades.

It is difficult to believe that such a constitution can have worked at all. But the proof of the pudding is in the eating.

Athens was a great and successful state, the greatest in Greece in the fifth century, and even after her disastrous defeat in the Peloponnesian War, still one of the major powers. Her army was not outstanding, but no worse than those of most contemporary states; her navy was incomparably more efficient. She governed an empire and managed her finances with notable success. As far as administrative efficiency went, Athens was superior to most cities, and if the Athenian people made some serious political or strategic blunders, so do all governments.

By and large the Athenian democracy also maintained social justice at home. Greek political theorists were inclined to argue that since democracy meant the rule of the majority, and in any city the poor were the majority, democracy in fact meant the rule of the poor over the rich, and therefore the exploitation of the rich by the poor. Some rich Athenians made this complaint about Athens – and bitterly, to judge from a speech of Isocrates:

When I was a boy wealth was considered so secure and respected that practically everyone pretended to possess more property than he did in fact in his desire to gain this repute; but now one has to prepare a defence to prove that one is not rich as if it were a great crime and to walk warily if one is to be preserved. For the reputation of wealth is a far greater danger than manifest crime.

The charge is at any rate grossly exaggerated. The normal peace-time expenditure of Athens was covered by mining royalties, customs dues, and other indirect taxes. A direct property tax was only raised occasionally for war expenses, and from the few figures available the average annual rate was to our ideas absurdly low – equivalent to an income tax of about sixpence in the pound. The richest citizens had also to perform in rotation what were called liturgies, public duties involving expense. Notably they produced the choruses, tragedies, and comedies at the great festivals, paying the actors, dancers, and singers and providing the costumes and scenery; and they served as captains of the war-ships of the fleet, and had to maintain them in seaworthy condition. There were some who grumbled at these burdens, tried to shirk them, and skimped their expenditure when they had to take them. But most rich Athenians, it would seem, took a pride in maintaining a smart ship, or producing a well-acted play, and many spent more than they were legally obliged to spend.

The democracy did more than provide a high level of administrative efficiency and social justice. It gave the citizens a rich cultural life. The state itself created the great public buildings which are still accounted among the world's masterpieces and adorned them with sculptures whose battered remains are today the chief pride of the British Museum. The state itself produced the festivals of music and drama for which Aeschylus, Sophocles, and Euripides wrote their tragedies and Aristophanes his comedies. The tolerance of the democracy allowed free range to speculation and discussion of new ideas, and Athens not only produced great thinkers of her own, but attracted philosophers and scientists from all parts of the world.

The best proof that the democracy satisfied all classes is that it lasted almost unchanged for two centuries. During those two centuries there were only two counter-revolutions, that of the Four Hundred in 411 B.C., and that of the Thirty in 403 B.C. Both were organized by small cliques of oligarchic extremists, under the stress of a disastrous war. At first they won some support from the upper classes, but within a matter of months they were overthrown by mass risings of the citizens, rich and poor alike, and the democratic constitution was restored. It was only when they were crushed by a foreign power, Macedon, that the Athenians were finally compelled to abandon their democracy.

Bibliography

Athens
JONES, A. H. M., *Athenian Democracy*, Basil Blackwell, 1957, reprinted 1960
Sparta
MICHELL, H., *Sparta*, Cambridge University Press, 1952
General
EHRENBERG, VICTOR, *The Greek State*, Basil Blackwell, 1960

4 Greek Literature after Homer

K. J. Dover
Professor of Greek, University of St. Andrews

Most Greek literature is lost. Out of nearly four thousand
plays produced at Athens in a space of two centuries, less than
fifty have come down to us intact. Of some fifty historians
who wrote during that same period, we have the works of
only three; of lyric poetry, only a tiny fraction is available to
us in readable form. The rest perished slowly in the closing
centuries of the Roman Empire, when the Graeco-Roman
cultural unity of the Mediterranean broke down, Christian
society made different demands upon the educated man, and
Christian theology absorbed intellectual energies. It was not
until the ninth century A.D. that interest in pagan antiquity
woke again in Byzantium; then, books which had survived
from an earlier age were sought out, studied, copied, and multi-
plied. Medieval Byzantium never again lost interest in the
pagan past; Byzantine culture was the bridge which led from
the Ancient Greeks down to the era of printing and thus to
our own day. We know a lot about what we have lost; part
of this knowledge is owed to quotations and references in the
surviving literature, and part to the papyrus fragments which
have been discovered in great numbers during the last seventy
years and have provided the same lively stimulus to the historian of literature as the uncovering of buried buildings and
pottery has provided to the archaeologist. On the whole it is
fair to say that the literature which survived to the end of the
Roman Empire and was brought to light by the Byzantines
early in the Middle Ages owed its survival to its quality; it
represented the authors who had for long been most read and
most admired. So it happens that Greek literature differs in

one striking respect from all modern literatures: practically all of it that is available for us to read is first-rate; time has swallowed up the rest.

The most striking characteristic of Greek literature is that we do not feel, in reading it and listening to it, that Greek writers were trying, in a primitive way, to do something which we have learnt to do better. Their response to people and things was in some ways simpler, in other ways more subtle, than ours. The Greek writer, like the Greek sculptor, was more interested in creating what ought to exist than in portraying what does; but his idea of what ought to exist was always based on an acceptance of human life as he found it. He was a perfectionist in technique, and intolerant of work that did not measure up to the highest technical standards; the idea that self-expression might be in itself artistically valuable would have seemed strange to him.

It is convenient to describe Greek literature in terms of three great stages or periods: the Archaic period, down to (roughly) 500 B.C.; the Classical period, from 500 to about 300 B.C.; and the Hellenistic period, thereafter to the end of the Ancient World. These periods correspond to similar divisions which suggest themselves in the political history of the Greeks and in their visual arts. The Classical period is the heart of Greek literature. It was during those two centuries from 500 to 300 B.C. that most types of literature took shape and grew to maturity. It was during the same two centuries that Athens became the cultural centre of the Greek world; and a very high proportion of Classical Greek literature – not of Archaic or Hellenistic literature – is Athenian.

The great achievement of the Archaic period was in lyric poetry. This poetry was designed for singing or recitation; some of it solo, with comparatively simple and repetitive patterns of verse, some for a chorus, with verse patterns which are sometimes extremely complex. The Greeks, like any other people, had always sung. The lyric poets were not so much inventing a new kind of poetry as transforming folk song into a literary art, and they were the first individuals in Europe who left short poems to posterity in writing. In this poetry we meet many elements which endured as characteristics of Greek poetry in general. One is the way in which myths about a heroic age – about Helen of Troy, the wanderings of Odysseus, or the strange fate of Oedipus – are taken for granted. These heroes and heroines were real and intimate to the Greeks; they were worshipped in the localities where they were believed to have lived or travelled, and many of them were the reputed ancestors of contemporary noble families. A second characteristic is a love of moralizing. When the two characteristics are combined, we have a myth used as an example or as an argument. The frequent use of the same myths, and the frequent pointing of the same morals, are saved from monotony by the Greek poet's very sharp eye for colour and movement, a capacity for complete absorption in a scene, a readiness to digress into details irrelevant to his ostensible theme, and an imagination which often takes an unexpected direction. Here is a typical solo lyric poem of Sappho, a woman who lived on the island of Lesbos about 600 B.C.; one of the verses is missing, and I have patched up the hole with a few words which accord with the drift of the poem:

> What is fairest on the dark face of earth?
> Some say, a host of horsemen; some say, soldiers;
> and some say, ships; but I say: what you love.
> This is easy to prove; who could not see it?
> She who surpassed mankind in beauty, Helen,
> left her kindly husband, and gave no thought
> to child or parents, sailing off to Troy.
> For Love so led her, and his will was hers.
> And Love puts Anaktoria in my mind.
> For I would rather see her lovely step,
> her sparkling face, than all the chariots
> of Lydia and men battling in full armour.

The greatest of the writers of choral lyric – in fact, the last great writer of choral lyric – Pindar, who came from Boeotia, lived in the early part of the Classical period. Most of his poems were composed to be sung at festivals or celebrations; for example, an annual procession to a particular temple, or an individual's celebration of a victory in the Olympic Games. Pindar's language is deliberately elaborate, and he has a certain liking for the oblique and the enigmatic. Here is a passage in which he is delicately approaching the subject of an exile, a friend of his, who wants to return to his native land; the poem is addressed to the ruler of that land, in whose power the decision on the exile's return lies:

> Lop the branches
> of a great oak
> with a sharp axe
> and mar its lovely shape;
> though its fruit is wasted,
> if ever it comes
> to a winter fire
> in after time
> it asks your judgement on its worth;
> or if ranged
> in a row of pillars
> it bears the weight
> of servitude,
> a mournful task
> in alien walls,
> leaving its own place empty.

But by Pindar's time poetry had begun to mean something besides lyric or epic. Not very long before 500 B.C. someone – we do not really know who – made a chorus and an actor represent and enact a portion of heroic legend instead of simply singing about it, and this created drama. In the hands of Aeschylus, an almost exact contemporary of Pindar and a profoundly original dramatist with a flair for the spectacular,

83

tragedy developed with remarkable speed. Aeschylus is one of the three great names of Athenian tragedy; the other two, Sophocles and Euripides, both died a few years before 400 B.C., some fifty years after Aeschylus. The subject matter of tragedy was occasionally historical – Aeschylus, for example, produced a play, only eight years after the event, about Xerxes' invasion of Greece – but usually it was heroic legend, and different dramatists would handle the same legend in different ways. So, for example, Aeschylus portrayed the murder of Clytemnestra (who had murdered her husband) by their son Orestes, in such a way as to involve in the action fearful supernatural forces. Sophocles accepted the story as the kind of thing that happened to heroes and heroines. Euripides, profoundly interested in the moral and aesthetic issues, aroused the pity of the audience for Clytemnestra and Orestes alike, and aroused also their mistrust of a tradition which represented a god as commanding so monstrous an action as matricide.

Although psychologically realistic, tragedy was often extremely formal in expression. The presence of a chorus throughout the play was the source of many dramatic conventions alien to our own practice, for it is not easy to fit a part for a chorus into every legend. Dialogue was often cast into the form of a strictly regulated debate, line answering line and couplet answering couplet. Here is a passage from the *Antigone* of Sophocles. It occurs at a moment of crisis; Antigone is threatened with death by Creon, the ruler of Thebes, because she has buried her brother Polynices. Polynices had attacked Thebes, and her other brother, Eteocles, defended it; both brothers perished; Creon gave Eteocles an honourable burial, but forbade anyone to bury Polynices. Part of the dialogue between Antigone and Creon, in swift and telling blow and counter blow, goes like this:

CREON: Your eyes alone see this, but not the people's.
ANTIGONE: They see it; fear of you has curbed their tongues.
CREON: You feel no shame that their way is not yours?

ANTIGONE: There is no shame in piety to kindred.
CREON: Is he no kin, that died in our defence?
ANTIGONE: He is my kin; our parents were the same.
CREON: Your pious gift was impious towards him.
ANTIGONE: The dead man's voice will not uphold that plea.
CREON: Not if you honour the impious no less!
ANTIGONE: It was no slave, it was his brother that died!
CREON: Wasting this land – which Eteocles defended!
ANTIGONE: What's that to Death? I did what Death demands.
CREON: The good demand more honour than the bad.
ANTIGONE: Does Death give that his blessing? Who can say?
CREON: No man that earned our hate earns love by dying.
ANTIGONE: I love with him that loves, but hate I cannot.
CREON: Go then below, and love the dead, if you must love. No
  woman rules me while I live.

Although heroic legend is full of battle and murder and
suicide, it was a dramatic convention that physical violence
should not be represented on the stage. The Greeks preferred
it to be described in a narrative speech by a messenger, and the
following excerpt comes from a long and powerful messenger
speech in the *Bacchae* of Euripides. It describes how Pentheus,
who had opposed the introduction into Thebes of the worship
of Dionysus, was torn to pieces by his own mother and her
sisters; they were inspired by Dionysus and believed that they
were destroying a wild animal (an actual feature, at some time
and places, of Dionysiac worship).

He touched her face, and cried, 'I am your son!
O Mother, I am Pentheus, whom you bore
in Echion's palace! Mother, pity me!
Do not, for my sin, murder your own son!'
Her lips were foaming, and her eyes in madness
twisted and rolled. Her mind was hers no more –
the god possessed her. Vain were Pentheus' words.
She grasped his left arm, planted firm her feet
on the poor creature's ribs, wrenched out his shoulder –
not by her strength; it was the god who filled

85

her hands with power. And on the other side
Ino fell to her work, tearing his flesh.
Autonoe and all the Bacchanals
pounced to attack, and a great noise of cries
was blended, as he screamed with all his breath,
they yelled in triumph. One bore off his arm,
and one his sandalled foot; and all his ribs
were bare and stripped. Then all the Bacchanals
with bloody hands played ball with Pentheus' flesh.

In comedy we enter a rather different world from this. What is called the Old Comedy – Aristophanes was the most notable of its poets – was firmly rooted in the events and fashions of its own day. An Aristophanic comedy does not have a 'plot' in the ordinary sense of the word; it builds wild fantasies on the basis of a topical idea, and its humour relies greatly on literary parody and satirical comment on living people. Here is a passage from the *Acharnians*, in which penetrating political criticism is blended with a delightful caricature of Greek ideas about the 'wondrous East'. An ambassador is reporting to the Assembly on his return from a mission to the King of Persia, and the interjections come from a hard-headed farmer Dicaeopolis. I have added what seem to me to be the appropriate stage directions:

AMBASSADOR [*pompously*]: You sent our mission to the King of
    Persia,
    [*a little hurriedly*] with an allowance of two pounds a day,
    [*previous manner*] twelve years ago.
DICAEOPOLIS [*anguished*]: The money!
AMBASSADOR [*affected and languid*]: We were exhausted
    by the long journey on the Caÿstrian plains,
    all under cover, lying in carriages –
    too pampered – it was very bad for us!
DICAEOPOLIS: It must have done a world of good to me
    to lie in muck, guarding the walls at home.
AMBASSADOR: They entertained us; we simply had to drink,

from gold and crystal goblets, such strong wine,
[*ruminatively*] . . . very good wine.

DICAEOPOLIS [*deep tragic voice*]: O city of our fathers!
You see how these men make a fool of you?

AMBASSADOR [*defensively*]: Persians have no respect except for those
who eat and drink the most.

DICAEOPOLIS: We only respect
those who can – you know what – front-ways and back!

AMBASSADOR [*pompously*]: In the fourth year we reached the Royal
Palace.
We found the King had gone, with a great army,
to the lavatory. And he relieved himself
for eight whole months upon the Golden Mountains.

DICAEOPOLIS: How long before he pulled his trousers up?
The full moon, I suppose?

AMBASSADOR: Then he returned
and entertained us, setting on the table
whole oxen baked in ovens . . .

In Aristophanic comedy there was no limit, in word or
action, to obscenity; the wording of the passage given has been
toned down in translation. It is unlikely that this absence of
inhibition is owed to the fertility rituals with which comedy
may have had an ancestral connexion, for the humorous poetry
of the Archaic period and vase paintings of scenes from daily
life are equally uninhibited. Comedy ridiculed gods as well as
men, for gods were regarded as enjoying dramatic festivals
with an essentially human enjoyment and had to take a joke
against themselves; the people who were the audience of
comedy were ready to condemn to death anyone who taught
publicly that the gods did not exist. Living men were not
only ridiculed but grossly slandered in comedy; Aristophanes
appears to have been free to bring any accusation, however
monstrous or cruel or indecent, against anybody.

In the latter part of the Classical period the sting went out
of comedy, and so did the fantasy, the obscenity, and the
blasphemy. By 300 B.C. the typical Greek comedy represented

typical Greek families and individuals involved in the strange operations of Chance. This was the kind of comedy which was later adopted by the Romans and so may be reckoned the ancestor of Shakespeare's *Comedy of Errors*.

Now, the lively ferocity which was so characteristic of the Old Comedy is strongly reflected in Greek oratory. To the average Greek, oratory was the most important and interesting type of prose literature, and the literary critics of Hellenistic times show a certain tendency to treat it as the standard by which other kinds of literature should be measured. To the modern reader it is perhaps the least congenial part, and certainly the least read and studied part, of Greek literature. The reason for this difference in taste and interest lies in the great differences between the Greek city state and the modern nation. Most Greek communities, whether they were democracies or confined political power to a small section of the citizen body, depended for their working on the direct and immediate persuasion of gatherings of people, and the Greeks naturally applied themselves with immense thoroughness, and with their usual gift for turning anything they handled into an art, to the technique of persuasion. A Greek speech, whether designed for a law court or a political assembly, is what a barrister's speech would be if the barrister were addressing a large jury with no judge in control and no possibility of cross-examination. The Greek orator is not concerned to tell us the truth; he is concerned to win – often, that is, to secure the downfall of his enemy or save his own skin, because it was always possible to prosecute men for political mistakes or improprieties, and the death penalty was inflicted very freely. To this end the orator will use invective, ridicule, exaggeration, and every means of swaying the audience's emotions or diverting its attention from sequences of thought which are unwelcome to him. Here is an excerpt from the speech of Demosthenes against his enemy Midias; the speaker is cleverly exploiting the jury's prejudices:

I understand that certain wealthy men are proposing to ask you, as a mark of gratitude for their services to the community, to acquit Midias. Now, I don't wish to say anything offensive about these gentlemen to you – that would be absurd – but I will tell you what you should consider and turn over in your minds when they put their request to you. Just reflect: if it should happen – pray God it will not; I am sure it will not – but if it should happen that these men, with Midias and others like him, were masters of our nation, and one of you, an ordinary man of the people, committed some offence against one of them – not the kind of offence which Midias has committed against me, but anything else you like – and were brought before a jury composed of *them*, do you think he would get any sympathy? Do you think he would get a hearing? They'd be so nice to him, wouldn't they? Would they lend an ear to an ordinary man's entreaty? Wouldn't they say at once, 'This scum, this pest, this man to commit an outrage and still breathe? He's lucky if we let him live!' Men who would deal with you in this way you must not treat in any other way. You must respect not their wealth or their prestige, but your own selves. They enjoy much from the possession of which no one debars them; let them not debar us from possession of that security which the law assures to all of us as our common heritage.

Oratory, as a literary art, was a product of Greek life; it had its roots in practical politics and in the law courts. But the Greeks were not entirely a practical people. They developed, to a higher degree than any people before them, the capacity for being interested in people and things. This curiosity of theirs manifested itself above all in history and philosophy. The first historians, early in the Classical period, seem to have been interested, characteristically, in genealogies and in the systematization of the legends of the heroic age. History, as we understand the term, was the creation of Herodotus. Herodotus took as the core of his subject the defeat by the Greeks of the great Persian invasion of Greece; but he treated this subject in a leisurely, discursive manner, going back sixty years for the antecedents of the invasion and digressing at great length to tell us, for example, about the animals of Libya or Egyptian religion or the geography of the Ukraine. Depending as he does on tradition handed down by word of mouth, he often seems to be giving us the raw material of history and not the finished product of the historian. He says on one occasion:

It is my duty to tell what is told; to believe it is no part of my duty,

a remark in which, I think, he does himself less than justice, for he can on occasion criticize traditions with acumen, though his fundamental belief in divine intervention sets a limit to argument from cause and effect. Here is a typical, lively passage in which he relates how Cyrus, king of Persia, was killed in battle against the Massagetai, a tribe of Turkistan, and their formidable queen Tomyris:

As Cyrus paid no heed to her message, Tomyris assembled all her forces and joined battle with him. This battle I judge to be the mightiest of all those ever fought between foreign peoples; and I learn that this is what happened. It is said that they began by firing arrows at each other from a distance, and then, when all their shafts had been shot, they fell to and came to grips, with spear and dagger. For a long time they were locked in battle, and neither side would flee; but in the end the Massagetai prevailed. The greater part of the Persian army perished on the field, and Cyrus himself died; he had been king for twenty-nine years in all. Tomyris filled a wineskin with human blood and sought the body of Cyrus among the Persian dead; and when she found it, she cast his head into the skin of blood. And she mutilated his body and insulted it, saying 'You have destroyed me, though I live and have conquered you in battle, in that you killed my son by treachery; but you, as I threatened, I will sate with blood.' Many stories are told of the end of Cyrus's life, but the most credible is this that I have told.

The Massagetai wear clothing similar to that of the Scythians, and have a similar way of life. They fight both on horseback and on foot, and both with arrows and with spears; it is their custom to carry battleaxes. . . .

The historian Thucydides, who began to take notes for a history of the great war of his own day just about the time that Herodotus was finishing, was a man with a very different approach to his task. He does more than 'tell what is told'; he digests his material and makes it his own; and his view of his work, as he expresses it himself, sounds peculiarly ambitious:

I shall be content if my work is judged useful by those who want a clear picture of what has happened and what is likely to happen in the future, mankind being what it is, in essentially similar form.

This belief in the practical utility of history is reflected in Thucydides' peculiar ability to analyse and describe the motives and feelings of armies and peoples and parties. Here, for example, is his comment on a group which had temporarily seized political power in Athens:

This was the form which they gave to their argument for popular consumption; but the majority of them, ambitious for personal advancement, had embarked on that course of action which, more than any other, brings to grief an oligarchy which has succeeded a democracy. From the first day, every member thinks that, so far from merely having equal rights with the other members, he should himself be at their head – whereas in a democracy a man bears the results of an election with greater equanimity, not feeling that he is worsted by his peers. What had the greatest effect on them was the strength of Alcibiades' position at Samos, and the fact that they did not really believe that the power of the oligarchy would last; therefore each individual strove to outdo all the rest, and to be acknowledged as champion of the people. Those of the Four Hundred who were most strongly opposed to such a policy, and were the leaders of the oligarchy. . . .

If Thucydides had interpreted his declared purpose too narrowly, he might have been a rather dull historian; but fortunately a historian's 'philosophy of history' does not always obtrude when he is intellectually excited by the process of discovering the facts, and Thucydides possessed to a very marked degree the Greek ability to find things interesting. For good measure, he was also an artist, and some of his narratives are of incomparable power. Curiously enough, although he stands quite near the beginnings of historical writing, Greek civilization did not produce, in the centuries that followed, another historian of the same quality. Possibly this was because after about 400 B.C. it was philosophy, not history, which attracted men of first-rate intellectual ability. It is significant that Polybius, the only man among the Hellenistic historians who can be compared with Thucydides in respect of historical technique (he is certainly not comparable in artistry), shows traces of philosophical preoccupations which are absent from Thucydides.

Philosophical writing began among the Greeks about the same time as historical writing. The earliest philosophers tended to express themselves in an oracular manner, imitating the poets – some of them, indeed, wrote in verse, continuing at a higher intellectual level an Archaic tradition of didactic and moralizing poetry – and throughout the first half of the Classical period the philosopher was expected to expound rather than to argue. Then, shortly after 400 B.C., Plato developed one of the most remarkable and fruitful ideas in the history of literature. He gave philosophy a dramatic form, and represented two or more characters arguing together, sometimes from irreconcilable standpoints, sometimes in cooperation. The main character is usually Socrates, who had not himself left any philosophical writings. The realistic conversational form of Plato's work, aided by the skill with which he sets the dramatic scene and leads us gently and naturally into the problem, gives us the illusion that we are ourselves taking part in a search for the answer to a philosophical question. Inquiry by literary historians into the ancestry of the Platonic dialogue has yielded very meagre results, and it seems essentially to be Plato's own invention. Here is a characteristic passage from the *Republic*:

GLAUCON: Socrates, do you want it just to seem that you've convinced us, or do you hope that you've really convinced us that being honest is better in every way than being dishonest?

SOCRATES: I'd prefer, if it were for me to choose, really to convince you.

GLAUCON: Well then, you're not achieving what you want to. Tell me: do you think that there's a kind of good which is acceptable to us not because its *consequences* are desirable but because we are glad of it for its own sake – enjoyment, for example, and the harmless pleasures, things which don't have any result later but are just enjoyable at the time?

SOCRATES: Yes, I agree that that kind of good does exist.

GLAUCON: Well, what about the good which we like both for its own sake and because of its consequences? Thinking, for example, and seeing, and health? We are glad of things like that for both reasons, aren't we?

SOCRATES: Oh, yes.

GLAUCON: Can you distinguish, then, a third kind of good, which includes physical exercise, and undergoing treatment when you're ill, and practising medicine, and making a living in general? We would naturally say that these procedures are tedious, but are to our advantage, and they're not acceptable to us for their own sake but because of the money one earns or whatever other consequences they have.

SOCRATES: Yes, this is certainly a third type. But what follows from that?

GLAUCON: In which category do you put honesty?

SOCRATES: I should say, in the best of the three, those which a man must like both for their own sake and for their consequences, if he's going to live the kind of life one wants to have.

GLAUCON: Well, that's not what most people think; they reckon it belongs to the tedious kind of good, which has to be pursued in order to earn a wage, or, for appearance's sake, to be well thought of.

SOCRATES: I know that's what people think, and Thrasymachus has been attacking honesty all the time on the grounds that it's that type of good, and he's been commending dishonesty, but I'm afraid I'm rather a slow learner.

GLAUCON: Well, now listen to what I've got to say, and see if you still think as you did. I think Thrasymachus gave up much too quickly; you had an effect like a snake-charmer on him. . . .

This brief survey of Greek literature has devoted far more space to the two centuries of the Classical period than to the eight centuries of the Hellenistic period. This does not mean that there were no good creative writers in Greek after 300 B.C.; the reason lies rather in the self-consciousness of the Hellenistic period and in its relation to what had gone before. Hellenistic poetry, as it were, fills in the corners which the Classical poets had left empty. At its worst, this approach to poetry meant that traditional themes continued to be treated within the framework of traditional literary forms, but were elaborated by the pursuit of detail and the extension of the poetic vocabulary, as for an audience more scholarly and knowledgeable, more detached and sceptical in its attitude to legend, and less responsive to the immediate impact of great emotional issues, than the audiences of Classical times. At its best – and the best of Hellenistic poetry is represented by Theocritus and Callimachus at the beginning of the period – it exploited moods and aspects of life which Classical poetry, comparatively speaking, had neglected. These poets combine an extraordinary technical virtuosity with what can only be described as playfulness. In prose, the outstanding original achievements of the Hellenistic age were in biography, literary criticism, and (late in the day) the romantic novel.

But the essential characteristic of the Hellenistic age as a whole was its own awareness and acknowledgement of the Classical period as a model and of the Classical authors as unsurpassable. When we today put Sophocles or Aristophanes or Thucydides or Plato in the centre of the study and enjoyment of Greek literature, we are simply recognizing what the Greeks themselves were quick to recognize. I say 'study' deliberately, because when we take up the work of a writer who belongs to any time or place other than our own we cannot always know what he is talking about unless we take the trouble to find out. But the freshness and directness of Greek literature are such that the reward of study is the intensification of enjoyment, and the barrier which two thousand years seemed at first to interpose vanishes.

Bibliography

The reader who wants to know more about Greek literature should first of all, and above all, read some of it, and only then read books about it. The translations which have been published in the Penguin Classics series are a good starting-point, and the Loeb Classical Library, in which the Greek and English texts are on opposite pages, offers a very wide range of authors. Also to be recommended are the translation of *Herodotus* by POWELL (Oxford), of *Thucydides* by CRAWLEY (London), of *Plato* by JOWETT (Oxford; revised edition in four volumes), of *Pindar* by LATTIMORE (Chicago), and of the *Greek Bucolic Poets* by GOW (Cambridge).

A high proportion of the most perceptive, scholarly, and interesting books on Greek Literature (as well as a fair proportion of the most extravagant and perverse) is in German, and A. LESKY'S *Geschichte der griechischen Literatur* (Vienna) gives the best modern conspectus of the whole subject. Among modern works in English, the reader is likely to find the following useful and interesting:

ARNOTT, P. D., *An Introduction to the Greek Theatre*, Macmillan, 1959

BALDRY, H. C., *Greek Literature for the Modern Reader*, Cambridge University Press, 1960

BOWRA, SIR MAURICE, *Greek Lyric Poetry*, 2nd ed., Oxford University Press, 1961

FLICKINGER, R. C., *The Greek Theatre and its Drama*, 4th ed., Chicago University Press, 1946

GRUBE, G. M. A., *The Drama of Euripides*, 2nd ed., Methuen, 1941

HUDSON WILLIAMS, H. L., *Three Systems of Education*, Oxford

LUCAS, D. W., *The Greek Tragic Poets*, 2nd ed., Cohen & West, 1959

PLATNAUER, M., (Ed) *Fifty Years of Classical Scholarship*, Blackwell, 1955, Chapters I–VIII

ROSE, H. J., *Handbook of Greek Literature*, 4th ed., Methuen, 1961

SNELL, B., *The Discovery of the Mind*, Blackwell, 1953

TAYLOR, A. E., *Plato: the Man and his Work*, Methuen, 1952

TURNER, E. G., *Athenian Books in the Fifth and Fourth Centuries B.C.*, H. K. Lewis, 1952

5 Greek Tragedy: Sophocles' *Women of Trachis*

Hugh Lloyd-Jones
Regius Professor of Greek, Oxford University

Greek tragedy is a form of drama with laws of its own, different from those of any other kind of drama, including those which its influence has helped to shape. We can see that these laws must have been conditioned by the peculiar circumstances of its origin, obscure as that origin unfortunately is. During the seventh and six centuries before Christ there developed in the Peloponnese a great tradition of lyric poetry written for performance by a chorus. Meanwhile on the coast of Asia Minor and in the islands of the Aegean other verse forms developed which were closer to the rhythms of ordinary speech. It was a certain Thespis, a native of the Attic deme of Icaria, who added to the choral lyric performances on a heroic theme a prologue and set speeches written in these more colloquial kinds of verse. These were delivered by a person called the *hypokrites*, which some take to mean 'the answerer', but which more probably means 'the interpreter'; if 'the interpreter' is correct, the *hypokrites* was thought of as interpreting the words and dances of the chorus with their accompanying music. Words, dance, and music were all the work of the poet, who in the earliest period was himself the *hypokrites*; that word became the regular Greek term for actor. About 534 B.C. a performance of tragedy became a regular feature of the festival held at Athens late in March of each year in honour of the god Dionysus.

These performances seem to have been developed into something which could properly be called drama by the great poet Aeschylus, who lived from about 525 to 456 B.C. Out of some eighty plays of his, only seven have been preserved complete; many fragments are known from quotations in other authors, and others from modern discoveries of papyri. He was the first to use two actors, each of whom might play more than one part; a third was added later, probably by Sophocles in the sixties of the fifth century. It became the practice for an officer of the state to choose each year three poets to compete for the tragic prizes at the Dionysiac festival. Each trained a chorus and actors, his expenses being paid by some rich citizen; each was required to exhibit a group of three tragedies, together with a satyr play, a shorter entertainment that contained a strong burlesque element. Performances took place in the open air, in the theatre of Dionysus, which stands on a slope of the Athenian Acropolis, inside the precinct of the god.

We are unable to form any clear notion of the development of tragedy before the second quarter of the fifth century. One surviving play of Aeschylus, the *Suppliant Women*, was until lately thought by most scholars to be as early as 500 B.C.; but a few years ago there appeared a new papyrus fragment which makes it almost certain that it belongs to the sixties of the fifth century. A few fragments give us a faint impression of Aeschylus' older contemporary, Phrynichus, whose lyrics had a soft and voluptuous beauty that shows marked affinity with the great lyric poets of Ionian Greece. Like other tragedians, Phrynichus took most of his themes from the heroic legends of the epic age. But he also wrote one tragedy about the sack of Miletus by the Persians in 494 B.C. and another about the defeat of their expedition against Greece in 480 B.C.; and on at least one occasion Aeschylus followed him in choosing a contemporary subject. *The Persians*, produced in 472 B.C., is the earliest surviving complete tragedy; in it Aeschylus followed Phrynichus in describing how the news of the defeat at Salamis was received at the Persian court. By modern standards this play is markedly undramatic; it can scarcely be said to have a plot; much of it consists of the lyrics sung by the

D

chorus of Persian elders, who express anxious foreboding at the start, extol the past victories of Persia, and bitterly lament the disasters of the campaign of Xerxes. The remaining six complete plays of Aeschylus all differ from *The Persians* in dealing with heroic legends and in forming part of trilogies upon continuous themes; three of them, *Agamemnon*, *The Libation-bearers*, and *The Eumenides* make up the *Oresteia*, the only trilogy that survives complete.

In most tragedies the chorus delivered four or five lyrics of some length, written in complicated metre and elevated style and sung and danced to the accompaniment of the poet's own music. The loss of this dance and music is much to be regretted, for they formed an important element of the performance. Choral lyric might express wild rejoicing or bitter lamentation, phrased in language that clearly owed much to the prayers and hymns used in the worship of the gods. In Aeschylus the chorus is often closely involved in the action of the play; among later dramatists, its connexion with this tended to be looser; but in general it supplied a kind of commentary on the action from a more exalted level than that of the actors. Dialogue was in metres simpler and closer to the rhythms of ordinary speech and in language less elevated than those of lyric, but it was still very far removed from the naturalistic dialogue of a modern play. Sometimes it was of an extremely artificial kind, with each character speaking one line or two lines at a time in alternation; but there were also conversations between actors who made longer speeches, and sometimes debates or altercations that might include speeches of some seventy lines each. Towards the end of a play, off-stage action might be reported by a messenger; and the messengers' speeches, like the debates and altercations, gave splendid opportunities for the displays of rhetoric which a Greek audience seems to have enjoyed as much as anything. The Greek poets seldom ended their plays upon a note of climax. They liked to bring their audience gently down from the highest pitch of emotional intensity, and tragic events are often followed by a scene of lamentation and then a quiet close. The actors of tragedy wore masks and an elaborate costume with flowing robes very unlike the everyday dress of the fifth century. No form of art could be less naturalistic than Athenian tragedy; Euripides, who is sometimes produced in translation as though he were a naturalistic dramatist, is even less of one than Sophocles.

A tragedy presented almost always an episode taken from the large body of heroic legend which the Greeks had inherited from their epic age; its characters are the heroes descended from the gods, and sometimes the gods themselves. The world of Aeschylus and Sophocles is as like that of Homer as they knew how to make it. But under the persisting influence of nineteenth-century romanticism, modern interpretation has tended to play down this affinity with the ancient epic. It has preferred to exaggerate the closeness of tragedy's relations to its contemporary world, and even to read into it ethical and religious notions which are not known to have existed in the fifth century B.C. Rightly perceiving the importance of the moral and religious ideas which tragedy presupposes, it has gone wrong by trying to make these out more complicated, more 'original', and more 'advanced' – that is, more like our own – than the facts give us any warrant to suppose. Evidence for this statement is supplied by all the most widely used handbooks on the subject written in English; and more than one distinguished modern dramatist has been deeply influenced by a conception of Greek tragedy which, however fruitful in its effects, is wholly untrue to facts.

Tragedy formed part of a festival in honour of a god. Each story from heroic saga is so told as to illuminate the relation of man to the gods and to the universe. The heroes are descended from gods, and gods may have their favourites among them; but it is the gods' own concerns, not those of men, that are uppermost in their minds. To their favourites they will give

99

help; but those who anger them by refusing them honour they will ruthlessly destroy. Over gods and men alike is Zeus, whose will is inscrutable but will always be accomplished; a stern and arbitrary ruler, but one whom mankind in general has reason to thank for maintaining in the government of the universe his own harsh justice. The man who wrongs another must be done to as he did; the foolish man, who fails to see that this is Zeus' law, will learn by bitter experience, he or his children after him. Wisdom for men consists in knowing their place, in remembering their insignificance in face of the immortal gods. The men we see in action are the great heroes of the epic world, occupied in the pursuit of glory by their valiant deeds against foreign enemies, robbers, or legendary monsters. The heroes are men favoured by the gods; yet even a hero may draw down on himself, in his pride, the anger of a god, perhaps of Zeus himself, and then the god destroys him.

Three of the Aeschylean trilogies that survive in whole or in part show the law of Zeus' justice at work in the history of one of the great families of heroic legend. The *Suppliant Women* is the first play of a trilogy which told how the fifty daughters of Danaus fled from their home in Egypt to the home of their ancestors in Argos, rather than submit to marriage with their cousins, the fifty sons of Aegyptus. The Argives tried to protect them, but were unsuccessful; the Danaids had to submit to marriage, but on the wedding night all but one of them murdered their bridegrooms. The one Danaid who spared her husband survived persecution by her father and sisters to become the ancestress of the kings of Argos. *The Seven Against Thebes* is the last play of a trilogy that told how the curse laid upon Laius, king of Thebes, destroyed in succession Laius himself, his son Oedipus, and his grandsons Eteocles and Polynices. When the play begins the sons of Oedipus have quarrelled over the throne, and Polynices with an Argive army is besieging his native city. Eteocles is, from one aspect, the heroic defender of his country against the foreign invader;

but from another he is the inheritor of the curse of Laius, and is bound to perish. The details of the lost plays are not known, but it is most improbable that the curse upon Laius was presented as an arbitrary decree of the gods. Laius had caused the death of Chrysippus, the son of King Pelops, and Pelops' curse upon him was fulfilled by the agency of Zeus' law of justice. So in the one complete trilogy, the *Oresteia*, the curse laid upon Atreus, King of Argos, by his brother Thyestes was accomplished by the workings of divine justice. Atreus' son, Agamemnon, the great ruler who led the Greek expedition against Troy, was at the outset compelled by the goddess Artemis to sacrifice to her his own daughter. In her desire for revenge his wife, Clytemnestra, plotted with Thyestes' only surviving son to kill her husband; and in the first play of the trilogy, *Agamemnon*, their purpose is accomplished. In *The Libation-bearers*, Clytemnestra and her lover in turn fall victims to the curse when her son, Orestes, returns to Argos to take revenge. *The Eumenides* takes its name from the euphemistic title, 'The Kindly Ones', given to the terrible daemonic beings who were the agents of Zeus' vengeance upon the killers of their own kin, more commonly known as the Erinyes. They pursue Orestes to avenge his mother's blood; Apollo, who through his oracle at Delphi has made known to Orestes the will of Zeus that he shall kill his mother, gives him protection. Orestes takes refuge in Athens, where the conflicting deities agree to submit the case for judgement by Athene presiding over the tribunal of her city, the council of the Areopagus. Both parties have a case, and in the end the knot is cut by an arbitrary decision of Athene. The Erinyes threaten revenge upon Athene's city, but are mollified by the promise of a special cult on the Athenian Acropolis. We have seen Zeus' law of reciprocal justice at work through three generations; but it is idle to suppose that any problem has been solved, or that the primitive custom of the vendetta is from now on replaced by the justice of the *polis*.

The other surviving play of Aeschylus, *Prometheus Bound*, describes how Prometheus, a god of an older generation than that of Zeus, the benefactor and according to the common legend the creator of mankind, was punished by Zeus for having given men fire. Nailed to a rock upon a solitary mountain peak in the Caucasus, where an eagle comes daily to feed upon his liver, Prometheus continues to defy his tormentor. His only weapon is the knowledge of a secret that he refuses to yield up in face of Zeus' threats; Zeus is one day fated to love a goddess whose son will prove mightier than his father. The play ends with Prometheus being swept down to Hades to endure further tortures while still proclaiming his defiance. We know that another play, *The Release of Prometheus*, followed this one; we do not know if the two plays came first and second in their trilogy or second and third, and we cannot be sure that the third play of the trilogy was ever written. Nor do we know the exact details of how Zeus came to acquiesce in his enemy's release. Some scholars hold that, during the immensely long interval between Prometheus' binding and his release, Zeus has become a reformed character, so that he regrets his treatment of Prometheus. It is likelier that in the end Zeus and Prometheus struck a bargain, in which Prometheus used his knowledge of the secret as a counter. The style and language of this marvellous play are in some ways markedly different from those of Aeschylus' other works; but the differences hardly suffice to establish the thesis of some scholars that it is not by Aeschylus at all: neither does the alleged contrast between the just Zeus of the other plays and the cruel tyrant of the Prometheus. Zeus maintains justice among men; but when his own power is threatened, he can hardly be expected, by ancient standards, to show special compunction for his enemies. Nor has he, in early Greek religion, the same special regard for mankind as, say, the Jewish or the Christian god, a fact which the comparison between Zeus and Prometheus helps to confirm.

The long life of the second great tragedian, Sophocles, almost spanned the fifth century; seven of his one hundred and twenty-three plays survive complete, and we have many fragments. His style and technique differ markedly from those of Aeschylus; but in their religious outlook the poets are less far apart. Much of the apparent difference may be accounted for if one bears in mind that a Sophoclean trilogy was not written on a continuous theme, but consisted of three separate plays, so that the poet had less space for lyric reflection upon the workings of the universe. Sophocles aimed to present a story from heroic legend against the unchanging background of the early Greek view of the gods and their relation to mankind. Facts which to us seem to have an important bearing on the theme may be neglected by the poet; his first concern was for the impact of the individual scene. Nowhere in the famous play *King Oedipus* are we told *why* Oedipus was fated to kill his father and marry his mother; so that some modern writers have inferred that Sophocles meant to depict the workings of an unjust and arbitrary fate and others have ingeniously invented crimes for which they suppose that he and his mother are punished by the gods. Had Sophocles been asked why Oedipus is ruined, he would have answered in terms of the well-known legend, used by Aeschylus before him; it was in consequence of the curse of Pelops, mentioned above. Had he been asked why his play made no mention of the curse, he would have answered that it did not form part of his subject. We see here a significant difference between his outlook and that of a modern dramatist.

King Oedipus has what seemed to Aristotle the perfect tragic plot. By modern standards of coherence and verisimilitude it would not pass muster; but it has a well-defined beginning, middle, and end; and a single, uninterrupted movement, gathering speed as the action proceeds, carries us rapidly towards the climax. But it was by no means usual for a Greek tragedy to have this character. One can hardly imagine a modern play with as little plot as Aeschylus' *The Persians*, or as Sophocles' *Oedipus at Colonus*, which describes how the aged Oedipus, after long wanderings as a blind beggar, came at last to Athens to die and to receive after death the honour of worship as a hero. Sophocles' *Ajax* describes in its first half how the great hero Ajax, angry with the Greek generals before Troy for having awarded the arms of the dead Achilles to Odysseus instead of to himself, set out to attack them treacherously by night. By an idle boast he had offended Athene, who visited him with an attack of madness, and instead of the generals and their friends he killed only sheep and cattle; when sanity returned to him, his shame drove him to suicide. The second part of the play is occupied with a long debate as to whether Ajax shall be accorded an honourable burial. At first the generals angrily reject the notion, but in the end the dead man's rival Odysseus persuades them to agree. This play has been severely censured as falling into two almost separate halves; but granted the importance in Greek eyes of proper burial and the wholly different notions of what constituted a dramatic plot which obtained during the fifth century, this censure seems misplaced. Other plays of Sophocles have plots more conformable to modern notions. The *Electra*, like Aeschylus' *The Libation-bearers*, describes how Orestes returned and killed his mother Clytemnestra and her lover Aegisthus. Sophocles concentrates on the tragic figure of the heroine, and unlike Aeschylus and Euripides in their plays on the same theme does not concern himself with the problem of whether Orestes was doing right or wrong. The *Antigone*, a play of the late forties, describes the conflict between the king of Thebes, who denies burial to Polynices as an enemy of his country, and the dead man's sister, who insists on discharging the religious duty of burying her brother. Some modern interpreters have argued that both parties are held by the poet to have right on their side; but though Antigone is impartially given all the haste and recklessness of a daughter of Oedipus, like him a victim of the curse, the king's action in withholding burial is plainly meant to be seen as an act of impiety towards the gods. The late play *Philoctetes* describes, with a psychological truth and sympathy hardly equalled in Greek literature, how the experienced Odysseus and the young and gallant Neoptolemus were sent in the tenth year of the Trojan War to fetch to Troy the great archer, Philoctetes, marooned on a solitary island by the Greeks at the start of their expedition, but now pronounced by a prophet to be essential to their victory.

The world presented in these dramas is a world not essentially different from that of Aeschylus; Sophocles could have described his plays, as Aeschylus did, as 'scraps of food from the great banquets of Homer'. Looking on the gods neither with grovelling acquiescence nor with powerless indignation, Sophocles accepts in all its harshness the archaic world order, with its stern reciprocal justice. His style and language are perfectly characteristic of the classical moment in Greek art and literature, between the Archaic and the Hellenistic periods. They preserve the strength and vigour of Aeschylus with only a little of his roughness; and they avoid the sometimes tiresomely neat and antithetical smoothness of Euripides. Sophocles' dialogue never departs from the grand manner, but it comes a little closer to ordinary language than the dialogue of Euripides, which the influence of rhetoric combined with an archaizing tendency makes stiffer and more formal. Lyrics occupy a far smaller portion of the play in Sophocles than in Aeschylus, and their content is in general less profound; sometimes they serve only to emphasize a passing mood or to comment on a general sentiment of no special importance that has found expression at the close of the scene which they separate from the next one. Yet Sophoclean lyric has a unique charm and beauty, and is without the mechanical and repetitious tendency that affects some of the lyrics of Euripides.

Passing from Sophocles to Euripides, his junior by some twenty years, we seem at first to be in a different world. The gods appear to have grown more remote; no longer they, but men's ungovernable passions, are the agents of tragic catastrophe. The actors debate moral issues in a brilliant rhetoric closely akin to that taught by the contemporary sophists; and we meet with occasional allusions to the cosmological speculations of the time, often expressed in a way that seems on the face of it inconsistent with belief in the Olympians. A closer examination reveals an outlook far less alien to that of the earlier poets than is commonly supposed. Like them, Euripides saw man as a being at the mercy of arbitrary forces which he is powerless to control; he was far from sharing the optimistic faith of some of his contemporaries that these could be overcome by the systematic application of human reason. Whether we call these forces by the names of human passions or whether we ascribe them to the power of gods is not, in the last resort, the most important question; nor can the case for regarding Euripides as an atheist by any means be regarded as established.

In polish and in clarity the style of Euripides surpasses that of both his predecessors. He has more control than they over his resources; but his resources are less rich than theirs. At its best his dialogue shows a dazzling dialectical brilliance; at their best, his lyrics have a delicate, almost romantic charm. But his dialogue can lapse into a weary and brittle artificiality and his lyrics into an ornate emptiness that suggests a libretto rather than a poem. The taste of the Hellenistic and Roman ages, not to mention that of many moderns, found him the least remote and the most congenial of the great tragedians, and nineteen of his ninety plays have been preserved; yet in his lifetime he won only four first prizes. We are often told that his cleverness and originality were too much for his contemporaries. Yet though he is beyond doubt one of the great dramatic poets of the world, those who think him comparable to his two great predecessors may reflect with uneasiness that in most aesthetic matters the fifth century judged more truly than the later ages of antiquity.

The surviving plays of Euripides are of unequal merit. Two plays of the poet's middle age, *Medea* and *Hippolytus*, are among the greatest of all dramas that depict the workings and consequences of passionate love. *Hecuba* and *Andromache*, and above all *The Trojan Women*, are rich in the effects of pathos for which Euripides was specially renowned in ancient times. The opening of *Ion* (like one exquisite chorus that survives from the lost play *Phaethon*) has a special gaiety and freshness; the satyr play *Cyclops* has a gusto that resembles the fragments of Aeschylean satyr plays now known to us from papyri; and *Heracles* has a sombre power. But as a work of art *The Bacchants*, a play written near the end of Euripides' life, stands out above the rest.

Dionysus comes to Thebes, where he was born as the son by Zeus of a mortal princess, Semele. The Thebans, led by his mother's sisters, have denied his divinity; it is his purpose to punish them and to make manifest his power. He presents himself as a mortal being, the leader of the women followers who have accompanied him, and is at once persecuted and imprisoned by the ruler of the city, his cousin Pentheus. Finally Dionysus escapes from prison by the use of his miraculous power and tempts Pentheus to go with him to witness the revels of the Bacchants on the mountains outside Thebes. There Pentheus is torn to pieces by his own mother and her sisters, who under the god's spell take him for a lion. Some critics have thought that Euripides is here vindicating the cult of Dionysus against atheism; others have taken him to be attacking the evil cult of Dionysus. Euripides, is neither 'for' nor 'against' Dionysus in this simple way; rather, he acknowledges his power, and sees the danger of resisting it. Steeped as he is in the rhetoric of his sophistic contemporaries, he can seldom resist a chance to allow his characters to debate a moral issue; but he seldom tries to force upon his audience the decision of such an issue, and we are forced to conclude that the methods of the sophists were more to his purpose than their opinions. Still farther is his thought from that of their modern writers who have tried to read into it their own liberal or humanitarian ideas.

The play singled out for special discussion here is Sophocles' *Women of Trachis*, a work of unknown date which by no means wholly conforms to modern notions of the dramatic. Further, the author's comment upon the action is implicitly, and not directly, stated. The play describes the events that led to the death of Heracles, the bravest among the heroes of Greece and the greatest benefactor of mankind. His mother was Alcmene, wife of the hero Amphitryon; but his real father was not Amphitryon, but Zeus himself. Against all manner of robbers, giants, and monsters, as well as human enemies, his mighty strength brought him victory. The jealousy of Zeus' consort, Hera, put him in the power of an envious king, who imposed on him a series of twelve gigantic and apparently impossible labours, which he discharged with triumph. After his death, according to the general belief, he became a god, and long before the production of the play he had been worshipped over the whole Greek-speaking world.

When the play begins Heracles' family home is in Trachis, to the east of central Greece; the chorus consists of young women of the locality, who give the play its name. It is Deianeira, Heracles' wife, who speaks a prologue which at once establishes its speaker's character and strikes the keynote of the action that is to follow. It is an old saying, she begins, that you cannot know whether a man is happy or unhappy till he is dead; but she knows, even while she is alive, that her fate is an unhappy one. As a girl she had been wooed by a terrible suitor, Achelous, the greatest river of all Greece, and had been rescued only when Heracles appeared to vanquish him in single combat. As Heracles' wife, she has lived a life of loneliness and terror while he has been away accomplishing his mighty labours; and now he has been gone for more than a year, and no news of him has reached home. She is now desperately anxious, and on the advice of an old nurse sends her son Hyllus in search of his father. At this point the young women who form the chorus appear and in the first choral lyric of the play appeal to the all-seeing Sun to bring news of Heracles, and then try to comfort his unhappy wife.

Suddenly one of the servants of the house appears; he brings great news. Heracles has slain King Eurytus and sacked his city of Oechalia, and is even now on his way home in triumph, laden with spoils. His envoy, Lichas, has been sent ahead to convey back the prisoners and to bring the news of victory. The chorus sings a short song of rejoicing, and Lichas enters, escorting a party of captured women. Deianeira is overcome with joy at the news of her husband's safety; but she feels pity for the prisoners and greets them kindly. To one girl of great dignity and beauty she speaks words of special sympathy. But now one of her own servants betrays to her that this girl is Iole, daughter of Eurytus; and that it is to ravish her from her unwilling father that Heracles has sacked Oechalia and put its defenders to the sword. Deianeira implores Lichas to admit all (lines 436–69).*

> No, by Zeus whose lightnings flash above the glens
> Of Oeta, do not cheat me of the truth
> For you will tell your tale to no mean woman,
> Nor to one who's ignorant of the human way
> Of not desiring the selfsame joys forever.
> Well, anyone who gets into the ring
> With Eros – like some boxer putting up his fists –
> Is mad, since love sways even gods at will,
> And, I know, sways me; why not, then, another
> Woman like me? So if I blame my husband,

* The translations are by Frances Lloyd-Jones, who has tried to keep as closely as possible to the idiom and word-order of the original.

A victim of this same disease, I'm surely
Mad, or blaming her, accomplice in a thing
That's no disgrace to them or wrong to me.
It cannot be . . . But if you learnt from him
Your lies, no pretty lesson have you learnt,
And if self-taught, though wanting to be gentle,
You'll turn out base. Come, speak the truth in full:
The name of liar brands the freeborn
Like a curse. Get away with lies – you cannot;
You've spoken to many, and they will tell me.
And if you're afraid, that fear is ignoble –
Since not to know would cause me pain indeed.
But what's so fearful in knowing? Has not
Heracles of all men had most paramours?
Never yet has one of them heard harsh or jeering
Words from me, and this one shall not either,
Though he dissolve in tenderness for her,
Because especially I pitied her
On seeing how her beauty has destroyed
Her life, and she, ill-starred, unwittingly
Enslaved and sacked her fatherland – but let
That go with the wind! To you I say: be false
To some other, but always true to me.

This speech breaks down Lichas' resistance, and he admits all, at the same time imploring Deianeira to keep her promise to treat Iole with kindness. Deianeira renews that promise, and goes into the house to fetch gifts for Lichas to carry back to Heracles while the chorus sings an ode in celebration of the power of love:

Mighty force of victory
The Cyprian carries off eternally.
As for the Gods – them I pass by
And of her cheating the son of Cronos I tell nothing
Nor speak of nocturnal Hades
Or Poseidon, maker of earthquake.
But to win as wife Deianeira,

Who the twin powers that clashed for her hand?
Who that enlisted in all blows, in all dust, in ordeals of battle?
The one was the force of a river, four-footed, high-horned,
A bull's horrid likeness,
Achelous from Oeniadae.
The other came from Bacchic Thebes
With bending bow, and spears, and club a-shaking,
Son of Zeus – these it was, who then entered
Together in combat for love of the bride.
And only the lovely Cyprian with them as arbiter.
There was a rattle of fists and of arrows
Commingled with clattering horns;
There was grappling interlocked, was a deadly crash
Of foreheads, and the bellowing of both,
And she a delicate beauty
Sat on the far-off hill, awaiting him to be her husband.
They fought as I say;
But the fought-over face of the maiden
Piteously waits for an end –
And suddenly must she go from her mother
Like a she-calf torn away.

Deianeira now comes out of the house, bringing with her
the gift she has prepared for Heracles. In spite of her promises
she cannot bear the thought of sharing him with a younger
and more beautiful rival; and she has remembered that she
has something that may help her to regain him. When she left
home with Heracles after their wedding, they had to cross a
mountain torrent; as ferryman they employed Nessus, one of
the mythical monsters called centaurs, half man and half
horse. Nessus took Deianeira first, and in midstream laid
wanton hands on her; in a moment he had in his chest one of
Heracles' poisoned arrows. Dying, Nessus told Deianeira to
take the clotted blood from about his wound and keep it as a
philtre she might use on Heracles, one that would make him
never again love any other woman. She did so; and she has

now anointed with the stuff a splendid robe which she gives to Lichas as a present to his master.

The chorus sings an ode full of rejoicing over the triumphant return of Heracles, such an ode as in Sophocles is often the prelude to disaster. Then Deianeira becomes a prey to second thoughts. She remembers that Nessus had no cause to do her kindness, and she anticipates the worst. Suddenly her son Hyllus bursts on to the stage, and in terrible words denounces his mother as his father's murderess. He tells how as soon as Heracles put on the robe, it clung to his body, causing the acutest agony. In appalling pain and rage, Heracles seized Lichas and hurled him from the top of the mountain on which he was sacrificing into the sea below; then he commanded Hyllus to convey him home, where he will presently arrive. Hyllus ends his speech with a yet fiercer denunciation of his mother. She makes no attempt to defend herself, but leaves the stage silently. After an ode of lamentation by the chorus, an ode contrasting sharply with the one before it, her nurse enters to announce that she has stabbed herself.

The chorus has hardly finished lamenting Deianeira's death when the dying Heracles is brought in upon a litter, attended by Hyllus and a doctor. He who has never before shed tears is now reduced by the poison to cries of agony and bitter demands for revenge upon his wife. In a scene of unmitigated horror, he implores Hyllus to fetch Deianeira to him, so that he may kill her. At last Hyllus manages to make his father realize that Deianeira had anointed the robe with the blood of Nessus, believing it to be a love charm; and Heracles at once realizes that all is over. Long ago his father Zeus has warned him that he will meet his death 'at the hands of one already dead'; and now the prophecy is fulfilled. Not one word more does he say about Deianeira; now that he knows he is to die, he has more important things to think of. First he makes Hyllus promise to place him on a huge funeral pyre, which he is to set alight. Hyllus agrees to the first part, at least,

of this request. Then he asks of his son a favour that puts him
to an even harder test:

HERACLES: Now you know the daughter of Eurytus?
HYLLUS: It is Iole you mean, I take it?
HERACLES: It is. This only, son, I ask of you –
　　To take that girl when I am dead and you
　　Would wish to reverence me with memory
　　Of your father's oaths – as wife; do not betray
　　Your father, let no other man take her
　　That's lain against my side, instead of you.
　　But yourself, my son, accept this marriage.
　　Consent! To have obeyed in greater things,
　　But not in little, makes all former credit vain.
HYLLUS: Oh, to be angry with sick men is base,
　　But to see your mind run so, what man could bear?
HERACLES: You sound as though you'll fulfil not one request.
HYLLUS: Whoever could, when she alone's the reason
　　That my mother's dead, and you are as you are.
　　Who, who could take her, that had not been cursed
　　By Furies? Better for me too to die,
　　Father, than to live with my greatest foe.
HERACLES: This fellow, it seems, will not respect the rights
　　Of dying men; but heaven's curse most sure
　　Awaits your disobedience to my words.
HYLLUS: Ah, soon, I fear, your sickness will be fully proved.
HERACLES: Yes, you are waking up my pain, which slept.
HYLLUS: Wretch that I am! – all is perplexity.
HERACLES: Only do right – heed him who begot you.
HYLLUS: Must I learn, then, to be wicked, father?
HERACLES: There's no wickedness in gladdening my heart.
HYLLUS: So you urge me to this act in righteousness?
HERACLES: I do, and call the gods to witness it.
HYLLUS: Then I'll do it, and not reject your plea.
　　My defence before the gods: your will. For none
　　Could be called vile obeying you, father.
HERACLES: You end this well. To words add speedily
　　The grace of deeds – before fresh spasms goad

And rend me, set me on the pyre. Make haste!
Come, lift me. Now comes respite from all pains,
The last and final end of the man I am.
HYLLUS: Nothing stays the execution of your will;
You command it and compel us, father.

Hyllus orders the bearers to take up the litter, and they leave
the stage. All that has happened, say the chorus in their final
words, has been the will of Zeus.

Has the poet given us any insight into Zeus' purposes?
Some scholars have failed to find any, for the poet's comment
on the action is not directly given; but in the light of our
general picture of Sophocles' world it should be clear enough.
Zeus has indeed brought about Heracles' end, and so has given
men one more reminder of his inexorable law of justice.
Heracles in his dealings with Eurytus and his family has
violated that law, a thing not even he can do and go un-
punished. To Hyllus all seems unrelieved disaster; only the
audience may remind themselves that, according to the
familiar legend, the great hero is to be carried off by Zeus at
the moment of death, to join the gods on Olympus.

Most modern critics, of which I quote one, have found 'the
action of the play disjointed, and the beauty of the play about
Deianeira tarnished by the incomprehensible appendix about
Heracles'. Even by modern standards, which are in any case
inapplicable, I find more unity in the play than this remark
suggests. Deianeira is indeed beautiful, but she is incidental;
the subject of the play is the death of the great hero, and his
death is the climax of its whole action. His callousness to his
wife is not ignored by the poet; nor, in a sense, does it go un-
punished, since it is bound up with the injustice towards the
house of Eurytus which costs Heracles his life. Must we, then,
consider Heracles as an unfeeling brute? How does an ancient
poet, writing in the Homeric tradition, conceive the hero who
wrestled with the Nemean lion, slew the hundred-headed
Hydra, brought up Cerberus from the mouth of Hades, and

held the sky upon his shoulders? Not as a gentle and chivalrous knight, but as a man of passionate appetites and violent temper; that is the uniform tradition of antiquity. Such a character accords well with the actions attributed to Heracles, actions which were held to have conferred immense benefits on the human race. Heroes, in the opinion of the ancients, were not to be judged by the standards that are applied to common humanity. Without their heroism, common humanity could not survive; yet the ancients did not expect that the ordinary man would find them comfortable company.

Bibliography

Ancient Greek is a highly inflected language, and its structure differs in many ways from those of modern European languages; and ancient Greek metre depends not on rhyme but on the recurrence of long and short syllables at fixed places in the verse. Consequently it is very hard indeed to translate Greek poetry with any real fidelity to the original. Either a translation is wholly unlike the original or it is a bad piece of English prose or verse. It is scarcely possible for verse whose metre depends on stress to reproduce the effects of verse whose metre depends on quantity; rhymed verse is particularly ill-suited for this purpose. Until the last fifty years most English poetry was written in rhymed verse, or at least used a line with a rigidly fixed number of syllables; and most translators rendered Greek poetry into English poetry of this kind without attempting to reproduce its characteristic poetical effects. The freer verse forms that are employed by most modern poets offer a somewhat better prospect of producing versions that to some extent reproduce the impression made by the original. The opportunity that this offers has been taken far better advantage of in America than in England, although LOUIS MACNEICE'S rendering of Aeschylus' *Agamemnon* (Faber and Faber) is a successful version in the modern manner.

The best versions available are included in *The Complete Greek Tragedies*, by DAVID GREENE and RICHMOND LATTIMORE (Chicago University Press), and a large selection of these appear in the same publisher's Phoenix Paperback edition: vol. 1: Aeschylus, *Agamemnon* and *Prometheus Bound*, Sophocles, *King Oedipus* and *Antigone*, Euripides, *Hippolytus*; vol. 2: Aeschylus, *The Libation-bearers*, Sophocles, *Electra*, Euripides, *Iphigenia in Tauris*, *Electra*, and *The Trojan Women*; vol. 3:

Aeschylus, *The Eumenides*, Sophocles, *Philoctetes, Oedipus at Colonus*, Euripides, *The Bacchants, Alcestis*.

Texts with translations printed opposite are available in the editions of the three tragedians in the Loeb Classical Library (though the translations of Sophocles and Euripides are very poor).

During the last eighty years many new fragments of tragedy have come to light through the discovery of papyri; some of these are of great interest. The Loeb *Aeschylus* (in its latest edition) has an appendix containing the recently-discovered fragments of this author; most of the other new fragments of tragedy will be found translated in the Loeb volume *Greek Literary Papyri*, edited by D. L. PAGE.

The best critical study of Greek tragedy in English is *The Poetry of Greek Tragedy*, by RICHMOND LATTIMORE (Oxford, 1958). *The Greek Tragic Poets*, by D. W. LUCAS (Cohen & West, 2nd ed., 1960) contains some useful information. Other books are:

DODDS, E. R., *The Greeks and the Irrational*, University of California Press, 1956 (also in a paperback edition)

GUTHRIE, W. K. C., *The Greeks and their Gods*, Methuen, 1950

ROSE, H. J., *Ancient Greek Religion*, Hutchinson, 1948

6 Greek Science

G. S. Kirk*

Reader in Classics, Cambridge Universiy

For hundreds of years the Greeks did not clearly distinguish science from philosophy, and in this lay both their strength and weakness as scientists. They simply set out to explain the world in all its aspects, no less. Most of the thinkers from the sixth century B.C. down to Socrates seem to have conceived that they could account for everything: how the world started, what it is made of, what is man's place in it. These early *physikoi*, physicists or students of the nature of things, possessed the vast aims and uninhibited imagination that have marked many of the great artists and thinkers of history. Yet although they have given their name to an important branch of modern science – physics, the study of the nature and behaviour of matter – they were hardly scientists in our sense. They lacked the methodical attention to detail, and the constant relation of theory to the observed facts, that made possible the spectacular development of science from the Renaissance onwards.

All through the history of Greek science we can observe both the strength and the weakness: their intense interest in the world in all its larger aspects, and their reluctance to focus on limited fields of vision; their magisterial attack on the greatest problems of being, and their pitifully inadequate supply lines of detailed, accurate, and relevant observations. It is often said that the early Greek thinkers did not bother about observation. That is an exaggeration. Of course they bothered, up to a point: what they were trying to explain was precisely the world of human observation and experience.

These men were capable of exact observation. Thales, for

* With a section on Aristotle by J. E. Raven.

example, was known for his practical ingenuity, and devised a method for measuring the distance of ships at sea; Anaximander recorded equinoxes and constructed some kind of map of the heavens; Empedocles used the wine-lifting pipette to prove the concrete existence of air. But their speculative flights went far beyond the control of their casual and unsystematic observations. One reason is that these thinkers were not simply trying to explain the world as it is, but rather the world as man needs it to be – unified, comprehensible, and ultimately sympathetic. This tendency to interpret the world in terms of human needs, to impose a social pattern on nature, can never be entirely eradicated from human thinking; but it was stronger for the Greeks than for the new scientists of the Renaissance or their modern successors. Admittedly there *are* certain kinds of regularity in our world, and it is with these that science must be largely concerned. Yet the earlier pre-Socratic thinkers sought not so much to observe and classify these regularities as to invent some all-explaining and universal principle of existence. Even the Atomists, Leucippus and Democritus, whose theory of matter looks at first sight like our own, were glib and superficial when it came to explaining the detailed consequences of atomic shapes and movements. The followers of Pythagoras, to take another example, used his discovery of the mathematical structure of the musical scale as the basis of an elaborate semi-mystical theory of a universe somehow entirely made out of numbers.

In spite of these handicaps the achievement of the pre-Socratic physicists is startling enough. Matter itself they came to regard either as continuous and capable of being infinitely divided, or as discontinuous and made up of individual atoms. Pythagoras and Heraclitus had turned their attention from the simple *identification* of matter to its structure and behaviour; Heraclitus at least seems to have supposed, reasonably enough, that the coherence of the natural world depended more on how matter behaved than on what it was made of. This was really quite a promising position; yet by the last quarter of the fifth century, physics, instead of advancing farther, was going into a decline. The most serious blow was dealt by Parmenides of Elea, who about 460 B.C. claimed to have proved by logic that essential change in matter is impossible. 'There is no such thing as Not-being,' Parmenides and the Eleatics argued in effect; 'so coming-into-being, or becoming, is impossible. Change involves becoming, so the phenomena of change and motion studied by the physicists can have no real existence.'

The deceptive simplicity of Parmenides' argument held his contemporaries and successors spellbound. Physicists like Empedocles and Anaxagoras did not challenge its logic, but they tried instead to meet it by devising systems in which *essential* change was avoided. These systems grew ever more complex, contradictory, and improbable; and, as a result, interest in the whole subject gradually declined. Socrates and his younger contemporaries turned to the study of human and social problems, which in an age threatened with decadence seemed to them of greater immediate urgency.

Plato, the great figure of the next generation, did little to revitalize science. The Academy which he founded at Athens was strong in mathematics, and subjects like the classification of plants were discussed there – but as exercises in logic rather than for their own sake. At the same time Plato further developed the Eleatic approach to nature, declaring that true reality must be a set of unchanging, immaterial, and imperceptible 'Forms', and that the physical world has no more than a kind of half-existence by virtue of its relationship with these Forms – a relationship which was unfortunately indefinable. Plato exhibits in a supreme degree the tendency to philosophical superiority, not to say snobbishness, and the aristocratic rejection of the apparently second best, which had already shown itself in the pre-Socratic period. There is a famous passage in the *Phaedo* where Socrates discusses the reason for his sitting in prison and not trying to escape: it is not, he says, because his sinews and joints are so arranged that he is in the sitting position – the real reason for his remaining there is that he thinks it best not to run away. The mechanical conditions are subsidiary to the mental purpose. This kind of motivation Plato applied to the universe as a whole. The truth is that when the Greeks needed a model for regularity in nature they found it in the planned intellectual activity of man, particularly of the artist or craftsman deliberately shaping his material to a preconceived end. They did not find it, as men have since the Renaissance, in the soulless regularity of the machine; they did not have many machines and they did not like the idea of machines as such. The mechanical elements in causation, like Socrates' sinews, were held to be subsidiary and unimportant, and, for Plato at least, to be beneath the detailed attention of the true thinker. This is partly an effect of living in a slave-owning society; for if slaves do most of the work, it is a short step to believing that the exact processes of production are uninteresting; and even those who did not own slaves seem to have regarded technology as unnecessary and unimportant.

Thus by Plato's time the dislike of mechanics, the apparent inconsistency and over-complexity of fifth-century physical theories, and the tendency to explain the world's regularity as due to some higher mind-like cause, had all coalesced to divorce science from philosophy. Plato calls his dialogue *Timaeus* no more than a 'reasonable story', but even so it is remarkable to see such an intelligent man arguing that the human head is more or less spherical because it is the most important part of the body and the sphere is the most perfect shape. Fortunately Aristotle, who was a member of Plato's Academy for twenty years and owed a very great deal to his teacher, reacted strongly against the other-worldly tendencies of Platonism, against those remote Forms, and reinstated the particular objects of our world as the true basis of reality. But even Aristotle took off from here in a sort of inflationary spiral. He observed and noted the orderliness of the natural world, the relationship of individual to species and species to genus, the regularity with which a man begets a man and not an acorn or a fish, and the apparent purposiveness of most of the organs of animals and plants. But these observations convinced him that the motive and directional force of nature is some kind of unconscious urge towards a complete and perfect reality. The only way in which this reality, the prime mover of the universe, could cause mechanical motion without itself being moved, and so infringing its own perfection, is by being loved. Thus Aristotle decided in one part of his writings, in a very theoretical and Platonic mood – a pre-Socratic mood, almost. Yet at least Aristotle the philosopher worked partly on the basis of materials provided by Aristotle the scientist. This was a man who rejected the common Greek ideal of what was intellectually respectable, and devoted a great part of his life to minute observation of the world of nature.

*

Aristotle* reacted so vigorously against the other-worldliness of Plato that he reinstated the individual objects of our own world as the true basis of reality; and you need only take a brief look at his *History of Animals* to understand just why that was so. Aristotle was the first, possibly even the only, ancient Greek with the true naturalist's passion for minute observation. His description of the habits of the cuttlefish in the island lagoon at Pyrrha; his concise but completely accurate account of the life cycle of the gnat; or his observations of the wryneck's tongue or the owl's eyes – all these conjure up a picture of Aristotle spending hour after hour out in the open air in absorbed contemplation of the creatures round about him. He apparently left the study of botany to

* Mr Raven's section begins here.

his pupil Theophrastus, whose *History of Plants* is a painstaking but not very exciting work. But since in the course of his biological writings he names one hundred and seventy species of birds, one hundred and sixty-nine fishes, sixty-six mammals, and about sixty insects (and many of his observations, incidentally, were never repeated until the nineteenth century) Aristotle can fairly be regarded as the founder of the four sister sciences of ornithology, ichthyology, zoology, and entomology.

Nor was he merely an amateur field naturalist; he was enthusiastically active in the laboratory as well. In various parts of his works one or more of the internal organs of over a hundred different creatures are described in sufficient detail to suggest dissection, and of these descriptions about fifty contain such reliable information that it is highly probable that Aristotle carried out the dissection himself. One animal that he certainly did not dissect was man; he makes a number of blunders about human anatomy which the simplest dissection would have eliminated at once. But on animals ranging from the cow and the deer to the lizard and the frog he almost certainly did practise dissection, and on two in particular, the chameleon and the tortoise, he must have gone so far as to employ vivisection. 'After being cut open along its entire length' he writes of the chameleon 'it continues to breathe for a considerable time; a very slight motion goes on in the region of the heart . . .' and so on. What *would* Plato have thought of a pupil who indulged in such activities?

With his extraordinary capacity for both generalization and detail, it is not surprising that Aristotle should have hit upon theories of lasting value – the recognition for instance that, since hybrids are normally sterile, the ability to produce fertile offspring is one of the marks of a genuine species; or the huge advance in a single step towards a complete classification of the animal kingdom. Yet even in Aristotle there remains a conflict between the philosopher and the scientist. His philosophical belief that the highest aim of every living thing is to embody as fully as possible the form of its particular species prevented him from arriving at a theory of evolution, to which, as a biologist, he yet seems at times to draw very close. And even in Aristotle there is occasionally the usual Greek addiction to *a priori* argument. Consider what he says on the thorny question of the sexes of bees, drones and queen bees – or, as the Greeks preferred to call them, king bees:

It is unreasonable to suppose that bees are female and drones male; for Nature never bestows an offensive weapon on any female, and yet, while the drones are stingless, all the bees have a sting. Nor is the opposite view any more reasonable, that the bees are male, and the drones female; for no males are in the habit of working for their families, and yet as it is the bees do.

As Arthur Platt, whose translation I quote, remarks in a footnote: 'This is an unlucky paragraph; for many females have offensive weapons, and many males work for their offspring.' But at this point even Aristotle himself was evidently none too sure of his reasoning; for only a page or two later he sums up his discussion of the problem with the admirable and revolutionary maxim: 'If ever the facts about bees are fully grasped, then credit must be given rather to observation than to theories, and to theories only if what they affirm agrees with the observed facts.' No single sentence could summarize better than that the essence of Aristotle's momentous contribution to science.*

*

Apart from being a great observational scientist, Aristotle was a tireless teacher and organizer. He founded his own school, the Lyceum, in Athens, and proceeded to organize something entirely new, a joint effort for an encyclopedia of all branches of learning: not only physics, metaphysics, astronomy, mathematics, and biology but also theology, medicine,

* Mr Raven's section ends here.

history, literature, politics, and ethics. So one could perhaps say that the scientific spirit declined in the first half of the fourth century B.C. and established itself on a new basis in the second half. An exception would be medicine, in which some sort of scientific method had been fairly widely practised from the fifth century onwards. The school of medicine founded by Hippocrates in the island of Cos spread its influence all over Greece. In terms of observation and record its methods were scientific: the great aim was accurate prognosis of the course of illness, so that the doctor could win the patient's confidence and be able to know how often to visit and what nursing to arrange. The Coan doctors did not deceive themselves about their power to cure the dangerous illnesses like tuberculosis or malaria; they relied on a sensible diet, good nursing, and the healing power of nature. Often these were not enough. The case-records, though, are impressive: 'In Abdera acute fever seized Pericles, continuous and accompanied by pain; great thirst, nausea, could not keep down drinks. He had some enlargement of the spleen and was heavy in the head.' This is the first day; his progress is reported on each successive day, with special attention to appetite, stools, and urine, until he recovered – a rare event among the records. Yet the Hippocratic school, too, had strong limitations. Their practice of detailed clinical observation did not prevent them from holding some very far-fetched theories about the processes of the body: in particular that its health was controlled by the ratio of four liquids or humours: blood, phlegm, black bile, and yellow bile, and that digestion was a kind of cooking.

Aristotle died in 322 B.C., a year after his former pupil, Alexander the Great. This was a time when the Greek world, after the Macedonian conquest, was still in travail, and when the independent city states were in decline. Literature, architecture, and art all take a turn for the worse; philosophy is preoccupied with making the individual feel at home in an insecure world; but science breaks out and begins one of its greatest periods. This happened to some extent in Athens, but much more brilliantly in Alexandria. In this fine new Hellenic city at the mouth of the Nile, Alexander's Macedonian general Ptolemy I founded not only a great library but also a great research institute called the Museum, both of which were expanded by his son Ptolemy Philadelphus. The interest in Alexandria was primarily in literature and science, not in philosophy in the old sense. Alexander's eastern campaigns had made available much new knowledge about plants, animals, peoples, and places. His massive sieges had produced a new technology of siegecraft and mechanics. The foremost settlers of Alexandria were Macedonian veterans, and for an ambitious and wealthy new city, set in a land of great technical achievements in building and irrigation, science was the thing both for prestige and for practical advantage.

This was the main setting for the resurgence of Greek science. Mathematics, the most theoretical of scientific studies, had already reached a high level in fourth-century Athens. In Alexandria Euclid produced his famous geometrical compendium around 300 B.C., and shortly afterwards came the more original work of Apollonius of Perga, notably on conic sections,* and the great geometrical achievements of Archimedes of Syracuse, for example his calculation of the value of π. Astronomy, too, had been less hindered than other branches of science by the lack of experimental method and by the prevailing eyebrow-lifting about anything smacking of manual work. The study of the heavens had been encouraged by religion and philosophy as well as by sheer curiosity and the practical requirements of sailors and calendar makers; one can go a long way without cameras and telescopes, and Nature herself obliged by setting up control conditions – eclipses and so on – at regular intervals. Aristotle's pupil Heraclides had argued from his remote colonial home on the Black Sea that the earth rotates on its axis, and that some at least of the planets

* See also pages 148 et seq.

revolve around the sun. In Alexandria, Aristarchus developed this idea into a truly Copernican theory. Yet this correct view of the universe was soon abandoned, for two reasons: first because it ran up against the powerful picture of an earth-centred universe built up by Aristotle; and secondly because not all observed phenomena could be easily explained on the theory that the sun is at the centre and the planets revolve around it. 'Saving the phenomena' – or accounting for observed facts – was a professed Hellenistic ideal, and a very scientific one, if strictly applied; but the truth is that the generalizing qualities of most Greek thinkers, and their unsystematic attitude to details and the immediate inferences that may be drawn from them, turned this ideal into one of saving *most* of the phenomena, or saving the most obvious ones and the devil take the rest. Thus Plato's successor Eudoxus, and then Aristotle, had argued that the motions of the heavenly bodies could be explained on the assumption of a system of concentric spheres; the geometry of this was ingenious even though it did not really explain all the planetary movements. When Aristarchus' account of the universe revealed difficulties, the great Hipparchus reverted to the earlier, Aristotelian system; he had the new idea of epicycles, or that each planet revolved on a little circle of its own, which itself revolved about the earth. Even as a purely geometrical solution this was still imperfect; but the world had to wait nearly two thousand years for Copernicus to re-establish a solar system and for Kepler to conceive that the paths of the heavenly bodies were elliptical not circular. *This* is the true theory to save the phenomena; Hipparchus could not think of it, not because he did not know the geometry of ellipses, but because the circular revolution of the heavenly bodies seemed to be guaranteed by the idea that the stars are somehow divine and perfect and that the circle is the perfect figure.

It is not easy to draw up a balance sheet of the strengths and weaknesses of Alexandrian scientists. At some points they improved on Aristotle: by the time of Heron, who lived most probably in the first century B.C., experimentation and scientific method were firmly established. Heron gives minute instructions for building apparatus to prove the possibility of an absolute vacuum. This was something that Aristotle could perfectly well have done, had he ever given any thought to the matter; instead he had worked out a series of general reasons for rejecting the void – as one consequence of which he continued all his life in the belief that bodies fall with a velocity equivalent to their weight, which again he could have disproved by the simplest experiment. But over a wide field of physics and astronomy the Alexandrians were content to follow the elaborate false picture which Aristotle had left them, with its absolute weight and lightness and its earth in its 'natural' place at the centre of the universe. And in some fields where Aristotle was more successful – in dynamics, for example, which he tried to reduce to quantitative and mathematical terms – his successors, on the whole, refused to follow him: the Alexandrian scientific tradition virtually ignored the science of dynamics – even Archimedes, who made part of his living by designing ballistic weapons. In this they seem to revert to the distant pre-Socratic past, in which motion had been largely taken for granted – it was there, it always existed, it was a kind of life or the activity of the divine.

Medicine was further developed by Hellenistic scientists. They practised dissection extensively, not on men but at least on monkeys, and acquired a good knowledge of bones, joints, and muscles; though their conclusions about the internal organs were still bedevilled by theoretical beliefs about vital heat and the four humours. There was an empirical and a dogmatic school, but the division applied to questions of medical treatment rather than to assumptions about the human constitution. Even so critical, learned, and practical a man as Galen, in the second century A.D., accepted the old dogmas. He lived in an age of codification and was one of its chief exponents;

so was the astronomer and geographer Ptolemy, who wrote a vast survey of current knowledge and reached some good new results, for example, about mathematical geography and the distance of the sun and moon, by aligning information collected from different sources. Yet these men, though they progressed in system, had lost the old imagination, just as Heron, in spite of his experiments in mechanics and pneumatics and his ingenious toys and religious gadgets, seems to have lacked the power of creative induction. The third century A.D. saw a grave economic and cultural decline in Egypt and the Roman empire at large. Alexandria and many other outlying towns of the Graeco-Roman world, from which so many of the great scientists of the first three centuries before Christ had come, sank into mediocrity, and the urge and opportunity for further scientific research disappeared. Thus the works of Galen and Ptolemy became crystallized as the last word, and dictated the trend of medicine and astronomy for over a thousand years to come. In a way it might have been better for the world if nothing quite so cut-and-dried had been to hand. Similarly the great corpus of Aristotle survived to become an absolute orthodoxy, supported as it now was, in its conception of a Universe moved by love of an absolute Being, by the new and totally unscientific force of Christianity.

It is unfortunate that the immediate legacy of Greek science was so sterile; that the brilliant men who lived in the two centuries after Aristotle were preoccupied with new fields of knowledge and were not more critical of his physics; it is unfortunate that Galen and Ptolemy happened to come at the end of a cultural era, and that such speculation as survived them became completely subordinated to Christian belief and doctrine. Yet the essential weakness of Greek science was an internal one, and this weakness was also much of its strength: its vision of physics as philosophy not mechanics, and its disregard of attainable minor discoveries in favour of unattain-

1. View across the Argive plain from Tiryns; the walls of the Bronze-Age citadel are in the foreground

2a (left). The theatre at Epidaurus, built in the mid fourth century B.C. The auditorium is cut out of the hillside and lined with stepped stone seating, partly enclosing the circular *orchestra* where the chorus performed, the other actors appearing on a low stage at the back

2b (right). The temple of Nike (Victory) at Athens. A small temple in the Ionic order, on a bastion of the Acropolis; last quarter of the fifth century B.C.

2c. The Acropolis of Athens from the south-east. Dominating the citadel is the Parthenon, a large temple in the Doric order built in the mid fifth century B.C. The Corinthian columns in the foreground belong to the temple of Olympian Zeus, built in its present form between the second century B.C. and the second century A.D.

3a (left). Athenian scent bottle decorated in the 'white-ground' technique. Woman holding bowl. Signed by potter Pasiades, *c.* 500 B.C. Found in Cyprus

3b (right). Athenian oil flask decorated in the 'red figure' technique. Young hunter. By the Pan Painter, *c.* 470 B.C. Found at Gela in Sicily

3c (below). Athenian mixing bowl, decorated in the 'black figure' technique. Dedicated on the Acropolis in the mid sixth century B.C.

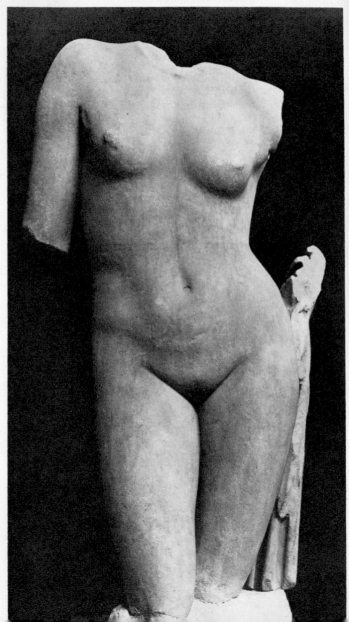

4. Marble torso of Aphrodite. Copy made under the Roman Empire from a Greek statue of the early fourth century B.C.

5a (left). Bronze statuette of a youth dedicated on the Acropolis of Athens. Late sixth century B.C. 5b (right). Bronze statuette of a discus thrower, probably from the Peloponnese. Second quarter of fifth century B.C. These show the contrast between the formal stance of archaic statuary and the relaxation into natural movement introduced by the classical revolution of the early fifth century

6a. Horsemen getting ready for the Pana-thenaic procession. A relief in Pentelic marble from the north frieze of the Parthenon. About 440 B.C.

6b. Marble head of Epicurus. A life-size copy, made under the Roman Empire, from a statue of the early third century B.C.

7a. Life-size bronze statue of a boy jockey, from a Roman ship wrecked off Cape Artemisium (Euboea). Late second century B.C. A fine example of the naturalistic trend in Hellenistic art

7b. The 'Barberini Faun'. Over life-size statue of a drunken satyr asleep, made at Pergamum perhaps in the late third century B.C. The right leg and left arm are the work of Bernini. The harmony of these restorations underlines the Baroque affinities of this side of Hellenistic art

8a and b. Coin of Syracuse, celebrating the defeat of the Athenian attack in 413 B.C. Head of Arethusa surrounded by dolphins and charioteer crowned by Victory. 8c. Coin of Athens, early fifth century B.C. Owl. 8d. Coin of Lysimachus of Thrace, *c.* 300 B.C. Head of Alexander the Great with the horn of Ammon

8e (left). A Greek papyrus. First sheet of a complete play (the *Dyscolus*) of Menander, recently discovered on some papyrus sheets, the surviving portion of a book produced in the third century A.D. It contains a statement of the contents of the play, the date of its first production (316 B.C.), and the dramatis personae. 8f (right). A medieval Greek manuscript. A page of a parchment manuscript of the early fourteenth century A.D., containing the works of some of the Attic orators. Codex Burneianus 95, f. 105 verso able major ones. For philosophy itself this attitude was not wholly unfruitful; for science, it was a terrible limitation. Yet even so the actual achievement was tremendous. If philosophy prevented it, at the time, from being more tremendous still, yet it was philosophy that elicited and cherished the greatest of all Aristotle's achievements, a workable formal logic. This was the tool that was to enable science to resume its advance from the Renaissance onwards, and to attain its true status neither as mechanics nor as pure philosophy but as 'experimental philosophy', the name given to it in England by the founders of the Royal Society.

Bibliography

COHEN, M. R., and DRABKIN, I. E., *A Source Book in Greek Science*, Harvard University Press, 1958

FARRINGTON, B., *Greek Science*, Pelican Books, 1953

HEATH, T. L., *Aristarchus of Samos*, Oxford University Press, 1913, reprinted 1959

JONES, W. H. S. (ed.), *Hippocrates*, vols. I, II, IV, Loeb Classical Library, Heinemann, 1923–

KIRK, G. S., and RAVEN, J. E., *The Presocratic Philosophers*, Cambridge (paperback edition), 1962

NEUGEBAUER, O., *The Exact Sciences in Antiquity*, Hamish Hamilton, 1962

SAMBURSKY, S., *The Physical World of the Greeks*, Routledge & Kegan Paul, 1956

The Greeks and their Philosophy

A. H. Armstrong
Gladstone Professor of Greek, Liverpool University

The Greeks invented the word 'philosophy', but it is not easy to give a short and simple answer to the question 'What did they mean by it?' It covered, in fact, a remarkable variety of mental activities, some of which we should not now think of as forming part of philosophy at all. In Chapter 6 you read about Greek science; but if an ancient Greek philosopher had been reading it he would have said that it was about philosophy, and he would have thought it very odd of us to separate the two. The Greeks distinguished philosophy from mythology – that is, telling the sort of stories about the gods and the world and how things began that the poets told; and some of them also quite early, perhaps from the time of Pythagoras, distinguished it from the activities that aimed at practical advantage, and held that what marked out a philosopher was the disinterested love of knowledge, that he wanted to know just for the sake of knowing and not for what he could get out of it. But if we really want to understand Greek philosophy we must be careful not to make these distinctions too sharp. We can now see when we read them that some of the early poets and storytellers (Hesiod or Pherecydes of Syros, for instance) were doing a certain amount of thinking about their traditional material, and that it was not always so very different from the thinking of the earliest philosophers, who were certainly influenced unconsciously by ideas which came from the oldest and most primitive levels of Greek religious thinking. And, though Greek philosophers did not as a rule expect or want to get any practical advantage for themselves from their philosophy, at least from the age of Socrates they were not unpractical in the sense of being uninterested in ordinary human life and its problems. Plato and Aristotle and many of their successors were intensely concerned to think out how men ought to live in communities, how their political and social life could be organized for the best. And practically all later Greek philosophers were mainly concerned with the quality of individual human life, with the search for moral and religious perfection. Philosophy in fact became more and more not just a mental activity, but a way of life, and an extremely demanding one: in the circle of the great Neo-platonist philosopher Plotinus, to become a philosopher had drastic practical consequences: it meant giving away all your property and living the life of an ascetic.

Greek philosophy, then, covered a great many different subjects and meant a great many different things to the men who practised it in the course of its long history. Before we take a quick look at some of the most important of them, it will be interesting to notice just how long that history was. It began at the beginning of the sixth century B.C. Our first fixed date is 585 B.C., the year in which there was an eclipse which Thales of Miletus, the first Greek philosopher, predicted. It is not so easy to decide when it ended. It would not be quite unreasonable to say that it has not ended yet. The works of the great Greek philosophers, above all Plato and Aristotle, are still read and their ideas quite seriously discussed by modern philosophers of a wide variety of different outlooks. And a philosophy whose ideas are still alive in the minds of living philosophers can hardly be called dead, or its history finished. But historians of philosophy, for reasons of practical convenience, have to divide their subject up more tidily than it is divided in real life, and make artificial stops in the continuity of living and thinking. And if we narrow our terms of reference, and, instead of saying just 'Greek philosophy', say 'pagan Greek philosophy as an organized study, with its own colleges and professors', we can easily find the date when it stopped. It is A.D. 529, when the Emperor Justinian closed the philosophical schools at Athens. This date gives us a life for Greek philosophy of over a thousand years. It began not far from the beginning of the development of classical Greek civilization, in the time of early archaic sculpture and architecture, a century before the beginning of Athenian drama. It ended in the full Byzantine civilization, when the Roman Empire had been officially Christian, with its capital at Constantinople, for two centuries. When Plato was a little boy, the Parthenon was still quite new. The last head of his school in Athens, Damascius, could have seen Justinian's Church of the Holy Wisdom at Constantinople.

What did the Greek philosophers think and talk and write about during this long period of over a thousand years? At first, mostly, about what the world is made of, how it came into being, and why it is like it is. These were the questions which interested the first Greek philosophers, the Milesians, Thales, Anaximander, and Anaximenes, and they continued to be of primary interest to all the philosophers of the period called pre-Socratic, the period, that is, which lasted till the influence of Socrates, through the circle of friends and admirers with whom he had talked at Athens, became dominant in Greek philosophy: it is worth remembering that the later pre-Socratics were contemporaries of Socrates himself. You have read about some of the more interesting of these early speculations about the physical world in the chapter on Greek science. But I should like to draw your attention to a few questions which the pre-Socratics tried to answer and which we should consider philosophical rather than scientific. First there is the question closest to physical science, whether the world is an ordered whole, a *cosmos* as the Greeks called it, and what is responsible for the order; if there is a cosmic law, is there any sort of a lawgiver? The idea of cosmic law and order appears in a simple form in Anaximander, and in a strange and striking form in that disconcertingly original thinker Heraclitus, whose thought seems to be dominated by the idea of a living order, a balance of opposing tensions, which persists through and governs the endless changes of things, a fiery rational principle which regulates the leaping flames of the great bonfire of the world:

This world order did none of gods or men make, but it always was and is and shall be: an everlasting fire, kindling in measures and going out in measures.

Thunderbolt steers all things.*

In Xenophanes, the first philosophical critic of the stories of the gods told by the poets, we meet the idea of a divine intelligence pervading and regulating the world:

Homer and Hesiod have attributed to the gods everything that is a shame and a reproach among men, stealing and committing adultery and deceiving each other.

One god, greatest among gods and men, in no way similar to mortals either in body or in thought.†

And Anaxagoras, the friend of Pericles, who was the best-known, the most influential, and the most unpopular of pre-Socratic philosophers in fifth-century Athens, put forward clearly the idea of a world-arranging Mind. For the Atomists order was the result of blind mechanical necessity, and not of any sort of intelligent arrangement.

Another question was that of the One and the Many. Have the many things in this world a single originating principle, and how did they come from it? This appears at the beginning of Greek philosophy in the Milesians, with their conception of a single living stuff from which all things come, and remains important to the end. Parmenides of Elea and his followers, the Eleatics, gave a most disconcerting twist to their answer to it. They insisted that reason shows us that only the One exists, and that our belief in the existence of the many things

* Translated by G. S. Kirk, Kirk and Raven, *The Presocratic Philosophers*, Cambridge University Press, 1961, p. 220.

† ibid., p. 169.

and the change and motion which our senses show us is quite irrational. This at once raises a set of philosophical questions of enormous and lasting importance – all the problems of knowledge and perception which have taken up so much of the time of later philosophers.

Then again we find appearing already in pre-Socratic philosophy that concern about the nature and destiny of man, and how he ought to live, which became dominant later. It was the answers given by Pythagoras and the Pythagoreans to questions about man which had the greatest influence on later developments. For them the soul was a divine being, fallen and imprisoned in the body through a series of reincarnations. It could get back to its original state through leading a life of ritual purity and virtue, and bringing itself into tune with the order and harmony of the universe, by understanding how all things were number. For, as Aristotle says of them,

They supposed the elements of number to be the elements of all things, and the whole heaven to be a musical scale and a number.*

With Socrates and Plato, the central preoccupation of Greek philosophy at Athens in the fifth and fourth centuries B.C. comes to be man, what he is, and how he ought to think and to live, as an individual and in community; this naturally led back to thinking about the gods and the universe, in rather a new way. In the lifetime of Socrates something which might be called higher education, for well-to-do young men of good family, appeared for the first time in Greece. It was given by the Sophists, travelling professors of the art of success in public life, charging high fees and claiming to produce quick and certain results. We really *know* very little about these men: Gorgias, Protagoras, Prodicus, Hippias, and the rest, but they seem to have been intelligent and morally respectable people on the whole, not altogether deserving the dubious reputation which Plato and Aristotle have given them. They were not

* Translated by J. E. Raven, ibid., p. 289.

serious thinkers, and, being professors of the art of success in society as they found it, were not interested in absolute religious or moral values. They generally seem to have accepted the already widespread idea that morality was a matter of the conventions of particular societies, though most of them held that you should conform to the conventions of the society in which you lived. Their attitude of mind is perhaps best summed up in the famous and much discussed saying of Protagoras:

The measure of all things is man, of the things that exist that they exist, and of the things that do not exist that they do not.*

Now this sort of moral relativism, whether in a conformist or a rebellious form, completely failed to satisfy Socrates, and his refusal to accept it brought him into disagreement with the Sophists and, ultimately, into conflict with Athenian society. It is impossible to be quite sure that we have ever got back to the real Socrates behind the writings of his friends and admirers. The Socrates we know best, the Socrates who has been disturbingly present in the minds and imaginations of Europe since the fourth century B.C., is the Socrates who appears in the dialogues of Plato; and Plato was not writing accurate history or biography; nor was the more prosaic Xenophon. Perhaps the things about him of which we can be surest are these: that he thought that the most important thing in life was for a man to know what he was and what he was for and to care for his soul so as to make it as good as possible; that he believed that 'virtue is knowledge' – if a man really knew what was good he would do it: that the method which he used for trying to arrive at this knowledge was that of endless rational argument and questioning: that he himself claimed to know nothing, and to be wiser than others only because he knew that he did not know, but that he never seems to have been in doubt about what he ought to do, and was so sure of his own vocation that

* Author's translation.

in the end he was ready to die for it. Perhaps we come nearest to the real Socrates in the *Apology*, the version Plato wrote of his defence before the court which condemned him to death in 399 B.C. Here are a few sentences from it:

> When the generals whom you chose to command me, Athenians, placed me at my post at Potidaea, and at Amphipolis, and at Delium, I remained where they placed me, and ran the risk of death, like other men: and it would be very strange conduct on my part if I were to desert my post now from fear of death or of any other thing, when the god has commanded me, as I am persuaded that he has done, to spend my life in searching for wisdom, and in examining myself and others. That would indeed be a very strange thing: and then certainly I might with justice be brought to trial for not believing in the gods: for I should be disobeying the oracle, and fearing death, and thinking myself wise when I was not wise. For to fear death, my friends, is only to think ourselves wise, without being wise: for it is to think that we know what we do not know.*

The Socratic dialogues of Plato are the greatest literary monument that any disciple ever erected to his master: and the greatest importance of Socrates in the history of European thought is that he set Plato thinking. Plato himself considered philosophical writing of little value or importance compared with oral teaching. But we know very little about the oral teaching which he gave in his school, the Academy; perhaps the best evidence of its quality is the thought of his independent and critical pupil Aristotle. But the dialogues which he wrote have influenced not only all later Greek but all European philosophy and to read some of them is still the best introduction to philosophy for ordinary intelligent people: they are easily available in good English translations. It is impossible to give any sort of adequate summary of what you will find in them. They are wide ranging, often puzzling, and not infrequently inconsistent. They deal with morals, law, politics, and

* *Apology*, 28–9, translated by F. J. Church in *The Trial and Death of Socrates*, Golden Treasury Series, Macmillan.

art, as well as with what we should call logical, metaphysical, and theological questions. They contain many brilliant, and often unfair, character sketches of fifth-century intellectuals and statesmen, some magnificent symbolic stories or myths, a great deal of very acute verbal analysis and critical thinking, and some quite shockingly bad arguments. Perhaps we can state their main purpose, the main purpose of all Plato's teaching activity, something like this. It was to persuade the small minority capable of philosophy to find out the truth about what really exists and to order their lives according to that truth, and, in the extremely unlikely event of their being given a chance to do so, to direct the whole lives of the communities in which they lived according to their own knowledge. In Plato's philosophy the central problems are about man and how he ought to live in the city, how the political, social and religious community life of a Greek city state ought to be organized so that all its members will be as good men as possible. For Plato, and Aristotle, the goodness of the citizens is the end and object of all political and social activity. But Plato looks for the answers to his problems about man in knowledge of what really exists, and what really exists is something unchanging, eternal, and divine, the world of Forms or Ideas with its ultimate principle the Good. It is according to this pattern that a good divine intelligence forms and rules the world, and it is here that man can find the cause and standard of the human goodness which he seeks: and he can find it because his soul is akin to eternal reality, and if he lives well and wisely in this world of body and change, he will return to the divine world of immaterial reality from which he came. Here is a description, in consciously imaginative and figurative language, of that world, from one of the greatest of Plato's dialogues, the *Phaedrus*:

Of that place beyond the heavens none of our earthly poets has yet sung, and none shall sing worthily . . . It is there that true Being dwells, without colour or shape, that cannot be touched; reason alone, the soul's pilot, can behold it, and all true knowledge is knowledge thereof. Now even as the mind of a god is nourished by reason and knowledge, so also is it with every soul that has a care to receive her proper food; wherefore when at last she has beheld Being she is well content, and contemplating truth she is nourished and prospers, till the heaven's revolution brings her back full circle. And while she is borne round she discerns justice, its very self, and likewise temperance, and knowledge ... And when she has contemplated likewise and feasted upon all else that has true being, she descends again within the heavens and comes back home.*

Aristotle, Plato's greatest pupil, kept a good deal more Platonism in his own thinking than is sometimes supposed. He shared his master's concern for the goodness of personal and community life, and his ideal of certain and unchanging knowledge. But, though he did not altogether reject transcendent realities, he thought that the objects of philosophic knowledge must be found in and through the world our senses show us, and not in an altogether transcendent world of eternal realities knowable only by the disembodied reason. He is a much tidier-minded philosopher than Plato, and is the greatest systematizer and arranger in the history of Greek philosophy. His philosophy is stiffer, tighter, and less universally attractive than Plato's; and his surviving writings are certainly very much less pleasant to read, being apparently sets of notes for lecture courses. None the less, the later Greek Platonists, like a great many other philosophers, found him indispensable and read and used him continually, though critically. Perhaps his best-known and most generally accessible contribution was in the field of moral philosophy. Anyone who wants to do some serious thinking about morality will find his most readable work, the *Nicomachean Ethics*, an excellent starting-point.

After Aristotle, Greek philosophy kept its concern for the ordering of human life on the basis of truth, but it became more

* 247 c–e., translated by R. Hackforth, *Phaedrus*, Cambridge University Press, 1952.

and more concentrated on the individual rather than the community. We should not exaggerate the sharpness of the change. The Stoics were very much concerned with the community, and rose to the vision of a universal society, a brotherhood of all mankind. And, though the Epicureans withdrew from the public, political community, they withdrew not into isolation but into their own little communities of friends. And far down in the history of Greek philosophy we find the greatest of the Neo-Platonists, Plotinus, wanting to found a Platonic city in the unfavourable environment of the later Roman Empire. But on the whole it would be true to say that the Greek philosophers after Aristotle were mainly concerned with finding the right way of life for individual men and giving them inward peace and security. The Stoics found this in absolute conformity and submission to the fiery divine reason which permeated the universe: this was virtue, the only thing which mattered. The power, and strangeness, of their faith comes out well in this prayer of the Stoic Emperor of Rome, Marcus Aurelius, to the divine universe:

Everything suits me that suits you well, O universe: nothing in your good time is too early or too late for me: everything is fruit for me which your seasons bring, O Nature: from you are all things, in you are all things, to you are all things. The poet says 'Dear city of Cecrops': will you not say 'Dear city of God'?

Meditations, IV, 23

The Epicurean universe was very different from that of the Stoics. It was the meaningless universe of the Atomists, and in it man had to depend on his own resources to reach inner peace by living according to the truth, without fear or great desire, with no help except that of a few like-minded friends. The Epicureans had a sort of confession of faith, the 'Medicine with Four Ingredients', which in its short form went like this:

God is nothing to be afraid of: death is nothing to worry about: good is easy to get: evil is easy to bear.

We are now beginning to see more clearly that the most interesting and important part of later Greek philosophy was the long development of a revived Platonism whose beginnings go back to the first century B.C. and which lasted to the end of organized philosophical teaching in the sixth century A.D. During these six centuries a great deal of critical and constructive thinking about all the major questions raised by earlier Greek philosophy went on in the Platonic schools. But their central concern soon became to find our way back to knowledge of and union with the God from whom we came by bringing our souls into likeness with him. The greatest of these later Platonists, and one of the greatest of all Greek philosophers, was Plotinus, who lived in the third century A.D. These quotations from his treatise *On Beauty* give some idea of the spirit of his philosophy, though not of his depth, precision and critical power:

Here the greatest, the ultimate contest is set before our souls; all our toil and trouble is for this, not to be left without a share in the best of visions. The man who attains this is blessed in seeing that blessed sight, and he who fails to attain it has failed utterly. A man has not failed if he fails to win beauty of colours or bodies, or power or office or kingship even, but if he fails to win this and only this.

But how shall we find the way? What method can we devise? How can one see the inconceivable Beauty which stays within the holy sanctuary, and does not come out where the profane may see it?

Our country from which we came is there, our Father is there. How shall we travel to it, where is our way of escape? We cannot get there on foot; for our feet only carry us everywhere in this world, from one country to another. You must not get ready a carriage, either, or a boat. Let all these things go, and do not look. Shut your eyes and change to and wake another way of seeing, which everyone has but few use.*

The line of development from Plotinus and his Neo-

* Author's translation, *Plotinus*, 1, 6, 7, and 8, Allen & Unwin, 1953.

Platonist successors leads on to Christian and Moslem theology and religious philosophy. But the influence of Greek philosophy on later thought is by no means confined to theologians or theistic philosophers. If you study philosophy of any period, including our own, with some historical intelligence and interest in the origins of the ideas you meet, you will keep on coming across traces of the Greeks. You will meet them so often, in fact, that you may be inclined to agree with my suggestion earlier, that the history of Greek philosophy has not ended yet.

Bibliography

ALLAN, D. J., *The Philosophy of Aristotle*, Home University Library, Oxford, 1952

ARMSTRONG, A. H., *An Introduction to Ancient Philosophy*, 3rd ed., Methuen, 1957; *Plotinus*, Allen & Unwin, 1953

BEVAN, E. R., *Stoics and Sceptics*, Heffer, 1959

BRÉHIER, E., *The Philosophy of Plotinus*, translated by J. Thomas, University of Chicago Press, 1958

BURNET, J., *Early Greek Philosophy*, 4th ed., A. & C. Black, 1930

CORNFORD, F. M., *Before and After Socrates*, Cambridge, 1932; paperback edition, 1960

FIELD, G. C., *The Philosophy of Plato*, Home University Library, Oxford, 1949

GRUBE, G. M. A., *Plato's Thought*, Methuen 1935, reprinted 1958

GUTHRIE, W. K. C., *Greek Philosophers from Thales to Aristotle*, Methuen, 1950

JAEGER, W. W., *Aristotle*, translated by R. Robinson, 2nd ed., Oxford University Press, 1948

KIRK, G. S., and RAVEN, J. E., *The Presocratic Philosophers*, Cambridge University Press, 1955; paperback edition, 1960

ROSS, W. D., *Aristotle*, 5th ed., Methuen, 1949

SAUVAGE, MICHELINE, *Socrates and the Human Conscience*, translated by P. Hepburne Scott, Men of Wisdom Series, Longmans, 1960

TAYLOR, A. E., *Plato: the Man and His Work*, 4th ed., University Publications, 1937; also Methuen paperback edition

8   Greek Mathematics and Astronomy*

George Huxley
Fellow of All Souls College, Oxford

The early history of Greek mathematics has to be recovered from statements of Plato and Aristotle and from quotations and allusions in later writers. Since not even one mathematical treatise by an Ionian or Pythagorean philosopher has survived, the gaps in our knowledge are very great; we do not know how and when the mathematical learning of the Egyptians and Babylonians was introduced to Greece.

The pre-Socratics

The history of Greek mathematics traditionally, and perhaps rightly, begins with Thales of Miletus, but it is far from certain that any of the mathematical discoveries attributed to him were his. Proclus in his commentary on Euclid's *Elements* asserts that Thales was the first to demonstrate that the circle is bisected by its diameter, but Thales can hardly have done so; even Euclid did not demonstrate the property, for he gave it as a definition in his first book.

Thales is reported by Herodotus to have predicted the year in which an eclipse of the sun would occur, and the eclipse is taken by many to be that of 28 May 585 B.C. If Thales really foretold the eclipse it was a very fortunate conjecture. There is no cycle for solar eclipses visible at any one place on the earth's surface, and all modern cycles concern the earth as a whole. There is no evidence that in 600 B.C. the Babylonians were able regularly to predict solar eclipses, and even if Thales made use

---

* Many Greek mathematicians were also philosophers and natural scientists. The other aspects of their work are discussed in Chapter 6 of the present book. Here we are concerned with the exact sciences only.

of Babylonian astronomy to predict the eclipse of 585 B.C., he could not have been certain that the eclipse would occur. If he was aware of a lunar cycle, that cycle would still not have enabled him to predict an eclipse of the sun.

To find out what an Ionian of Thales' time could have known about mathematics and astronomy the correct procedure is not to examine first the often unreliable reports of later writers, some of whom wrote as much as one thousand years afterwards, but to study Egyptian and Babylonian mathematics of his period. In Near Eastern mathematics we find no trace of the axiomatic method and the analytical proofs that characterized Greek geometry from the fourth century B.C. onwards. The Babylonians and Egyptians were chiefly concerned with mensuration and with algebraical problems; in the latter the Babylonians achieved great numerical skill as early as 1800 B.C. They had simple formulae for determining the areas of triangles and the volumes of some solids. One cuneiform text gives a value for π of $3\frac{1}{8}$, and the Egyptians had the formula for the area A of the circle: $A = (\frac{8}{9}d)^2$, where d is the diameter. An Ionian could have had access to such elementary knowledge at Greek outposts, for instance at Al Mina in Syria or at Naucratis in Egypt, or perhaps at Sardis in Lydia, which according to Herodotus was visited by many 'sophists'.

The achievement of Eupalinus of Megara in constructing a tunnel one kilometre long through a hill at Samos, in which the excavators seem to have worked simultaneously from both ends, shows that the art of mensuration was well developed in Greece in the second half of the sixth century B.C. In the same period Anaximander of Miletus set up at Sparta a gnomon or vertical marker of a sundial. He probably made use of Babylonian knowledge, for Herodotus reports that the Greeks learned from the Babylonians of the celestial sphere and the gnomon and the twelve parts of the day. Anaximander conceived the earth to be like a column drum, three times as wide as it is deep. With great insight he abandoned the idea that the earth must have some support, and argued that it stayed still because of its equilibrium. This was a clear advance on Thales' notion that the earth floated on water.

In the fifth century B.C. the Pythagoreans of southern Italy busied themselves with arithmetical speculations and number mysticism. One of them, Hippasus of Metapontum, may well have been the discoverer of incommensurability; he may have made the discovery by comparing the diagonal of a regular pentagon with its sides, for the pentagram or five-pointed star, of which the pentagon is a part, was studied by the Pythagoreans. We do not know who discovered the irrationality of $\sqrt{2}$.

Zeno of Elea is stated by Plato to have been about forty when Socrates was a young man; Zeno, then, was active about 450 B.C. He is chiefly remembered for his paradoxes of motion, one of which, the *Achilles*, well illustrates his approach to the problem of infinitesimals. Zeno asserted that Achilles will never overtake the tortoise which he pursues: 'for', Aristotle reports, 'the pursuer must first reach the point from which the pursued started, so that the slower must always be some distance ahead'. Therefore, it is argued, the slower will never be overtaken. Aristotle refuted this argument by saying that when the slower is in front he is not overtaken, but he will be overtaken in the end if he gives the pursuer a finite distance to go through. Mathematically this amounts to the statement that Achilles overtakes the tortoise after he has travelled a distance represented by the infinite series $1 + \dfrac{1}{n} + \dfrac{1}{n^2} + \ldots$; this series converges to the sum $\dfrac{n}{n-1}$. Zeno did not admit that an infinite series could have a sum, so that *Achilles* was for him a deep mathematical puzzle: to philosophers it is still of great interest.

Democritus, who was born about 470 B.C., is supposed to

have written a book on irrational lines and solids, and if the attribution of the book to him is right, the irrationality of the square root of 2 had been discovered before his time. Like Zeno, Democritus was interested in the problems of infinitesimals. He asked: if a cone is cut by a plane indefinitely near the base, are the surfaces forming the sections equal or unequal? If they are unequal they make the cone irregular, as though it had many steps; but if they are equal, then the cone will have the property of a cylinder, being made of equal circles. Another considerable mathematician of the fifth century B.C. was Hippocrates of Chios. He is supposed to have discovered that circles are to one another as the squares on their diameters, and to have reduced the classical problem of duplicating the cube to that of finding two mean proportionals in continued proportion. After Hippocrates the problem of duplicating the cube, the so-called Delian problem, was always treated as one of finding two mean proportionals.

Some details of early Greek number theory are to be found in the *Introduction to Arithmetic* of Nicomachus of Gerasa (*c*. A.D. 100). Most of them are of small mathematical interest. When numbers were represented by dots, composite numbers could be expressed by a geometrical arrangement of dots – three and ten are triangular numbers, four and nine square numbers – but primes could only be represented by straight lines. Hence Thymaridas of Paros is said to have called primes rectilinear numbers. Much of this simple number theory is attributed indiscriminately to 'Pythagoreans'.

Plato and Aristotle both understood the strength of mathematics as an educational discipline (unlike many a modern self-styled 'Platonist'), but neither of them was a truly creative mathematician. Both were fond of mathematical illustrations. In Plato's *Theaetetus* it is stated that Theodorus, a teacher of Plato, proved that $\sqrt{3}$, $\sqrt{5}$, . . ., were irrational, 'taking all the separate cases up to the root of seventeen square feet, at which point, for some reason, he stopped'. We are not told how Theodorus worked, and many ingenious conjectures have been made about his method. There is no evidence that he knew a general theorem enabling him to adapt the traditional proof of the irrationality of $\sqrt{2}$ to other numbers, and from the context it is quite likely that he had to set out a separate proof in each case. The most reasonable explanation of his stopping at $\sqrt{17}$ is that he had become tired. Theodorus also studied irrational numbers, and, besides, gave a construction for the octahedron and icosahedron. These, with the cube, pyramid, and dodecahedron, constitute the five Platonic solids, so called because they are discussed by Plato in his *Timaeus*.

To Philolaus, a Pythagorean contemporary with Socrates, is plausibly attributed a system of the world. In the centre of the universe is a central fire called the Hearth or the Watch Tower of Zeus. Around the central fire the earth, moon, sun, five planets, and the sphere of the stars move. Between the central fire and the earth there is a counter earth. We do not see the central fire and the counter earth, because the inhabited part of the earth always faces away from them. The system accounted for the apparent rotation of the heavens, but it was quite incapable of explaining the seeming irregularities in the motions of the planets. There was no observational evidence for the counter earth: it was introduced to bring the number of bodies in the universe to ten, which in the view of the Pythagoreans was a perfect number. This forcing of the phenomena to fit their numerical preconceptions was severely criticized by Aristotle in his discussion of the Pythagoreans. While Philolaus was speculating, Meton's observations had led him to the discovery of a nineteen-year lunar cycle. Meton reported the discovery at Athens in 432 B.C., and Babylonian astronomers had recognized the existence of the same cycle at about the same time. It is noteworthy that the Athenian archons, who were responsible for the state calendar, seem to have paid no attention whatsoever to Meton's discovery: whereas cyclical intercalation was in use at the latest from 381

B.C. onwards in Babylonia, there was none in the Athenian calendar. Therefore it is most unlikely that the Mesopotamian nineteen-year cycle was introduced as a result of Meton's discovery. On the contrary, cyclical intercalation may well have begun in Babylonia earlier than the time of Meton, for even before 480 B.C. Mesopotamian intercalations were much more regular than any that were ever made in the Athenian calendar. Pericles was fully in sympathy with the exact science of his day, and had not the Peloponnesian War intervened, it is possible that he would with Meton's help have attempted to reform the Athenian calendar.

Eudoxus and Euclid

Eudoxus, a contemporary of Plato and a mathematician of the first order, discovered that the motion of the planets can be explained as the combination of uniform rotations of concentric spheres about inclined axes. Eudoxus had to explain two observed facts: first, that the planets from time to time become retrograde, and reverse the direction of their movement; and second, that the retrograde motion deviates from the ecliptic. The motion in latitude is always within fixed limits, and the planet has a certain mean motion in longitude enabling it to traverse in a given period the whole ecliptic. Eudoxus combined these motions by making the planet trace upon the surface of a rotating sphere the curve called by him in his book *On Velocities* the Hippopede or Horse-fetter (Fig. 1).

The curve is most simply described as the intersection of the sphere with a cylinder touching it internally. The two loops of the curve extend along the ecliptic, and their length represents the extent of the motion in latitude. Each planet required a separate system of concentric spheres; in one version of the machinery there were, according to Aristotle in the *Metaphysics*, fifty-five spheres in all. Eudoxus also developed the

FIG. I

theory of ratios which is the foundation of the fifth book of Euclid's elements.

About the middle of the fourth century B.C. Heraclides of Pontus taught that the earth rotates. Later Aristarchus of Samos (c. 280 B.C.) went farther towards explaining the phenomena by supposing that the sun and the fixed stars are immovable, but that the earth is carried round the sun, at the same time turning on its axis. The conjecture that the earth has motion was taken up a hundred years after him by Seleucus of Seleucia near Babylon, and then neglected for over a millennium and a half. Aristarchus is not known to have produced mathematical arguments for his heliocentric hypothesis.

The axiomatic method developed by Eudoxus and his contemporaries was perfected by Euclid in his *Elements*. He drew heavily on the ideas of Eudoxus and *Theaetetus*, and made more rigorous the demonstrations of other geometers, as Proclus remarks. That there had been considerable dissatisfaction with the traditional methods of Greek geometers is suggested by a statement of Archytas of Tarentum, a friend of Plato, to the effect that arithmetic, and not geometry, alone gave valid proofs. Euclid lived at Alexandria about 300 B.C., in the time of the first Ptolemy; to the king's question whether there was a shorter way to the Elements, he is reported to have answered that there is no royal road to geometry. This great mathematician also wrote on astronomy, optics, and conic sections. A good example of the economy of Euclid's thought is his proof that there is infinity of prime numbers. In modern notation, let 2, 3, 5, . . ., p be the aggregate of primes up to p, and let $q = (2 . 3 . 5 \ldots p) + 1$. Then it is either a prime, or divisible by a prime between p and q. In either case there is a prime greater than p. Therefore the number of primes is infinite.

The Eudoxian system of homocentric spheres was modified by Callippus, but after him it was neglected by serious mathematicians because it so obviously was contradicted by the phenomena. The great changes in the brightness of Venus and Mars showed that those planets could not possibly remain at a constant distance from the earth. Autolycus of Pitane (c. 300 B.C.), the author of a treatise, extant in two versions, on spherical astronomy, is said to have tried without success to explain the changes in brightness. Some of Aristotle's successors were also puzzled by the variable size of the moon; central eclipses are sometimes total and sometimes annular, which shows that the moon does not keep at a constant distance from the earth, as the homocentric theory requires. Mathematical astronomers very soon abandoned the Eudoxian system in favour of an eccentric or epicyclic theory, but homocentric spheres long continued, owing to the authority of Aristotle, to exercise their peculiar fascination upon philosophical minds convinced of the inherent perfection of circular motion.

Eratosthenes, Archimedes, and Apollonius

With Eratosthenes of Cyrene begins a golden age of mathematics. It lasted for less than a century, but Eratosthenes, Archimedes, and Apollonius advanced the study of geometry as no Greeks before had done, or were to do afterwards. Eratosthenes was called Pentathlos, an all-round athlete, because of the breadth of his knowledge. He was a poet, historian, literary critic, geographer, and mathematician, and he followed his teacher Callimachus as head of the Museum at Alexandria. He also had the name Beta, which means that he was second in several different disciplines, a high compliment. Archimedes had great respect for his powers, and sent him problems which he would not have wasted on a second-rate mathematician. An ancient critic of great discernment called a poem of Eratosthenes in all respects above criticism. Eratosthenes, then, was not only a scientist and an accomplished poet, but also surpassed his contemporaries in the extent of his learning. It is certain that he had a powerful and widely ranging intellect.

The principle of the 'sieve' of Eratosthenes is still used in constructing tables of primes, up to a moderate limit N. We write down the numbers 2, 3, 4, 5, 6, . . . , N, and strike out successively 2^2 and then every even number, 3^2 and every multiple of 3 not struck out, 5^2 and every multiple of 5 not struck out. Continue the process until the next remaining number, after that whose multiples were struck out last, is greater than $\sqrt{N}$. The remaining numbers are primes.

Cleomedes in his book *On the Circular Motion of the Heavenly Bodies* (*c*. 50 B.C.) describes how Eratosthenes calculated the size of the earth. Alexandria and Syene in Egypt are on the same meridian. At Syene at midday at the summer solstice the sun is directly overhead, and a sundial there will throw no shadow. At the same hour at Alexandria a sundial will throw a shadow because Alexandria lies farther to the north. Lines produced from the vertical gnomons of both sundials are radii of the earth, and meet at the centre O (Fig. 2). S is Syene, A Alexandria. If α is the angle ABC made by the sun's rays with the gnomon at Alexandria, $\alpha = \angle ABC = \angle SOA$, because the rays are parallel. The arc SA, the distance from Syene to Alexandria, is known to be 5,000 stadia* and the angle α at

* The Roman unit of length, the stadium, measured 606·953 feet, or 185 metres.

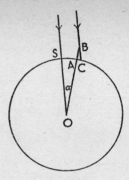

FIG. 2

Alexandria was found to be one fiftieth of four right angles. Therefore the circumference of the earth was, according to Cleomedes, 250,000 stadia. Eratosthenes' result is said to have been 252,000 stadia: the true figure is about 242,000. Amongst his other works were a treatise on the placings of the stars (from which an extant work that goes by his name is derived); a lost treatise on mathematical means, which Pappus includes in the so-called *Treasury of Analysis* with works by Euclid and Apollonius; and a work on the philosophy of mathematics called the *Platonicus*. His mechanical solution of the Delian problem he dedicated to his royal patron Ptolemy.

Archimedes of Syracuse was so great a mathematician that it seems impertinent to praise him. As an engineer and geometer he surpassed all the ancients in originality and brilliance. In all his work, whether in his *Sand-Reckoner*, a system for the expression of extremely large numbers, or in his study of conoids and spheroids, or in his analysis of the properties of spirals, or in his examination of centres of gravity, there can be seen the economy and the beauty that are the marks of mathematical genius. To Eratosthenes he sent his *Method*, the text of which was recovered by Heiberg at Constantinople in 1906; this work shows how he solved problems in quadrature and cubature, and explains what conditions are needful for their rigorous proof. His *Cattle Problem* was also communicated to the mathematicians at Alexandria in a letter to Eratosthenes. The problem, a difficult exercise in indeterminate analysis, is extant in an elegiac poem; we need not doubt that the verses are the work of Archimedes. Eratosthenes must have been delighted to receive them. Another friend of Archimedes was the astronomer Conon of Samos, who distinguished the Lock of Berenice in the heavens.

Much of Archimedes' work is known only from Arabic translations. An Arabic source states that a well-known formula for the area of a triangle, first found in Heron's *Metrics*, was discovered by Archimedes. Let a, b, c be the lengths of the sides of any triangle, and let $s = \dfrac{a+b+c}{2}$; then the Area $A = \sqrt{s(s-a)\ (s-b)\ (s-c)}$. Archimedes' beautiful construction for a regular heptagon also survives in Arabic only. It was discovered in a treatise of Al-Bīrūnī (of Chorasmia, 973–1048) on the construction of a regular nonagon. Thābit Ibn Qurra (of Baghdad, 834–901), the earliest known Arabic translator of Archimedes, had seen the original treatise in Greek, and had complained of the poor state of the text; but the proof can be recovered. To construct the heptagon let the diagonal BC of the square $ABDC$ and the transversal $DTEZ$ be drawn in such a way that the triangles DTC and ZAE are equal in area (Fig. 3). Draw a perpendicular from T to BA at K. Next construct a triangle AKH such that HK is equal to KB and AH is equal to AZ. Then circumscribe a circle about the triangle BHZ. BH will then be equal to one side of a regular heptagon inscribed in the circle. The remaining sides of the heptagon can next be drawn. Archimedes regularly covered his tracks, and it is very difficult to see how he hit on this construction for the side BH. We have here one of his many finished theorems, in which few hints are left of the method by which they were found. Such theorems have led some

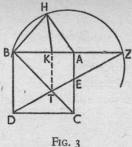

Fig. 3

scholars to suppose that Archimedes and his contemporaries had a very powerful analysis similar to modern analysis and that they worked out their results analytically before dressing up their theorems in geometrical form. But if such an analysis existed, no trace of it survives. Archimedes is one of the few ancient mathematicians whose life is well known to us. That is due to the historians' accounts of his defence of Syracuse against the Romans, and to his own memorable character that made him a legend in his lifetime. He is said to have been killed by a Roman soldier while engaged in the contemplation of a diagram. Upon his tomb his friends and relatives placed at his request a drawing of a cylinder circumscribing a sphere, with an inscription giving the ratio which the one bears to the other. Cicero found the tomb and repaired it.

Apollonius of Perga in Pamphylia is best known for his *Conics*, a systematic treatise in eight books; three survive only in Arabic and one is lost – though Edmund Halley conjecturally restored the eighth book with great probability with the help of some lemmas in Pappus. The *Conics* was still a standard textbook in the time of Newton, who made thorough use of it in the first book of the *Principia*, adapting and developing many of the Apollonian theorems, in order to determine the elliptical orbits of planets. There is no astronomy in the *Conics*, but Apollonius himself was a very great astronomer, and he must have been aware of possible astronomical applications of his theorems. Before him the conic sections had been studied by many geometers, notably by Menaechmus (c. 350 B.C.) and by Euclid. The original impetus towards the study may well have come from astronomy: the end of the shadow of a gnomon traces out a conic in the plane, and in the pre-Apollonian theory of conics it is always assumed that one generating line of the cone is perpendicular to the intersecting plane, just as the gnomon is perpendicular to the plane on which the shadow falls. Apollonius also studied geometrical optics. A fragmentary text mentions his discussion of the focus of the parabola, and shows that he applied his knowledge of conics to the theory of burning mirrors, a subject that had also interested Archimedes.

The astronomical work of Apollonius was of profound importance for the later development of ancient astronomy. It is known almost entirely from Ptolemy's treatment of it in the *Almagest*, but Ptolemaeus Chennus (c. A.D. 100) remarked that Apollonius was called epsilon, since the figure ϵ is related to the figure of the moon which he examined very accurately, and a later source mentions tables of lunar and solar eclipses compiled by him. The *Almagest* gives a clear insight into the theory of planetary motion according to Apollonius. CS (in Fig. 4) is the radius of an epicycle, and C is its centre. If CO rotates about O, and CS remains parallel to the fixed direction OA, then the resultant motion of S can also be understood as a motion on an eccentric circle of radius MA and eccentricity OM. The proof that eccentric and epicyclic motions were equivalent allowed centres of motion to be located outside the centre of the earth. Apollonius cannot have failed to see that any one of the four vertices of the parallelogram $CSMO$ may be taken as a centre of motion, and from there it was a short step from geocentric to heliocentric motion.

Apollonius also wrote a number of special treatises, the loss of which is greatly to be deplored. Several of them, including

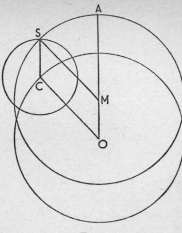

FIG. 4

his *Tangencies*, formed part of the *Treasury of Analysis*; he wrote a book called the *General Treatise* – perhaps a study of the axiomatic method and a forerunner of modern studies of mathematical foundations; and he also advanced the theory of irrational numbers. There are several references to his work *On Unordered Irrationals* in an Arabic translation from Pappus.

A notable successor of Apollonius was Diocles, the discoverer of the curve named the cissoid, so called because it resembled a leaf of ivy (*kissos*). To construct the cissoid, draw a tangent *AB* touching a circle at *B* and perpendicular to the diameter *OB* (Fig. 5). Draw lines from *O* to points on the tangent, and lay off from *O* on each the length of the segment lying between the circumference of the circle and the tangent. The locus of the points so determined is the cissoid. The curve is symmetrical to the axis *OB*, has a cusp at the origin, and has as asymptote the tangent to the circle, *AB*. Since the curve was discussed in Diocles' book on burning mirrors, he may have been interested in its properties as a reflector; but Eutocius, who describes the construction of the cissoid, states that it was

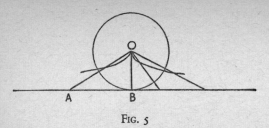

FIG. 5

used by Diocles to solve the problem of finding two mean proportionals, that is, the duplication of the cube.

Nicomedes, a critic of Eratosthenes, and perhaps a contemporary of Apollonius, constructed an instrument for generating the curve called conchoid or cochloid. Here we give the geometrical construction. Let O (Fig. 6) be a fixed point and OA its distance from a fixed line. Pass a pencil of rays through O, and lay off on each ray from its intersection with the fixed line in both directions a segment x. The locus of the points so determined is the conchoid. When x is greater than OA there is a node (as in Fig. 6). Eutocius states that Nicomedes used the curve for duplicating the cube: the conchoid may also be used for solving another classical problem of ancient geometry, the trisection of the angle. The problem of trisection may well have originated in the theory of sundials, where it is required to construct one twelfth of the arc of the sun above the horizon,

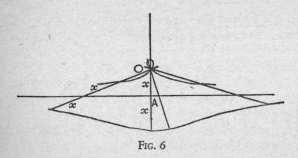

FIG. 6

that is, the equivalent of one 'seasonal hour'. This conjecture is supported by the fact that Pappus used the conchoid to trisect an angle in his commentary on the *Analemma* of Diodorus of Alexandria, a writer on sundials (*c.* 50 B.C.).

Hipparchus and Posidonius

Hipparchus of Nicaea in Bithynia wrote at least fourteen treatises on astronomy, mathematical geography, and mechanics, but of them only one survives, the commentary on the astronomical poem of Aratus (*flor.* 276 B.C.), which was in turn based upon the *Phaenomena* of Eudoxus. Ptolemy gives a list of vernal and autumnal equinoxes taken from the work of Hipparchus *On the Displacement of the Tropical and Equinoctial Points*; the observations range from 162 to 126 B.C., and so the working life of Hipparchus is securely dated to the middle of the second century B.C. Most of his observations were made at Rhodes. Ptolemy described him as hard working and with a passion for truth – qualities essential in an astronomer. His works show that he was also an astrologer.

Astrology originated in Babylonia. The earliest known cuneiform horoscope is dated in 410 B.C., and by the beginning of the fourth century Greeks were becoming aware of astrological doctrine. By the second century B.C. the practice had become fashionable, and the Stoics did much to popularize it. Hipparchus and Ptolemy were both astrologers. From the time of Hipparchus onwards astronomy and astrology were closely connected studies, and so they remained until Kepler and even later.

The greatest discovery of Hipparchus was the precession of the equinoxes. He compared his own determinations of the longitudes of certain stars with those of Timocharis, who had observed Spica in 294 and 283 B.C. and found it to be eight degrees from the autumnal equinox. Hipparchus found the angle to be six degrees. To Ptolemy, and presumably also to

Hipparchus before him, precession is a slow rotation of the sphere of the fixed stars around the poles of the zodiac. Other Greek writers who refer to precession are Proclus, who denies that it occurs, and Theon of Alexandria.

Posidonius the Stoic attempted to estimate the circumference of the earth by a method different from that of Eratosthenes. He related a given fraction of the great circle of the fixed stars to the known distance between two points in the same meridian of the earth. Let AB (Fig. 7) be an arc of the circle of the fixed stars, CD an arc of the earth's circumference, EF the two points of observation on the earth's surface (both being on the same meridian), and α, β stars directly overhead at E, F respectively. Then

$$\frac{\text{Arc } EF}{\substack{\text{Total circumference} \\ \text{of earth}}} = \frac{\text{Arc } \alpha \beta}{\substack{\text{Total circle of} \\ \text{celestial sphere}}}$$

Both circles have a common centre O. Therefore the angle EOF subtends proportional arcs. The arc $\alpha \beta$ can be determined as a proportion of the celestial sphere, and the arc EF is known. Therefore the circumference of the earth can be found.

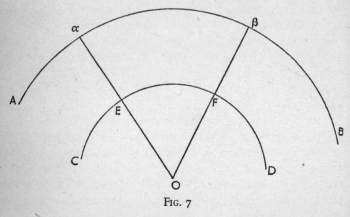

Fig. 7

Posidonius found that the star Canopus was on the horizon at Rhodes, while its elevation at Alexandria was equal to one forty-eighth of the celestial circle. By taking the distance from Rhodes to Alexandria to be 5,000 stadia, Posidonius calculated the circumference of the earth to be 240,000 stadia. Later he took a lower value for the distance from Rhodes to Alexandria, 3,750 stadia, and obtained a figure of 180,000 stadia, keeping the value $\frac{1}{48}$. This less accurate result was accepted by Ptolemy.

Later Greek mathematicians

From the second century B.C. onwards Greek mathematicians were less interested in advancing axiomatic geometry, and devoted themselves more to mensuration and to trigonometry. The work of Heron of Alexandria is typical of these tendencies. His date is not certain; he lived later than Apollonius and earlier than Pappus, and he may well have been active in the second half of the first century A.D. – in the *Dioptra* the lunar eclipse used for determining the distance from Rome to Alexandria seems to have been that of A.D. 62. Heron was not a great mathematician, but he was tireless in collecting the ideas of others. His *Metrics* is concerned with the determination of areas and volumes, and belongs rather to the traditions of Babylonian mathematics than of Greek axiomatic geometry. Heron's aim is to provide useful numerical examples, without proofs, for engineers and surveyors. His work was very popular with Roman and medieval authors, but much of it is mathematically trivial. To the historian of technology his descriptions of pneumatic machines, systems of gears, and lifting devices are of great interest. He also wrote on optics and commented upon the *Elements* of Euclid.

With Pappus, however, there was a genuine revival of geometry (*c.* A.D. 320). He was not simply a commentator, though he had read very widely in the great Hellenistic texts: the *Collection*, a work of high quality, contains a number of exciting theorems not found elsewhere, and some original lemmas to earlier treatises. One of his most interesting constructions shows how a spiral may be drawn on the surface of a sphere. It is proper to call Pappus the last great geometer of antiquity. The decline of mathematical studies under the Roman Empire is not easily explained. The schools of Alexandria and Athens did not lack good textbooks of the greatest Hellenistic geometers. One explanation may be that there were few people willing to study the texts, and fewer still ambitious and able enough to improve upon what they had been taught. Nobody thought, for instance, of developing a projective geometry from the abundant material ready to hand in Apollonius, and the theory of numbers never progressed beyond the stage to which Euclid and Apollonius brought it. The historian must be content to state what happened, and confess his inability to give reasons for the stagnation.

Greek algebra is chiefly known from the *Arithmetica* of Diophantus. His date is very uncertain, but he quotes Hypsicles who lived about 150 B.C. and is quoted by Theon of Alexandria whose date is fixed by the solar eclipse of 16 June 364. Only six of the original thirteen books of the *Arithmetica* are now extant. They are concerned with notation, the solutions of simultaneous and quadratic equations, and with the elementary theory of numbers. A typical problem is the division of a given square number into two squares, that is – $x^2 + y^2 = z^2$. The study of Diophantus led Fermat to note in 1637 in his copy of Bachet's edition his famous claim to have proved that when m is greater than 2: $x^m + y^m = z^m$ has no integral solutions (except the trivial ones where one of the variables is 0).

Simultaneous equations had been studied, long before Diophantus, by the earliest Greek algebraists. Thymaridas of Paros is credited with a rule called the *Epanthema* or 'bloom' for solving n simultaneous equations connecting n unknowns.

Diophantus admitted only positive rational solutions, and he generally does not find more than one solution, whether integral or fractional. His work does not contain any systematic theory of equations: no general solution is offered for the equations of the first degree $ax \pm by = c$. It is first found in the Indian mathematicians Āryabhaṭa (*c.* A.D. 500) and Brahmagupta (*c.* A.D. 625).

Ptolemy

The great intellect of Ptolemy dominates the history of ancient astronomy. Of the man very little is known. He was active in his Egyptian observatory between A.D. 127 and A.D. 150, and in addition to his works on astronomy, astrology, and mathematical geography, he wrote books on optics, geometry, and mechanics. The *Mathematical Composition*, better known by its medieval name of *Almagest*, a corruption of the Arabic definite article *al* and Greek μεγίστη 'greatest', is a masterpiece of exact scientific analysis. He undertook to improve the lunar theory of Hipparchus, and set himself the herculean task of representing completely the celestial motions by means of a mathematical model. The *Almagest* is a mathematical abstraction, not an attempt to represent the true physical system of the world. It was a very successful abstraction: the Hipparchian–Ptolemaic description of the solar orbit by means of an eccentric model produces errors in longitude far below the accuracy of ancient astronomical instruments. The distances of the planets are not nearly so well represented, but no direct measurement of the distances of the planets was possible for the ancients. Ptolemy paid especial attention to the correct representation of planetary longitudes, but he had great difficulty in accounting for their latitudes. His planetary theory made good use of an empirical fact, well known to Babylonian astronomers of the Seleucid period, that the number of sidereal rotations of a planet added to the number of conjunctions equals the number of years. Thus Mars in seventy-nine years completes forty-two rotations in longitude and comes into conjunction with the sun thirty-seven times, as is stated in cuneiform texts and in the *Almagest*. In an epicyclic model (Fig. 8) α is the angular distance of the centre of the epicycle from the apogee (the 'mean longitude'), β is the angular distance of the planet from the apogee of the epicycle, and γ is the longitude of the mean sun. Then $a+\beta=\gamma$ as for an exterior planet. This relation was known to Apollonius.

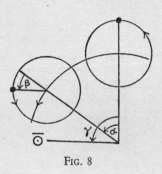

FIG. 8

Ptolemy's motives in studying astronomy were two. He desired the certain and unchangeable knowledge which only arithmetic and geometry provide, and he felt an overwhelming veneration for the heavenly bodies, regarding them as divine. Astrology and astronomy were inseparable constituents of his thought: exact science was his religion. This outlook is reminiscent of the astronomical mysticism of Plato's *Republic* and *Timaeus*, but Ptolemy was a far greater mathematician than Plato, and unlike Plato he was conscious that there can be no progress in theoretical astronomy without exact observation. Ptolemy's tables appended to the *Almagest* well illustrate his painstaking procedures. They were used for centuries afterwards by astronomers and astrologers, and the commentary of Theon of Alexandria upon them survives. To the same tradition belong the numerous Byzantine and Islamic astronomical tables, rich storehouses of evidence for ancient and medieval astronomy which have barely been explored.

Ptolemy denied that the earth moved: he argued that if the earth rotated everything that is not attached to it would be thrown up and fall back towards the west. To anyone ignorant of the law of inertia this may have seemed a cogent argument. Ptolemy's geocentric model enabled him to represent the planetary motions with far greater economy than Copernicus in the *De Revolutionibus*, who needed about twice as many circles in his heliocentric system.

Greek astronomical instruments included the water clock, which was also used by the Babylonians, and the astrolabe. The armillary astrolabe is a system of concentric rings representing the chief circles of the celestial sphere, and fitted with sights for taking observations. Ptolemy's zodiacal armillary enabled the latitude and longitude of a celestial body to be determined with respect to the ecliptic, and, in the *Almagest*, *astrolabos* means an armillary. Another type of astrolabe is the plane or planispheric, the use of which was common in late antiquity. Before the plane astrolabe could be invented, the discovery had to be made that in stereographic projection circles are kept as circles in the plane. In the *Planisphaerium* of Ptolemy use is made of the circle-preserving property of stereographic projection.

A new insight into Hellenistic astronomical methods has been given by the recent examination of a fragmentary astronomical computer of the first century B.C., recovered from a wreck off the island of Anticythera. The most extensive piece of the inscription upon the mechanism is part of a parapegma (an astronomical calendar) similar to one written by Geminus, who worked in Rhodes, probably about 77 B.C. One line refers to the Callippic and Metonic cycles of seventy-six and nineteen years respectively, and the next the eclipse cycle of 223 lunar months. The purpose of the device was to represent mechanically by pointers and dials the known cyclical relations of the heavenly bodies. Nothing in Heron would have suggested that such a machine existed; the discovery and interpretation of the device serves as reminder of how little is known about Hellenistic technology.

Spherical trigonometry was developed relatively late by the Greeks, and solely for astronomical purposes. By the time of Menelaus, however, who worked in Rome about A.D. 98, it was known that a spherical triangle is determined by its angles. The progress of trigonometry in general had been held back by the Greeks' lack of a convenient algebraical notation. Instead of using one formula for the solution of the general triangle, they divided each triangle into two right-angled triangles and solved them separately. Another characteristic of their trigonometry was the use of chords in a circle of radius 60 instead of trigonometrical functions. Hindu astronomers were the first to transform tables of chords into tables of sines. Ptolemy's command of spherical trigonometry enabled him to solve right spherical triangles in which an angle and one side, or two sides, are given. He could thus, for instance, determine the declination of the sun for a given longitude, given the inclination of the ecliptic.

The aftermath

Hellenistic exact science owed as much to the Babylonians as to the Greeks, and its influence extended to India, to the Arabs, to Persia, and indirectly to medieval Europe. In Byzantium the Hellenistic tradition was for long moribund, but it never died completely; astrology supported the continued study of theoretical astronomy, and elementary mathematics was studied with greater interest when Indian methods of calculation came to be known in Constantinople. The technical terms of Arabic astronomy were well known there. A history of the origins, transmission, and adaptation of Hellenistic science will be one of the most exciting chapters in the history of ideas, but it cannot be written properly yet. That the understanding of Hellenistic science has increased appreciably in the present generation is largely due to the devoted efforts of one man, Otto Neugebauer. His book *The Exact Sciences in Antiquity* is by far the best introduction to the mathematics and astronomy of the Hellenistic age.

When Theon's daughter Hypatia was murdered by a Christian mob, the mathematical tradition in Alexandria ceased; Hypatia had herself been a considerable mathematician, and had enjoyed the respect of learned men. At Athens the Academy still existed: there Proclus wrote his commentary on the first book of Euclid's *Elements*, and his astronomical work, the *Hypotyposis*. In A.D. 529 Justinian commanded the Academy to be closed, but mathematical studies lived on in Constantinople. Isidore of Miletos and Anthemius of Tralles, the architects of Hagia Sophia, were both mathematicians; Anthemius wrote a book on burning mirrors, and the so-called fifteenth book of Euclid's *Elements*, a work on regular polyhedra, probably belongs to the same period, since the Isidore mentioned in it is almost certainly the Milesian architect. An example of the returning current of Indian knowledge is the *Arithmetic after the Indian Method* of Planudes, who lived about A.D. 1300. About the same time Georgius Pachymeres wrote a *Tetrabiblon*, which draws on Euclid, Nicomachus, and Diophantus. The Hellenistic traditions, then, were not quite dead in the Byzantium of the fourteenth century; but there is little evidence of originality and vigour in Byzantine mathematical texts.

Mathematics is an activity that makes heavy demands upon its practitioners, and like most worthwhile studies Greek mathematics and astronomy demand effort and perseverance. The danger of superficial mathematical surveys, such as this, is that they make the subject seem less complex and demanding than it really is. Fortunately the Greekless, but mathematically

literate reader is not debarred from studying the greatest
Greek mathematicians and from entering into their reasonings.
There exist many good editions and translations of the Greek
geometers (the astronomers are not so well served). The
personalities of most Greek mathematicians are shadowy, but
we can still share in the pure intellectual delight of their
theorems. That is what makes them truly contemporary.

The most precious bequest of the Greeks to our own civilization is the habit of rational, disinterested inquiry. Their
rationality is most serene and most powerful in their mathematics. The same regard for truth that characterizes the exact
science of our own day lies at the centre of the Greek mathematical tradition. From the Eudoxian theory of proportion to
the number theory of Dedekind, from Diophantus to Fermat,
and from Apollonius to Newton, the unbroken tradition of
exact inquiry can be discerned.

Bibliography

BULMER-THOMAS, I., *Selections Illustrating the History of Greek Mathe-*
matics, 2 vols., Harvard, Loeb Classical Library, 1951

DICKS, D. R., 'Thales', *Classical Quarterly*, N.S. 9 (53), pp. 294–309,
1959; *The Geographical Fragments of Hipparchus*, University of London
Classical Studies, The Athlone Press, 1960

DIJKSTERHUIS, E. J., *Archimedes*, Munksgaard (Copenhagen), 1956

DREYER, J. L. E., *A History of Astronomy from Thales to Kepler*, Dover
Books (New York) reprint, 1953

HARDY, G. H., and WRIGHT, E. M., *An Introduction to the Theory of*
Numbers, Chapters 1 and 2, 4th ed., Oxford University Press, 1960

HEATH, SIR THOMAS, *Diophantus of Alexandria*, 2nd ed., Cambridge
University Press, 1910; *Apollonius of Perga: Treatise on Conic Sections*,
Cambridge, 1896; reprinted, Heffer, 1961; *Archimedes*, Cambridge,
1897; reprinted together with its supplement *The Method of Archimedes*
(Cambridge, 1912) in a paperback edition by Dover Books, 1960;
Aristarchus of Samos, Oxford University Press, 1913; reprinted, 1959;
The Thirteen Books of Euclid's Elements, 2nd ed., 3 vols., Cambridge
University Press, 1926; *A History of Greek Mathematics*, 2 vols., Ox-
ford University Press, 1921; reprinted, 1960

KIRK, G. S., and RAVEN, J. E., *The Presocratic Philosophers*, Cambridge University Press, 1957

KLEIN, F., *Famous Problems of Elementary Geometry*, pp. 44–7 (on the cissoid and conchoid), Dover Books, 1956

NEUGEBAUER, O., 'Apollonius' Planetary Theory', *Communications on Pure and Applied Mathematics*, **8**, pp. 641–8, 1955; 'Mathematical Methods in Ancient Astronomy', *Bulletin of the American Mathematical Society*, **54**, II, pp. 1013–41, 1948; *The Exact Sciences in Antiquity*, 2nd ed., Hamish Hamilton, 1962; 'The Equivalence of Eccentric and Epicyclic Motion according to Apollonius', *Scripta Mathematica*, **24**, pp. 5–21, 1959

PRICE, D. J. DE SOLLA, 'An Ancient Greek Computer', *Scientific American*, **200**, 6, pp. 60–7, June, 1959

WAERDEN, B. J. VAN DER, *Science Awakening*, Nordhoff (Groningen), 1954

9　　The Visual Arts of the Greeks

Martin Robertson
Lincoln Professor of Archaeology and Art,
Oxford University

In the visual arts, as in so much else, the Greek achievement
marks a turning-point, a revolution. Starting from the common background, the basic approach to representation, which
unites the various and varied arts of the Near Eastern Bronze
Age, Greek artists found a way of looking and showing which
became the way of European art ever since. The change can,
in a sense, be fixed to a precise point in time: the first few
decades of the fifth century B.C., which saw the deliberate
sloughing of certain ancient conventions in representation,
and the triumph of the new, Greek, vision – the moment we
designate as the change from archaic to classical. The seeds of
change, however, are there in Greek art long before; and the
archaic art of the seventh and sixth centuries takes much of its
fascinating character from the tension between inherited convention and the new vision. The tension endures, too, trans-
muted, in the mature phases of Greek art. Even in the Hellenistic age no Greek artist ever pursued naturalism for its
own sake as his single aim; the concept of a realizable ideal
always pulled him the other way. Yet this concept never
established itself in the form of an accepted body of rules,
such as those which make Egyptian or Byzantine art over long
stretches of their existence so static; the essential character
of Greek art lies in its perpetual development. A Polyclitus
might establish what he felt an ideal canon of proportions, and
he and others might accept it, but only as a framework within
which to develop; and even then a Euphranor or a Lysippus
would come to revise the canon.

Bronze Age and Dark Age

Greek architecture, sculpture, and painting in the accepted sense of 'Greek' took shape between the tenth and seventh centuries B.C. There was a great art in Bronze-Age Greece, and we know that over much of the country during much of that period Greek was spoken; but, while culturally and artistically the non-Greek-speaking civilization of Minoan Crete and the Greek-speaking civilization of the Mycenaean mainland make a loose continuum, there is an almost total break in material culture and artistic tradition in the dark centuries around 1000 B.C. during which the transition from bronze- to iron-using took place in Greece.

The art of Minoan Crete, typified in the frescoes that adorned its labyrinthine palaces, does indeed differ strangely from any other Bronze-Age art, in its vivid, impressionistic handling, and its concern, apparently, with Nature for its own sake; and it is arguable that the spirit of this difference in some way foreshadows the Greek revolution; but there is scarcely a trace of a direct connexion in artistic tradition. A possible example is on seal stones. Like classical gems in medieval Europe, Bronze-Age seal stones certainly survived in use into archaic and classical times; and it is perhaps no chance that, while most Greek art is dominated to a singular degree by the human form, in gem engraving (and in the daughter art of die cutting for coins) there is a wonderful display, comparable to that on Minoan and Mycenaean seals, of vividly observed animals.

In the later, Mycenaean, phase of this Bronze-Age culture, when the dominant powers were the Greek-speakers of the mainland, the representational arts tend to become rather more formal than before, rather nearer to the Bronze-Age norm. The most splendid example is also typical: the heraldic relief of lions confronted over a column which still stands above the main gateway of the upper citadel at Mycenae. The column is of a form found in actual Mycenaean architecture and apparently derived from Crete. In another way, it looks forward to the Doric column of classical Greece; for though monumental Greek architecture is in spirit and intention something quite new, in detail connexions can be traced with the lost world of the Bronze Age.

The tendency towards formalism and stylization, which distinguished the Mycenaean from the Minoan phase, becomes ever more marked in the period of decline. It can be perhaps most clearly traced in the painted pottery, which is always a flourishing craft in Greece from Neolithic down to Hellenistic times, and is of peculiar importance in the Dark Ages, the centuries of transition around 1000 B.C. The term 'Dark Age' is unfashionable since archaeology threw so much light where none was before; but it seems to me a proper designation of this period, not only because so much of what then occurred is still dark to us, but because it was manifestly a time of impoverishment, isolation, and cultural decline: a dark age to live in as well as to study. Writing fell into disuse; at least there is no evidence whatever for its employment in Greece during more than three hundred years, between the latest texts that we have in the Linear B script and the earliest in the alphabet adapted from the Phoenicians. In the visual arts sculpture and figure painting die out altogether, and monumental architecture too. Building, mainly on a small scale and with cheap materials, continues, and the everyday crafts: metal working, mainly for utensils, tools, and weapons; no doubt carpentry and weaving, which have left no trace but may have sustained a trickle of artistic tradition; and pottery, still painted but with ever more formalized and simplified designs and declining technical quality.

The beginnings

The revival from which Greek art stems begins somewhere within this dark time, perhaps a little before 1000 B.C.; but dating in this period is very uncertain. The change is first detectable on painted pottery, in an improvement in technique, the introduction of new shapes and the modification of old ones, and the scrapping of old decorative motives (ultimately derived from the naturalistic floral and marine designs of Minoan art) in favour of purely abstract patterns. These are mainly rectilinear or composed of concentric circles or semicircles drawn with compass and multiple brush; and the new shapes show a similar taste for clear definition of parts and precise, even calculated, forms, which recurs constantly in Greek art.

This new style, known by the clumsy name of Proto-Geometric, seems to have originated in Athens and to have spread thence over other parts of the Greek world; and Athens remains the leading centre of fine pottery production in the succeeding 'Geometric' period, which takes its name from the style of pottery decoration: an elaborate system of abstract, mainly rectilinear patterns disposed in graded zones over the surface of the vase. The most important of these patterns (it recurs constantly) is the maeander or key pattern, which was to take such firm root in Greek artistic tradition that the French call it *une grecque*. It is capable of very simple or extremely complicated variations; and as used by the potters of this time it is normally drawn in outline and hatched, a rather broad band which, with the other pattern bands, makes a net of unemphatic design over the whole surface of the vase. This apparent desire to make the decoration further define the clear-cut shape of the vessel seems to remain a fundamental principle in Greek vase decoration.

In early Geometric, as in the Proto-Geometric from which it is derived, animals are only very rarely introduced and we have no human figures at all. It is not till an advanced stage of the Geometric style, probably in the eighth century B.C., that figure scenes are introduced on Athenian vases: first perhaps battle-pieces on some shallow two-handled cups, in a thin, sketchy silhouette; then on the vases which give the figure style its character – huge vessels, not made for use but to place on graves. Their floors are pierced, to pour libations, and a plain stone sometimes stood beside them. It is as though, the art of sculpture having been lost, when with returning prosperity Athenians wanted monuments for their graves they monumentalized the principal art they had, that of decorated pottery, by creating huge pots and adorning them with figure scenes. The scenes chosen reflect the destination of the object: mourning round the bier, the procession to the tomb, battles by land or sea.

The figures are in silhouette and most carefully adapted to fit in with the surrounding geometrical ornament: the chest a triangle; the arms matchsticks which, when raised in mourning extend the sides of the triangle or set a rectangle above it; head and legs approximating slightly more, but still very remotely, to their actual appearance in profile; the eye indicated by a dot in the middle of the reserved circle of the head. Men are sometimes distinguished by longer chins (beards) or by wearing swords; women by longer hair and sometimes by two little marks for breasts. It is curious that Greek art, the first art in which illusionism, or at least a sustained attempt to discover means of conveying the actual appearance of things, was to become a central aim, should have started from this point of extreme abstraction, beside which earlier and contemporary arts of Egypt and the Near East are highly lifelike.

During the eighth century the Geometric style is extended to other media, especially metal work: little bronze figures, cast solid, of men and animals, especially horses; and figures and reliefs decorating big bronze tripod bowls – a form of cooking pot by origin, now glorified to be a prize at religious festivals and games, like those at Chalcis where Hesiod gained one for his poetry, which he dedicated to the Muses on Mount Helicon; or the more famous games at Olympia, traditionally founded in 776 B.C. Many have been found, there and at many other sanctuaries.

Influence from the East

During all this time, though there was certainly much movement among the Greeks themselves about the Aegean, they seem to have had little contact with the world outside. Certainly Greek art of this period takes its own development, almost untouched by foreign influence, and imports from abroad are rare. During the later eighth and the early seventh century the picture changes completely. This is the colonizing age, when Greek cities were thickly planted in Southern Italy and Sicily and more thinly over a wide area of the Mediterranean and Black Sea coasts. Trade with foreign peoples and a receptive attitude to foreign ideas accompanied this movement. The alphabet was learnt from the Phoenicians and improved upon; and in the same way imported works of Oriental art were copied, adapted, and outdone by Greek craftsmen.

The principal surviving imports and direct copies are in metal (mainly bronze) and ivory; and textiles and embroideries were no doubt also vehicles which carried this influence. None of the Eastern countries with which the Greeks were at this time in contact had a tradition of painted pottery comparable with the Greek; so that the foreign motives taken over by Greek potters are translated into their technique and medium and absorbed into the tradition, and there is a clearer continuity between the Geometric and Orientalizing styles in pottery than in metal-work. In bronze the old tripod bowl gives place to a new type: a big bowl supported on a conical stand, the bowl is adorned with heads of griffins and handle-attachments in the form of human-headed birds, male and female; the latter were to live on in Greek art as sirens and harpies.

The exact sources and nature of Oriental influence on Greek art at this time are exceedingly difficult to determine, but direct contact was perhaps mainly with the arts, themselves hybrid, of the Syrian coast; the northern part of this area deriving its styles mainly from Assyria and Urartu, and more remotely from the Hittites, the southern (Phoenicia and Palestine) from Egypt. The difficulty is well illustrated by the standed cauldrons with griffin heads and siren attachments. Precise parallels to the complete object are at present lacking from any Eastern source, as are griffin heads of exactly the Greek type; but the general form is widespread in the Near East, and many of the siren attachments found on cauldrons in Greece are of a style impossible to parallel in works of certainly Greek manufacture, and seem to be Syrian imports. The griffin-head type may have been developed in Greece out of eagle heads used in this position on some Eastern bowls. Certainly the best examples, of magnificent quality, are in a purely Greek style closely paralleled in contemporary vase painting, with their feeling for form defined by line and their combination of heraldic pattern and vivid life.

Geometric bronzes were cast solid, and so are the siren attachments. Some griffin heads are beaten out of thin sheets of bronze, a technique used in other bronzes of this time, notably some shields in a very Oriental style found and evidently made in Crete. The best griffin heads, however, are in another new technique, no doubt, like the last, learnt from the East: hollow-casting by the *cire perdue* method, which was to have a miraculous future in the hands of Greek sculptors. We know little about the centres of production of bronze work in Geometric and Archaic Greece, but griffin heads spoiled in the casting have been found on Samos, where many were dedicated in the sanctuary of Hera; and at Olympia, where many were also dedicated; they were no doubt likewise made.

Geometric pottery had been produced in many centres of Greece, but the only strong and consistent style of figure-drawing had been in Attica. This style absorbed Oriental influences and was transformed by them. The earliest vases of the so-called Proto-Attic style preserve the old geometric arrangement in zones, but the patterns are now largely reduced to various forms of zigzag, loosely drawn to form a shimmering background to the figures, whose silhouettes are filled out into swinging forms or broken down into outline, often filled with dots or fine hatching. The subject-matter too is extended and the fauna increased by real creatures like lions and imaginary ones like sphinxes – winged lions with human heads, male or female. Soon the subordinate zones are contracted, and the main picture spread to cover much of the base; and since the vases themselves are still often very large, this means drawing on a far bigger scale than hitherto. The use of outline increases, and when black silhouette is used it is enlivened with incised detail and added colour, a purple-red, a yellow, and a white.

Attic vase-painting throughout most of the seventh century is exceedingly experimental. It lacks the clearly defined standards of earlier and later work and it is often difficult to distinguish good from bad, but it has a tremendous vitality which led on to supreme achievements.

It makes an interesting contrast with the contemporary vase-painting of Corinth, called Proto-Corinthian. Corinthian Geometric was of very high technical quality and great refinement: pots of delicate make and generally small scale, finely decorated; but there is almost no figure work, and the pattern systems are simple and limited. In the Orientalizing period the taste for a small scale is preserved, and after a brief period of experiment with outline Corinthian potters develop a beautifully controlled style of figure-work in a technique which was later to become generally adopted by Greek potters – 'black-figure'. In this the figures are drawn in silhouette, not thin like that of Geometric but filled out and rounded, with detail finely incised and discreetly added in purple-red and occasionally yellow (in later black-figure, red and white are the colours added). With their tense, swinging curves, the animals which make up most of the repertory of Proto-Corinthian vase painting are closely allied at their best to the finest contemporary bronze-work, griffin-heads and others.

When human figures are introduced, the scenes are often clearly defined as mythological, as likewise in contemporary Attic. Some scenes on Geometric vases and bronze work can be given a mythological interpretation, and it is conceivable that even the funerals and battles of the grave vases are meant as legendary analogues rather than contemporary scenes. Possible evidence for this is the form of shield carried by the warriors, which apparently does not correspond to anything in actual use, but could be a misunderstood rendering of a type current in the Bronze Age. This could be a parallel to the confusion of Bronze-Age and later armament and tactic which has been perceived in the Homeric poems. It is, however, only in the seventh century that undoubted mythological scenes, in much variety, become a staple part of the subject-matter of Greek art.

Some of the finest Proto-Corinthian vases decorated with figure-scenes in the second and third quarters of the seventh century are not in normal black-figure, but show a brown colour for men's skin and a certain amount of outline drawing. A similar polychromy is found on some vases produced in other centres. It recalls the conventions of Egyptian painting, and is found again on a few fragments of painting not on vases that survive in Greece from the later seventh century. There can be little doubt that this development shows Greek vase painters influenced by wall painting; and so brings us to a new phase: the revival of the monumental arts in Greece.

The first temples; the Doric order

The first phase of Oriental influence on Greece took the form of import of small-scale Eastern works and imitation and absorption of motives and ideas found on them into the existing crafts of Greece. The next phase must have been the visits made by Greek artists to Egypt and other foreign lands, whence they brought back the idea of monumental art. The earliest Greek sculptures, at least, are certainly directly influenced by Egyptian concepts, and wall painting surely was too. The architecture seems rather an endemic development, owing more to surviving Mycenaean remains.

The type of building which sets the character of Greek architecture is the temple. This was unknown to Bronze-Age Greece, where holy places were normally either shrines in palaces or natural features – groves, caves, mountain tops. The Greek temple, however, bears little resemblance to any Oriental type, but seems to derive from the *megaron* or hall of Mycenaean palaces. This was a rectangular room, entered at the centre of one short side through a porch and anteroom, and with a central hearth that had four columns surrounding it which presumably supported a flat ceiling with a smoke hole. Bronze-Age kings were always in one way or another intimately linked to the religion of their people, and with the disappearance of monarchy during the Dark Age it is not surprising that a religious aura should cling to the decaying palace-halls. There is a little evidence suggesting the use of actual Mycenaean halls as Greek temples; and the earliest temples of which traces exist (some apparently from the ninth or even the tenth century; several from the eighth) seem impoverished versions of this form. They are small rectangular or apsidal rooms, entered from the centre of one end, sometimes through a porch, sometimes, perhaps normally, with a central 'sacrificial pit', which in certain examples had a column in front of and behind it. Actual examples survive only as foundations – dressed stone footings; the rest of the building was constructed from more perishable materials – timber with sun-dried brick or, in the apsidal examples, stone rubble. Models exist, however, which show a high-pitched roof, seemingly timber, with thatching in some cases, and a big smoke hole in the front gable.

A mid-seventh-century Cretan temple shows an attempt to translate this type into more monumental terms, with dressed stone and sculptured decoration; but the future was with a new form, created about this time in timber, and re-created in stone, perhaps not before the early sixth century, as the Doric temple.

This, in its most typical form (there are many and important variations) is a long narrow room with a porch at the east, a corresponding false porch at the back, a surrounding colonnade, and a very low-pitched roof with gables (pediments) at either end. The columns support a plain beam, the architrave or epistyle, and above this comes the frieze, consisting of a triglyph over each column and one over each interval with metopes between. The triglyphs represent the ends of original crossbeams (plain or sculptured slabs), the metopes the gaps between them; and there are many traces of the timber origin of the style: the triple grooving which gives the triglyphs their name, and especially the peg-like members which appear on the architrave under the triglyphs and on the underside of the cornice which crowns the frieze below the roof.

This type of building, if not a totally new departure, is at least a radical remodelling of the old type, and in one respect shows a profound breach with tradition. The central hearth or sacrificial pit disappears, and the building is focused internally on the cult statue of the deity, looking out from the back of the room through the eastern door. The sacrificial function of the pit is taken over by an altar outside the building. Independent open-air altars had existed earlier, but now they become regularly associated with temples, and are often set opposite the eastern door. Henceforward sacrifice and ritual take place outside, and the building becomes strictly the house of the god, who is impersonated in the statue. Thus from its beginnings the new form of temple is associated with the rise of large-scale sculpture; and after its re-creation in stone it becomes itself one of the principal vehicles for sculpture in relief.

In its timber phase this type of temple was sometimes adorned with painted terracotta metopes, set in the spaces between the wooden beam ends. Surviving examples of these, damaged and fragmentary, are among the rare remains of Greek painting other than those on pottery that have come down to us. They come from temples in Aetolia, an area of Greece always before Hellenistic times rather provincial, and at this period evidently under the cultural domination of Corinth. They closely resemble in colouring the little polychrome vases from Corinth, and share with them a bold overlapping of figures which contrasts with the usual style of composition on painted pottery. All figures, it is true, still have their feet planted on the base line of the picture, and so are kept in the surface plane, and this remains the constant convention in painting and relief sculpture throughout the archaic period; but the overlapping gives a kind of suggestion of space which hints at the revolution of the classical age.

The Greeks called the new style of architecture Doric, and the invention of one of its most striking features, the pediment or low gable, was traditionally assigned to Corinth. Certainly it seems to have been evolved in the mainly Dorian Peloponnese, though it soon spread all over the mainland and to the western colonies. The Ionic style of eastern Greece was of later and more gradual development, and we shall return to it. A very early temple, on the Ionian island of Samos, was given in the eighth century the form of a very long narrow room with a surrounding colonnade, but we know nothing of the elevations of this building. The room had also a row of columns down the centre, a feature difficult to combine with either a central hearth or a cult statue but which is nevertheless found also in a seventh-century temple on the mainland. It is evidently part of the attempt to monumentalize temple architecture before a technique for bridging wide spaces had been mastered.

The early type of temple seems to be derived from the Mycenaean *megaron*; and the first Doric architects seem to have looked back again to the same source, taking inspiration from the remains which no doubt still stood in some places. At least the Doric capital in its earliest forms is most easily explained as derived from Minoan–Mycenaean prototypes, and the flutes (the narrow concave grooving that runs the height of the column) are now known to have been used on wooden columns in at least one Mycenaean palace.

The earliest sculpture

Direct Egyptian influence is most unmistakably seen in a type of statue which appears at the beginning of Greek sculpture and remains constant throughout the archaic age: the so-called *kouros*, or youth. This figure, standing four-square, with absolutely no bend, turn, or twist, left foot forward, arms firmly at sides or lifted forward from the elbows to hold offering or attribute, had existed in Egyptian art for many centuries; but from the beginning there are certain differences. Such Egyptian statues are normally kilted and sometimes bearded; the Greek are always youths, and always naked, except that when they first appear, about the middle of the seventh century B.C., they often wear a belt.

The earliest marbles come from the great sanctuary of Apollo and his sister Artemis on the island of Delos: these are some fragmentary *kouroi* and a complete figure of a woman, dedicated by one Nicandra of Naxos, of very primitive style. Here again a tight-drawn belt makes an accent at the waist in the otherwise plank-like plainness of the clothed body. The male figures, being naked, have rather more defined forms, but there is almost no interest in anatomy and the main accent here too is provided by the belt. These figures have heads of a very individual type: a triangular face with high-set eyes under a low forehead with straight fringe and the hair falling in a wig-like frame on either side. This style is also found in a great number of small-scale works in terracotta, bronze, ivory, gold, and other materials, from Corinth, Argos, Sparta, Crete, and Rhodes, as well as in limestone sculpture from the Peloponnese and Crete. The spread of the style has been variously accounted for, but perhaps the most natural explanation is that it was the first style of monumental Greek sculpture, created by one artist or a small group of artists. It has been appropriately called Daedalic, after Daedalus, the first name in the tradition about Greek sculpture. He is associated with Athens and Crete, but it is impossible to disentangle him from mythology. Delos lies in the centre of the Cyclades islands, the primary source for fine marble in Greece, and the first school of marble sculptors certainly arose there, but they may have been anticipated by artists in the coarser stones of Crete and the Peloponnese, or anywhere in wood.

Small works from Athens do not belong strictly to the Daedalic style, and there is no large sculpture from there of the earliest period, but near the end of the seventh century begins a series of magnificent *kouroi*, some dedicated in a sanctuary of Poseidon at Sunium, others placed on graves in Athens itself. In these, and in contemporary works from all over Greece, the belt is sloughed and the pattern of the statue built up from anatomical detail – highly schematic in observation and rendering, but the beginning of one of the great interests of Greek art. Heads of many statues from this time, especially in areas where the Daedalic style had flourished, show a survival of the 'mask and wig' effect of that style; but the Attic pieces, especially a magnificent head from the Dipylon cemetery, have quite a new grasp of structure (the relationship of the face to the skull) and of sculptural form. From now on Attic artists are leaders in the development of Greek sculpture.

What do these figures represent? When *kouroi* were first

discovered they were called Apollo. The early cult statue of Apollo on Delos, of wood, a later one in the same material at Thebes, and a bronze at Miletus were certainly of this form; indeed any archaic artist wishing to represent the young god must have shown him thus. It may be, too, that some of the statues dedicated to him at Delos and his other sanctuaries are meant to represent him; but, taken all together, the evidence strongly suggests that the majority of dedicated statues were thought of neither as the deity nor the dedicator (though some certainly do represent the latter) but were simply as it were themselves: servants or companions for the god. Those placed on graves were probably conceived as standing in some sense for the dead; but in their lack of individual attributes and their unvaried youth they are more than one remove from any idea we have of a personal representation.

Early schools of sculpture

We hear in ancient writers of early schools of sculptors: pupil following master (often son following father) in one city or another of Greece. But the works we have can seldom be associated with recorded names, and in most cases not enough survives to form a clear picture of local styles. One big division is marked: between the sculpture of mainland Greece and that of the cities and islands of the Asia Minor coast (East Greece). The sculptors of the Cyclades, after their early leadership, while tending to reflect now Eastern, now Western styles, preserve a fairly distinct character. From the early sixth century onwards a varied but always provincial sculpture begins to be produced in the Greek settlements of southern Italy and Sicily.

On the mainland the naked male figure is for a long time the principal sculptural type: it is four square, with clearly defined front, side, and back views, and the pattern built up out of sharply defined anatomical detail. Female figures (practically always clothed) are comparatively rare and retain a simple and rather primitive character. There are early *kouroi* from east of the Aegean, but they seem to be mostly either imports from the West or rather soft characterless imitations. It is hardly before the sixth century that East Greek sculpture develops its own character, distinct in two important respects from that of the mainland. In all archaic Greek sculpture the natural forms are built on a strongly abstract basis; but whereas in mainland work it is the shadow of the rectangular block that one feels around the figure – planes meeting at lightly rounded angles – in East Greek work the rounding is something far more profound. The abstract basis is a sphere or an ellipsoid, a cylinder or a cone. With this goes a liking for smooth and subtle transitions, which contrasts with the emphasis, in mainland sculpture, on clear-cut division of parts. The second difference, which works in with the first to give East Greek archaic sculpture its particular character and influence, is one of subject matter. The male nude, the basic statue-type of the mainland, provides few of the best works of East Greek sculptors. There are some male figures in the *kouros* pose but clad – a type very rare on the mainland – but the greatest works are all clothed female figures: the forms partly revealed by clinging garments (completely smooth or covered with a surface pattern of folds) or concealed by stuff that hangs in forms of its own.

Works in this style are found on Samos and at Miletus as well as other places; and small ivory carvings at Ephesus perhaps take it back into the seventh century. These seem to be partly the work of Oriental craftsmen who settled in the city, partly of their Greek pupils; and elements in the East Greek style far down into the sixth century seem to owe something to Oriental ideas. In mainland Greece the phase of Oriental influence had been absorbed long before. In East Greece, contacts with the peoples of Asia Minor – Phrygians, then Lydians, finally the Persian conquerors – are far more sustained and complex.

Sculpture in sixth-century Athens

There is one great exception to the statement that we have not enough material from any archaic city to form an idea of its sculptural style: Athens. This is due to the historical circumstance that the arts were greatly encouraged there during the sixth century, and that the innumerable monuments then set up on the Acropolis and in the lower city were cast down by the Persians in the double sack of 480 and 479 B.C., and their fragments thrown into walls, terraces, and the foundations of new buildings after the Athenians' return.

Not all the material that has so been preserved is evidence for Attic style. Inscriptions show that East Greek, Cycladic, and Peloponnesian artists worked at Athens, and some surviving fragments can certainly or probably be identified as theirs; but from the mass of material a distinctive Athenian style does emerge. The wonderful feeling for form visible in the Dipylon head remains paramount, made softer and subtler by increasing skill and by the influence of East Greek work.

It is from the dedications on the Acropolis that we know best the type of female figure which we call *kore* (girl). Most of these examples are no doubt Athenian, but some are certainly East Greek, some Cycladic, and the type is found in many parts of the Greek world. It is a natural development of the interests shown earlier by sculptors in East Greece, and it was probably there that it was created. Early statues of girls in all parts of Greece stand with the feet together and the arms at the sides or one laid against the breast with a flower or bird in the hand. The new type, created about the middle of the sixth century, has the left foot forward, an idea presumably adapted from the *kouros*, and the left hand holds the skirt to the side and slightly forward, pulling it tight over the legs to reveal their form and letting a swag of stuff hang loose in its own folds. The upper part of the body is clad in a clinging undergarment, visible on the left shoulder, and a heavy upper garment brought diagonally over the right shoulder and under the left arm, with ends hanging loose under the right elbow; the right forearm is raised with an offering in the hand. There are many variations, but this is the usual scheme, and is clearly a deliberate creation: a type to correspond to the *kouros*, and one which would give maximum play with revealed and concealed forms, loose and clinging drapery. It is not a form that stands the rough treatment of time well, and few examples exist that do not suffer from ugly fragmentation; nor perhaps was it ever a very happy creation, leading at the best to virtuosity, at the worst to triviality. There are beautiful works among them, but it is noteworthy that the most satisfying statue of a girl from the Acropolis is not of this type but on the old model (feet together; simple, with a symmetrical garment, belted and almost without folds) yet treated with all the new subtlety and feeling for the relationship of body and clothes learnt from East Greek sculptors.

These girls dedicated to Athena are the clearest example of statues which represent nothing but themselves. They are not the goddess, since they bear none of her attributes (spear, helmet, aegis), as some other figures from the Acropolis do; nor are they the dedicator, since some of them stand on bases whose inscriptions show them to be the gift of a man. There are, however, statues which probably or certainly do represent the dedicator. A beautiful figure of a man with a calf on his shoulders – one of the first real groups in Greek art – stands like a *kouros* but has a beard and a cloak. These features must be meant to show that this is not the usual anonymous figure but an Athenian citizen, Rhombos, whose name appears on the pedestal. In a dedication at the Samian Heraeum the fact is beyond doubt. A long base bore several figures, standing, seated, or reclining, inscribed with their names, one also with the sculptor's name, Geneleos, another with the formula of dedication – evidently a family group.

Archaic relief and architectural sculpture; the Ionic order

On tombs in Athens from the later seventh century onwards were sometimes placed, instead of statues, tall narrow pillars of rectangular section, at first bare except for the inscription and a capital which supported the figure of a sphinx. During the first half of the sixth century it became the practice to adorn the slab with a figure of the dead in low relief; and later (the type lasts down till nearly the end of the century) the sphinx and capital are replaced by a decorative finial in the form of a palmette.

In Egyptian and other pre-Greek arts the basic conventions of low-relief sculpture are identical with those of drawing and painting and in some respects almost the opposite of those of sculpture in the round. The independent statue is conceived as a self-contained being, whose most important aspect is naturally the front view: one approaches it face to face as one would a person; and side and back views, though having an aesthetic validity of their own, are definitely subordinated to the front. Drawing, painting, and relief are essentially in these arts vehicles for narrative; and the figures in them are concerned with one another and with what they are doing. They, therefore, do not face the spectator but present him with an unconscious profile. This distinction is preserved in archaic Greek art; and it is noteworthy that, while the statues on graves are exactly the same ideal youths as those dedicated to the gods, the profile figures on the Athenian gravestones, though nothing like portraits as we understand them, are much more particularized. The dead person is shown in armour or with athlete's gear, bearded sometimes; and sometimes there is a little predella at the bottom representing him in action.

Low relief is used also for dedications at this time, and

sometimes in the decoration of buildings; but in this last context there gradually develops during the archaic period a new art form: sculpture in high relief. In the earlier arts of Egypt and the Near East, the depth to which the background of a relief is cut back varies. It is sometimes quite deep, but the conventions remain those of low relief and drawing, and the forms are more or less flattened out against the flat background. In archaic Greek architectural sculpture there is at the beginning what seems to be a confusion between the conventions of low relief and those of sculpture in the round: and these are finally developed into a fusion, a new art in which figures are given their full three-dimensional values, like statues, but are grouped against the flat background in a two-dimensional composition.

We have seen that the Doric temple in stone was in existence by the early sixth century. Its wooden predecessors had sometimes painted (sometimes also moulded) terracotta decoration in the gables and the metopes; in the stone version stone reliefs took the place of these. In low relief for graves and votives, as in free-standing sculpture, the Greeks had taken over from earlier arts existing types with their age-old conventions; but the Doric temple, as we have seen, has no close connexion with any foreign form and there were no conventions for its decoration. Moreover, both metopes and pediments were high above eye level, and there would be a natural tendency for a sculptor to deepen his relief so that the design should stand out more sharply. At first, however deep the background is cut, the surface of the figures tends to preserve a flattish plane parallel to that of the background, together with the inorganic relationships of contemporary drawing. Full-face shoulders and breast are set on profile hips, the transition is slurred or ignored; yet the heads, which in low relief or drawing would almost always be in profile, are often turned out towards the spectator, in defiance of the narrative content, as though the sculptor felt that a carved head ought always to look at one.

187

The concern with anatomy which appeared, we saw, in the *kouroi* of the later seventh century, continues throughout the sixth, and its progress can be traced most easily in statues of the *kouros* type. By the end of the century sculptors have mastered the structure of muscle and bone as it appears in the naked male body; but this structure is shown, as it were, in an abstract and ideal way, with none of the tensions, the contrast of taut and relaxed muscles that would appear in a human figure even if he stood in the rigid *kouros* pose. Similarly, in low relief and drawing, the growing knowledge of anatomical forms is reflected, but the problems of contrapposto and movement are not tackled. In architectural sculpture, however, the artist gradually finds himself carving figures with the full three-dimensional values of statues in the round but shown in movement and action, and these further problems are absolutely forced on his attention. The art of high relief is one of the great creations of archaic Greece, and is of central importance in the development that leads on to the classical revolution.

It is in the gables and metopes of Doric temples and treasuries in mainland Greece and the western colonies that this development can mainly be traced and, no doubt, mainly took place. Most of these sculptures, like the buildings themselves, are in limestone. It is only in the last quarter of the sixth century that marble begins to be used in these areas for architecture and architectural sculpture, but, east of the Aegean, it was employed earlier for both. Limestone sculpture seems normally to have been completely covered with washes of colour, the skin of men was brown or red, of women, white. In marble, at this time, the naked parts were left in the polished stone, with colour applied to hair, eyes, lips and parts of the clothes.

We saw that in free-standing sculpture East Greek artists made an important contribution to development during the sixth century. During the same period their contribution to architecture, the creation of the Ionic order, was no less significant. Like the Doric, the Ionic is clearly derived from timber construction. The basic form of the temple is the same, though there is a good deal more variation in plan; and throughout the sixth century there is altogether much more variety and experiment – it settles to a rigid rule much less soon than Doric. It differs from Doric throughout in having far more carved ornament, perhaps partly because it was, from the beginning of its stone phase, developed in marble, which takes a sharper finish than limestone. The columns stand on elaborately moulded bases and are crowned by capitals of complex design; the architrave is stepped in three sections; and junctions (the top of the architrave, the foot of the walls) are commonly marked by narrow bands of carved ornament. An important difference, derived from the timber prototype, comes at frieze level, where, instead of triglyphs and metopes – large beam ends with correspondingly large spaces between – are found the 'dentils', which evidently derive from small, close-set rafter ends, and offer no field for sculpture. A desire to have figured sculpture at this level (perhaps provoked by the example of Doric) leads often to the introduction, either below the dentils or in place of them, of a continuous carved band, the Ionic frieze, a feature for which there is no ready-made place on a Doric building. There is a marked tendency, in such friezes of the archaic period, to keep the relief low.

The classical revolution in sculpture

By the end of the sixth century the old conventions were beginning to be hampering to Greek artists. There are good works among the late *kouroi* and *korai*, but many of the latter are all fussy prettiness, while the former, with their carefully observed anatomy, have an empty, academic character, as though the form no longer offered the artist any problems which really challenged him. We have seen that in architectural sculpture artists had already begun to integrate their anatomical observations with the representation of action and complicated poses. It was, nevertheless, an act of great courage and incalculable significance to abandon the old idea of an image, standing as an image, and replace by it a figure standing as a man stands, with all the subtle interplay of taut and relaxed muscles, the balance of lines and masses released from the four-square shadow of the block. If certain artists had not taken that step, Greek art might have sunk into the decorative dullness of Achaemenid or late Egyptian. There is a view that the Greeks set European art on the wrong road for two thousand years. If that is what they did, this is the moment at which they did it; but the way to Michelangelo and Titian seems to me, like that which the queen of fair Elf-land took True Thomas, 'a bonny road', and I am glad they chose it.

We do not know by whom or where the change was first achieved, but statues on the new model were being made in Athens before 480 B.C. At least, among the figures from the Acropolis, and almost certainly part of the debris of the Persian sack, are remains of two such figures in marble: an almost complete one known as the Critian boy, and a marvellous head (whose neck shows that it was turned and inclined) called the fair-haired boy, from the yellow paint well preserved on the hair when it was found. In the Critian boy, the relaxations from the *kouros* pose are very slight but quite definite: weight on one leg; hips, therefore, not quite level; the slightest of twists in torso and neck; so that suddenly it is alive – an image not in the stamp of an image but in the likeness of a youth.

The other head shows better another quality of the new movement, its seriousness. Archaic faces often smile; a device, we are sometimes told, used by the primitive artist to give life to the features. There may be something in this explanation, but the gay effect – pure joy of living – is surely no accident; nor is the grave regard of the fair-haired boy. Archaic faces, one might say, are extrovert, classical introvert. So, one of the latest *korai*, dedicated by a certain Euthydicus, is known as *La Boudeuse*, from the contrast of her almost sullen expression with the smiling norm. This work is closely related to the fair-haired boy, and is perhaps from the same master hand. Here, however, the sculptor has not broken with the ancient principles of structure. The figure conforms strictly to the archaic idea of a statue; it follows the conventional scheme of a *kore*; only, together with the smile, the artist has suppressed all the virtuosity and prettiness which that scheme was designed to invite.

In these works we see the act of transition from archaic to classical. They must have been made very close to the time of Marathon, perhaps in the ten-year respite between that attack and Xerxes' invasion, anyway within the period of the Persian wars; and it was against that background of threat and triumph that the change from archaic to classical art was accomplished. Such events can never be the causes of such changes; and this change, we have seen, was long prepared; but the tensions of the time may have done something to precipitate it. The repulse of the Persians left a profound impression on the Greeks, and perhaps had a catalytic effect on their literature and art.

The beginning of bronze statuary

The figures from the Acropolis which we have been considering are of marble. Large-scale bronzes were dedicated there before the Persian sack, but while broken marble was thrown into terraces and foundations broken bronze was melted down to be used again. We know of one pair of bronze statues which stood in the market place at Athens and were carried off by Xerxes to Persepolis: the Tyrannicides Harmodius and Aristogeiton made by Antenor, who had earlier carved a large *kore* in marble dedicated on the Acropolis. They were replaced after the Athenians' return by Critius and Nesiotes, probably Antenor's pupils. Antenor's were returned to Athens after Alexander's conquest of Persia, but both sets have perished. We have, however, marble copies of the later pair, made under the Roman empire, and it is from a resemblance to these that the Critian boy takes his name.

Small bronze statuettes cast solid are a feature of Greek art from Geometric times, and we saw how, in the seventh century, Greek craftsmen learnt the art of hollow casting and practised it in the griffin heads for cauldrons. It seems to have been only in the mid sixth century, however, that they mastered the skill of hollow casting large-scale statuary. The names of Rhoecus and Theodorus, who were also architects and built the great temple of Hera on Samos under Polycrates, are associated in later tradition with the beginning of this art. From the second half of the sixth century we have several pieces of bronze statuary, mostly under life size, but one bronze *kouros*, over six feet high, certainly dates from well before the end of the century. These figures conform entirely to archaic conventions, as practised in stone sculpture, but the arms of the *kouroi* are free of the body – a natural development in the technique of modelling in clay and wax for casting, as against carving from the block. Some late archaic marbles show the same thing, perhaps under influence from bronze work. Antenor's bronze Tyrannicides, which like their successors were perhaps over life size, must like them have been portrayed in action; and there is evidence for late archaic groups in marble in which the figures were so shown. We saw that in architectural sculpture artists had felt free to experiment away from archaic conventions; and evidently this freedom, at the end of the archaic age, was extended to free-standing groups of action figures, while the single, substantive statue remained locked in the traditional form.

Architectural sculptors had the technical aid of the background, to which the figures either remained attached or (in the case of pediment figures, which were often carved completely free) to which they could be fixed to support them. The technical problem of producing free-standing marble figures in complicated pose and action presented difficulties to artists of this transitional period which were largely avoided in the use of bronze, with its far greater tensility and the possibilities of casting a statue in several pieces which could afterwards be joined, and of balancing it by weights put in the feet or in any other part of the hollow metal.

Perhaps partly for this reason bronze became the most popular medium for the great sculptors of the fifth century. It was usual to practise marble carving as well, but most of the masterpieces from that time of which we read in Greek and Latin writers were in bronze. Whatever the cause, the consequence is that our knowledge of Greek art in the classical period has not the same basis as in the archaic. Few archaic statues can be connected with famous names, but the marble of which they are made was the material in which all sculptors normally worked, and many of them are certainly masterpieces of their time. From the fifth century, the marbles that have come down to us are mainly architectural decorations, which, though they must often have been designed by leading artists, were certainly normally executed by hired hands, artisans paid by the piece; and reliefs for tombs or reliefs dedicated in sanctuaries, among which there are great works, but which were certainly in the main the work of comparatively humble craftsmen who specialized in this field of production. The great bronze works have almost all perished, owing to the convertibility and value of the material. Those that survive have done so largely through the accident of their early loss in shipwreck, landslide, or the like.

The shipwrecks took place when the objects were being looted for collectors in Rome or Constantinople; and many masterpieces of the classical age, marble as well as bronze, must have gone to those cities before they perished. The interest, however, which inspired the looting, was also responsible for another activity which does a little to repair the losses. Later taste for the most part ignored archaic art, or borrowed its formulae for decorative fancies. Classical art, however, was vastly admired; and those citizens of the Roman empire who laid claim to taste but could not afford originals liked to have copies (generally in marble, which was cheaper than bronze) of old masterpieces in whatever material. Thousands of such copies survive, many repeating each other so exactly that it is clear that they were pointed off by a partly mechanical process from casts of the same original. A certain number of these can be related, surely or with greater or less probability, to the works of famous artists recorded by ancient writers. Aesthetically, of course, these copies are no substitute for the lost originals, though they vary greatly in quality and the best are beautiful. There is a temptation to limit our interest in Greek art to what actually remains: the works of the archaic age, and from the classical the fresh and often lovely marbles from temples and tombs; but one cannot understand the historical importance of this historically immensely important art without considering also the traditions about the great masters of the classical age, and the copies of their works which survive.

Early classical statuary and sculpture

By a lucky chance a few great bronzes do remain from the early classical period: notably the charioteer of Delphi and the bearded god (Zeus or Poseidon) from the sea off Cape Artemisium. The charioteer formed part of a group dedicated by the Sicilian prince Polyzalus of Gela, to commemorate a chariot victory at the Pythian games, probably in 478 B.C. There was a four-horse chariot, the charioteer standing in it, with perhaps another figure, and possibly more figures outside the chariot; but only a few fragments, together with parts of the marble base bearing the dedicatory inscription, were preserved for us with the charioteer by a fall of rock. The figure has an almost archaic simplicity of pose, just relaxed like the Critian boy into a natural stance. His long tunic, belted high, falls in deeply cut columnar folds, a favourite form in clothed figures of this time, part of the reaction against late archaic elaboration and prettiness.

The god from the sea is an action figure. He strides out, looking along his left arm stretched before him, with the right arm back; the hand once held a thunderbolt or trident for the throw. The whole figure is designed in one plane (or rather would fit into a narrow space between two parallel planes) above all to be seen in profile – from front and back the outstretched limbs telescope; and this is a distinction which holds good generally in classical, especially early classical sculpture. 'Repose statues', simple, substantive figures of gods or men, not in any action but standing quietly, derive from the ancient concept of a statue as a being, designed above all to be seen from the front, met face to face. 'Action statues', whether parts of groups or alone, are conceived primarily in relation to the action they are performing, the event in which they are taking part; and are, therefore, often designed primarily to be seen in profile, the traditional aspect for narrative art. A striking example is the Discobolos (discus thrower) of Myron, a famous work of which we have full-size marble and small bronze copies. Here, even more than in the god from the sea, the figure is designed for a harmonious effect in side-view, which as one walks round it is gradually lost in a jumble of foreshortened limbs.

Myron, who seems to have flourished in the mid fifth century, came from Eleutherae on the borders of Attica and Boeotia and worked in Athens. We hear of sculptors from all over the Greek world at this time, Sicily included, but the impression given by the literary tradition is that the formative role in the development of bronze statuary was played by the artists of Argos and Sicyon in the north-eastern Peloponnese. We cannot connect any original or copy of this period with any of the names of artists in these schools which have come down to us; but it is probable that the god from the sea belongs to one of them, and certain copies of repose statues closely resemble it in style and must reflect works of the same origin. One is a youth, resembling the Critian boy in pose, but over life size and with the easy classical rhythm more pronounced. Two fine copies exist, one in the British Museum known as the Choiseul-Gouffier Apollo, the other in Athens, called the Apollo from the Omphalos. The copies differ; that in Athens is more sensitive in handling (a warning of the difficulty of judging from copies); but they share a dignity and beauty, an essential character, which can only derive from the original. Another copy from what must have been a marvellous work of this school is a heavily draped female figure, with skirt deeply fluted like the charioteer's and veiled head, a goddess known as the Hestia Giustiniani. There is another heavily draped and veiled woman, of equal beauty with the Hestia, but the swathing cloak is rendered in smooth, flat planes meeting at sharp angles, and the face is in a different style; the product one would say of the same time and spirit but a different school. She is known as 'Amelung's goddess' from the scholar who reconstructed the type from scattered copies of body and head, now proved by later discoveries to belong together. There is reason to think that the statue stood in Athens and represented Europa.

The cities of southern Italy and Sicily, which produced lively but provincial sculpture throughout the archaic age, continued production into the classical. Small terracotta reliefs from Locri suggest that it was there that was made the most beautiful of all low-relief marbles of this time, one of the masterpieces of Greek art, the so-called Ludovisi Throne – a three-sided relief of uncertain purpose. On the main face there is Aphrodite lifted from the sea by two helpers, on one short side a naked flute girl, on the other a swathed matron burning incense. The most impressive production of Sicily are metopes from a temple at Selinus, carved in local stone but with the flesh parts of the female figures added in imported marble – this is still perforce a provincial art. Of the four which survive fairly complete, two show rather conventional fights, a third a moving confrontation of Artemis with Actaeon torn by his dogs, the finest a veiled Hera standing before a seated Zeus – a noble example of classical quietness.

The acme of this early classical phase of Greek art is to be found in the sculptures, about contemporary with those at Selinus, which decorated the Temple of Zeus at Olympia and were completed soon after 460 B.C.; but before turning to those we must consider the development of painting.

Archaic painting and vase painting

The black-figure technique, perfected in Corinth in the first half of the seventh century, became before the end of that century the accepted manner for vase painting in Athens also; during the sixth century Attic black-figure became first the leading and then the only important style of vase painting in Greece. The technique of the best Athenian vase painting of this time reaches an extraordinary level of quality. The clay is an orange colour, the black hard and shiny, the incised lines exceedingly sharp and fine. White is used normally for women's skin and other details, and yet others are in a deep cherry red. These colours, especially the white, have not always lasted well, but when they have the decorative effect is most striking. Black-figure is essentially an art of decoration, a ceramic art which tells us little about contemporary developments in free painting. It is, however, a wonderful art in its own right. The artists' own pride in it is perhaps reflected in the frequent signatures, alike of painter and potter. From these we learn that sometimes the same man made a pot and painted it, sometimes a potter and a painter worked regularly together, sometimes a potter worked with many painters or a painter with many potters; and we also learn, since one will sometimes name a father whose name we meet elsewhere as a potter himself, that the craft sometimes ran in families.

The greatest of these painters (he was a potter too) was one Execias, who flourished in the third quarter of the sixth century. Archaic narrative art is as a rule directly concerned to portray action, to tell a straight story. Execias strangely anticipates the classical spirit in a liking for quiet scenes and in his power of imbuing them with a sense of emotion; he portrays a state of being rather than tells a story. Black-figure, however, is a racalcitrant medium for such a mood. Only a very great artist like Execias can compel it to that end. Vase painters took part in the classical revolution, but not with the black-figure technique.

During the first half of the sixth century Corinthian figured vase painting remains a rival to Attic. Corinthian painters employ black-figure, but not so strictly as the Athenian: there is more outline and a freer use of red and white, not simply as adjuncts to the black but on equal terms with it. The effect is probably nearer to that of free painting, and there is a tendency to more complex overlapping and massing of the figures in composition than is usual in Attic. We have precious remains of wooden panels from near Sicyon, which date from after the middle of the century, when figure painting on Corinthian vases had died out, and they do show a similar character, though with a lighter and clearer effect. The ground is white, and the figures are drawn in outline, red for women, black framing a pinkish wash for men, with washes of other colours (red, blue, grey, yellow) for clothes and the rest. The heights of the figures are more varied than is common in vase painting, but here, as in vase painting and in relief, all feet are on the base line still and there is no indication of depth or of modelling.

Up to the late seventh century little Attic pottery was for export, whereas quantities of Corinthian are found abroad, especially in the western colonies and in Etruria. During the early part of the sixth century, Athenian potters seem to have been trying to capture those markets, and succeeded so well that fine figured pottery ceased to be produced in Corinth after about the middle of that century. Sparta and various East Greek centres continued to make painted pottery of a rather provincial kind, mainly for local use; and two good black-figure wares arose after the demise of Corinthian, the so-called Chalcidian, perhaps made in one of the western colonies, and the 'Caeretan hydriai', probably the work of a Greek who settled in Etruria. These too, however, died out before the end of the century, leaving Athens unrivalled; but by this time the principal technique used in Athens was no longer black-figure.

It seems to have been about 530 B.C., in the generation of Execias' pupils, that the new 'red-figure' technique was invented. In principle it is simply a reversal of black-figure, with the figures left in the colour of the clay and the background painted with the shiny black; it is at first simply a decorative variation on the old technique, with black- and red-figure often used on the same pot. It proved, however, to have certain great advantages. From a purely decorative point of view, the larger area of black emphasized more than before the surface of the pot, a thing Greek potters had liked since Proto-Geometric times; and the background to the figures could spread over the whole pot, integrating pot and picture in a way which was hardly possible in black-figure. At the same time, for purposes of representation it has the advantage that inner detail, instead of being engraved, is drawn with a brush or pen in black or black thinned to brown – a subtler, suppler line which brings vase painting close to free painting. Thus in the second generation one finds practitioners of the new technique developing a style to suit it, spreading the figure work at the expense of the subordinate ornament, making less play with surface pattern, using added red very discreetly and white hardly at all (women's skin is no longer differentiated from men's).

The two techniques flourished side by side; some painters practised both, some specialized in one; but the general changes that came over Greek art during the late sixth century tipped the balance decisively in favour of red-figure. The concern with movement and contrapposto, developed in high relief, which we saw penetrating free sculpture and paving the way to the break with archaic convention, penetrates drawing too at this time, and we find efforts really to represent the twists and turns of bodies in action, the appearance of foreshortened limbs. For this kind of drawing the supple red-figure line proved much more suitable than the engraved silhouette of black-figure, which is best when most formal. Good artists continued to use black-figure for a while, but after the end of the century only occasionally, mostly for the special prize oil jars at the Panathenaic games; the old technique is employed, otherwise, only for the mass production of small vases.

Some leading red-figure vase painters of the late sixth century have left us their names, with expressions of rivalry which suggest that they felt themselves pioneers in the experiments of the new age; and the red-figure of those years and the first decade or two of the new century is perhaps the acme of Greek vase painting. The experiments are concerned purely with the rendering of individual figures in movement. The technique, with its shiny black ground isolating the figures, discourages any attempt to suggest the space in which they move and are related. No such attempt is made, however, in contemporary low relief nor in occasional drawings that survive in other techniques; and it is clear that no breach with the tradition of drawing as purely surface decoration was yet envisaged. That break was made by Greek painters in the generation after the Persian wars, in the seventies and sixties of the fifth century, and so the revolution which had been begun by sculptors of works like the Critian boy was carried a stage further.

The revolution in painting

The revolution in painting is associated with the name of Polygnotus of Thasos, who worked for Cimon at Athens, together with the Athenian Micon, and at Delphi. Their famous wall paintings are all gone, but we have descriptions, and there are vases which evidently echo their great innovation, which was to break the tyranny of the base line: to set figures up and down the field on indications of broken ground which may conceal parts of them. This is the beginning of the idea of a picture not simply as narrative decorating a surface, but as a feigned window on the world. It is clear from the descriptions and the vase imitations that this was a very cautious and limited departure; but to make it was no less bold and no less far reaching than the earlier action of the sculptors.

The most elaborate imitations are in red-figure, which as we have seen is by its nature unsuited to this departure, since the isolation of the figures against the unmodulated black of the shiny ground denies even the limited illusion of space aimed at by the great painters. There is however another technique employed mostly on smaller vases – mainly at this time within the shallow bowl of wine-cups – which must bring us nearer to the actual appearance of the lost wall paintings: the 'white-ground'.

A white slip had been used from Geometric times in some Greek vase-fabrics, and in the second half of the sixth century some Athenian black-figure painters used to cover the orange clay with it for a change of decorative effect. Late in the century some red-figure artists sometimes draw in outline on a white ground, adding washes of thinned glaze, purple-red and sometimes yellow; during the first half of the fifth century the practice is continued, with the outlines in thinned glaze and some increase in the range of colour washes, various browns and reds. The technique continues, with further modifications (matt outlines; blue and green added to the colours), to the end of the century, but never becomes other than a side-line of red-figure, perhaps because it was felt to be basically less suited to the primarily decorative purpose of vase painting; but with it we must stand very close indeed to the appearance of contemporary free painting.

We saw that the earliest classical sculpture has a withdrawn, inward character, opposed to the love of life and action in archaic. Polygnotus, by all accounts, seems to have carried this mood furthest, choosing to represent actions by the moment before or after the event, and composing his pictures out of groups of figures sunk in their own thoughts. It was perhaps this tendency, as much as an interest in spatial composition as such, which led him to his revolutionary advances, since to create an interesting composition in these terms is very difficult if all figures are anchored to the base line of the picture. This side of the new art comes across clearly in some of the vase paintings, as it does also in the sculptures of the temple of Zeus at Olympia.

The Temple of Zeus at Olympia

Zeus had been worshipped at an altar in the sacred grove at Olympia from time immemorial. His consort Hera had a temple there from at least the seventh century; and from the early sixth the god had had an image in it beside hers; but he himself had no house there until after the Persian wars. The decision to build a temple for him at this great and ancient sanctuary is a breach with tradition like so much at this time. It followed hard on the Persian defeat and must be connected with feelings of Greek unity, a theme which the sculptures of the buildings seem designed to illustrate. The temple, however, was built out of booty won by the Eleans in a war with neighbouring Pisa, and we know that it was finished by 457 B.C. because on the apex of the eastern gable the Spartans made a dedication for their victory at Tanagra in that year over the Athenians and their allies. These stones have a sermon in them.

The revolution carried through in the first half of the fifth century by sculptors and painters passed architects by. Classical Greek architecture is basically no different from archaic: the same rectilinear structure designed primarily for external effect; the same system of detailed forms derived ultimately from timber construction. A wonderfully subtle scheme of refinements is evolved, and a great deal of delicate variation is introduced in individual buildings, but there is no revolution. The temple of Zeus at Olympia is fallen, but the remains show it to have been a perfectly typical Doric building. Like most temples west of the Aegean it is in limestone once covered with marble stucco, but the sculptures are in marble.

The metopes of the outer colonnade were left plain, and only the six above the inner porch at the eastern end and the corresponding set above the false porch at the back were carved, with adventures of Heracles – perhaps first forming the canon of the Twelve Labours. The series began at the north end of the western set with the traditionally first adventure, the Nemean lion, and ended at the north end of the eastern set with a local story, the cleaning of the Augean stables. In these two, and in one other of each set, the hero is accompanied and aided by the patroness of heroes, Athena. In the lion metope and that with the Stymphalian birds, the sculptor has not shown the actual adventure but the moment of quiet succeeding it. In the first the boy rests exhausted, head on hand; in the other he brings the bodies of the birds to Athena. Both show the early classical, Polygnotan mood; in the second there is unmistakable influence from the new pictorial style: Heracles, fully carved in the round, stands on the base line, while Athena, in rather lower relief, sits up on a rock – a form of composition which recurs in many Polygnotan vase paintings. The same combination of high and low relief, echoing the new spatial ideas of paintings, is found in a magnificent action metope, where the fully realized body of the hero crosses the flattened one of the bull he is taming. Here the two figures, straining outwards, turn their heads back towards one another – a motive that was to become a favourite rendering of strife in classical art.

Of the pediments, the eastern shows another quiet Polygnotan moment, this time before the action, the preparation for a chariot race in which Pelops was to win his bride and found his fortunes. The other gable has a scene of violent action, the fight of Centaurs and Greeks at the wedding of Peirithous. This one is dominated by Apollo in the centre, the other by Zeus himself. Apollo, like Athena and Heracles, was a child of Zeus. He was also lord of the two other greatest interstate sanctuaries, Delphi in central Greece and the Ionian island of Delos. Athena was especially connected with Athens, and the Athenian hero Theseus played a leading part in the battle with the Centaurs: Apollo here is flanked by Theseus and his bosom friend Peirithous, king of the Lapiths in Thessaly, where the action takes place. The defeat of the Centaurs seems often to be used as a symbol of Greek civilization triumphant over barbarism, as are the labours of Heracles, the universal Greek hero. The *venue* of Pelops' chariot race is local to Olympia itself; but Pelops is the eponymous hero of the Peloponnese. The net of subject matter seems to be deliberately cast to suggest the unity of Greece against the background of the Persian wars.

The treatment of the Pelops theme illustrates another aspect of the classical mood. It is a barbarous story, full of treachery and blood guilt, but it was told about this time by Pindar (in an ode celebrating a victory at Olympia) in a carefully purified form. The sculptor cannot be so explicit as the poet, but he makes it clear that his intention is the same.

The pictorial influence evident in some of the metopes can also be seen in the battle of the west pediment. The last archaic gables, those of the temple of Aphaea at Aegina carved in the early fifth century, show likewise battles dominated by a deity (Athena) and make an interesting contrast with the Olympia scene. At Aegina every figure is completely finished in the round and completely separate from any other. At Olympia groups of twos and threes are carved in one, contained in a single harmonious contour line and only roughly finished behind. In two cases the back half of a Centaur is not carved at all but deemed to disappear behind the neighbouring group: a purely pictorial idea. There can be little doubt that, though sculptors took the lead in making the break with archaic convention, and resumed it again in the fully classical phase, Phidias and Polyclitus are being greatest names in art after the middle of the century, in the intervening period developments in painting were of the first importance.

The Parthenon

The Parthenon, built and decorated between 450 and 430 B.C., makes at many levels an instructive comparison and contrast with the temple at Olympia. If that represents the concept, however imperfectly realized, of Greek unity, the Parthenon stands for imperial Athens. In the quarter of a century following the expulsion of Xerxes' army from Greece, the Maritime League, which under Athenian leadership freed the islands and the cities of the Asia Minor coast, was gradually transformed into an Athenian empire. It was out of the revenues, and out of the pride, of this empire that the Parthenon and much else was built.

The Parthenon, entirely of marble, is among the least conventional of Doric temples. The refinements (the breaking down of apparently straight lines into curves of an extraordinary subtlety) are carried further here than anywhere else, and there are significant oddities of plan. Instead of the more usual six columns at the ends there are eight, and this, with the fact that the columns are slenderer in relation to their height than those of the Zeus temple (this is a general tendency of development), means that the proportions of the whole are quite different. Thus, although the Parthenon is larger than the other, the metopes are actually slightly smaller, and very much smaller in relation to the whole. The interior arrangements are also unusual, with a longer eastern and shorter western room, each entered through a very shallow porch. The main (eastern) section is thus much wider in proportion to its length than is usual in a Greek temple interior; and this is probably because it was designed from the start to house the forty-foot statue of Athena by Phidias. His other gold and ivory colossus, the Zeus of Olympia, was made for the already existing narrow temple-chamber, and though judged the greater work was thought to be cramped by its setting.

The decoration of the Parthenon was exceedingly rich. As well as the gables all ninety-two metopes of the exterior were carved; and above the porches and all round the building within the colonnade ran a continuous carved frieze in the Ionic manner. The subject-matter of the decoration is as limited as that of the temple of Zeus is widespread. Here Athena and Athens are all: the goddess's birth is depicted in the east pediment; in the west, her strife with Poseidon for the land of Attica; a great procession of Athenian citizens in her honour on the frieze. The metopes, not all of which can be interpreted, certainly show a wider range of subjects; but some of them – battles of gods and giants, Greeks and Amazons, Greeks and Centaurs – were repeated on the shield and sandals of the great statue of the goddess within.

The metopes are of very varied quality, and include work poorer than any found in other parts of the building. They were probably the first of the sculptures to be executed; and the very large team of craftsmen that must have been employed had not then been brought to the fine and harmonious level reached as the work went on. The gables are probably the latest. The statues from them are meticulously finished all round, in contrast to those at Olympia, but there are some closely knit groups which recall the principles of design employed there. For intrinsic sculptural quality the best of them perhaps surpass anything at Olympia, but we cannot say whether the complete compositions were as satisfying. A great deal is lost, including the centres of both, though in each case there is some record of the design. The Athena and Poseidon at the west were moving away from each other and looking back, in the 'strife motive' already noticed.

The subject matter of the frieze is an astonishing innovation. On all earlier and most later temples the decorative themes are drawn exclusively from myth and legend. Here we have a scene of human life: the great Panathenaic procession which took place every four years to bring to the ancient olive-wood image of the goddess, fallen from heaven in Erechtheus' reign, a robe woven by the daughters of Athenian citizens. The gods appear, in two groups at the east end which isolate the little central scene at the centre with preparations on the Acropolis for the robe's reception; but the participants in the procession itself are entirely mortal. It is not, however, a representation of the procession as it ever actually took place. The choice of episodes is very incomplete; some of the figures are shown in ideal nudity (as often in Greek art); and the faces are all ideal: it is an imagined ideal version of a recurrent actual event. Nevertheless, this introduction of a mortal theme into temple decoration is something most exceptional, which could hardly have happened elsewhere than in Periclean Athens.

Pausanias, in his guide book to Greece of the second century A.D., tells us that the eastern pediments at Olympia were the work of Paeonius and those at the west of Alcamenes. There are, as we shall see, difficulties in accepting these attributions, and some have felt that the style of the sculptures is so unified that they must all be from the design of one 'Olympia Master'. This does not seem to me demonstrable; and similarly, though Phidias surely had some say in planning the decoration of the

Parthenon and was a unifying influence on it, one cannot be sure that all or any of the detailed designs were supplied by him. In the case of a much smaller temple put up at Epidaurus to Asclepius early in the next century, there is inscriptional evidence that three or four artists were engaged on the two gables and the two sets of acroteria (free-standing statues above the gable angles), each gable and each set being by one man. The execution in all cases will certainly have been by hired workmen, an arrangement proved by inscriptions for one fifth-century building, the Erechtheum on the Acropolis at Athens.

Phidias is the greatest name in the history of Greek sculpture, but he is a shadowy figure now. Of the colossal cult-statues, the enthroned Zeus and the standing Athena, built up in clay, plaster, and wood and veneered with ivory and gold, we can form no picture. Phidias' studio at Olympia, in which he worked on the Zeus, has lately yielded fascinating finds: clay moulds, apparently for beating the thin gold of the drapery in; moulds for coloured glass, with fragments of glass and ivory; bronze tools; and a cup with the master's name scratched on the bottom – evocative, perhaps informative on technique, but marginalia in the history of art. For the Athena we have wretched little marble souvenirs produced under the Roman empire, which indicate that its design was, as perhaps one might have expected in a colossal cult-state, more formal, nearer to archaic rigidity than in most statues of the time. Some of these little figures give a sketch of the Amazon battle on the shield; and these have allowed the identification of some Roman marble reliefs, with splendid groups and figures, copied therefrom. Equally moving and beautiful are some reliefs in a related style showing the slaughter of the children of Niobe, a theme illustrated on the throne legs of the Zeus whence no doubt these are copied. It is in these reliefs that we can come closest now to Phidias. Some of the Roman copies from statues of this time probably reflect originals by him, but none has been identified with any certainty, though one would gladly accept the lovely Athena which Furtwängler thought was his Lemnia – a dedication on the Acropolis by the Athenian colonists of Lemnos. The quiet figure stands with simply-falling draperies in the tradition of early classical statues like the Hestia, but more delicate and easier, her bare head slightly bent. Classical artists eschew expression in the face but marvellously restore it in a posture, in the angle of a head.

Of Phidias' great rival, Polyclitus of Argos, we know more. We are told that he was deeply interested in working out a system of ideal proportions, and that, when in a figure called the Doryphorus (spear bearer) he had reached what he felt to be his goal, he wrote a book on the subject, taking this statue for text. The book (called the *Canon*, a name sometimes also applied to the statue) is lost, but the fact that Polyclitus wrote it is of great interest. His contemporary Ictinus, one of the architects of the Parthenon, wrote a book on that, as Theodorus had done long before on the temple at Samos. We shall see that a fifth-century painter wrote on his own work, and the fact is recorded of architects, sculptors, and painters in the following century also. This intellectualization of the creative urge, the feeling that it should be possible to find rules for beauty and in particular to express it in mathematical terms, is of fundamental importance in Greek art.

Polyclitus appears to have worked almost exclusively in bronze and to have specialized in the athletic male nude. We have marble copies of the Doryphorus and other works, some of which have a beauty which must convey something of the original's character, and they tell us a good deal about his approach to the art. They stand in poses which derive from that of the Critian boy and the Choiseul-Gouffier Apollo, but the proportions are heavier and the contrast between taut and slack muscles, bent and straight limbs, more pronounced and most carefully balanced. The musculature, too, is unnaturally emphasized, mapping the body and carrying the rhythms of the structure into the pattern of the torso. The facial type is distinctive, and often given a tender beauty by the subtle inclination of the head; when the heads are copied alone and set straight, as they sometimes are, the effect is entirely lost.

This Polyclitan type left a powerful stamp on Greek sculpture in succeeding generations. It looks as though he set out to establish, and in some degree succeeded in establishing, a rule much freer than but analogous to the archaic conventions within which classical sculptors could work. The element of freedom is illustrated in his own work by the Diadumenus (a young athlete binding his head with the victor's ribbon), of which we have copies. This is a gentler work than the Doryphorus, with rather looser structure, evidently later and showing that the theoretician was also a sensitive artist who could modify his system as he developed.

Doryphorus and Diadumenus are over life size. Polyclitus also made a number of smaller bronzes of athletes, which at this time became a regular type of dedication at Olympia by victors in the games. These, as inscriptions show, were deemed to represent the dedicator; but the faces (we know them in copies) are as purely ideal as those of the youths on archaic tombs, or of the figures or groups on the marble grave reliefs which were now coming into fashion in Athens.

Architecture and sculpture in late fifth-century Athens

In 431 B.C. broke out the disastrous war between Athens and Sparta which, hot or cold, dragged on, involving most of Greece, till Athens, decisively defeated, surrendered in 404 B.C. The Parthenon was complete before the outbreak, but work was still proceeding on the Propylaea, the monumental and very beautiful gate building of the Acropolis. The central feature of the complex is composed of an inner and an outer porch at different levels, and these are flanked by porticoes and rooms. The exterior, on both faces, is Doric, and in his imaginative design the architect, Mnesicles, shows again (like those of the Parthenon) what variety can be introduced into the seemingly rigid scheme. Between the porches was a columned hall in the Ionic order, the forms treated with unusual largeness and simplicity so that they fit perfectly with their Doric surroundings.

The building was left unfinished, and the other two temples raised on the Acropolis during the fifth century are purely Ionic, with all the traditional elaboration of the style. The first, a little temple of Victory on a bastion outside the Propylaea, probably belongs to the first phase of the war or to the beginning of a period of uneasy peace which lasted from 421 to 416 B.C. It is decorated with a frieze, mainly occupied by battle-scenes in which first appears a motive much used later: the flying cloaks of fighting figures, whose rhythmical arabesques fill the background and bind the composition together. On a larger scale and of more striking character is a balustrade, apparently added later in the century, round the edge of the bastion, decorated with seated figures of Athena and with Victories variously engaged, some leading bulls to sacrifice, the most famous and beautiful shown adjusting her sandal. These display the favourite drapery style of the period: garments clinging to the body so as to reveal its form almost as though naked but covered with an elaborate play of sharply cut folds, while other draperies hang or blow loose with a life of their own. It is a revival of the interests of late archaic sculptors, manifested in the *korai*, but transformed by the new naturalism. The treatment here shows an extraordinary virtuosity.

The second Ionic temple of the Acropolis, the Erechtheum, was certainly begun in the period of peace, probably soon after 421 B.C., but was finished after an interval in the last years of the second phase of the war. The abandonment of Doric in favour of Ionic at Athens in this period may have had propagandist overtones: Athens claimed to be the mother city of Ionia, while Sparta was the acknowledged leader of the Dorians; but whatever the reason it suited the aesthetic tendencies of the time, which are all towards elaboration and prettiness. The Erechtheum in particular is loaded with marvellously fine and beautiful ornamentation, though the design, of an awkward complexity for religious reasons, has none of the mastery visible in the Propylaea.

Fragmentary inscriptions survive concerned with the erection and decoration of the building, and they supply most interesting information. In particular it is made quite clear that the execution of the frieze was in the hands of workmen paid by the piece and evidently following a design supplied to them. One section is of a group harnessing a chariot, a single subject the design of which can only have been the work of one man, but for which payment to a number of named workmen is recorded. Each takes a figure, for which he is paid sixty drachmai, and one name recurs for two figures at opposite ends of the group. The frieze is exceptional in that the background, instead of being painted (that of the Parthenon frieze was painted red), is of dark marble, and the figures were carved separately in white marble and attached to it.

The inscription dates the frieze to the second period of the building; probably to the earlier phase belong the maidens of the south porch. In these figures the draperies are heavy and columnar, masking the massive forms though broken by one knee. This style is clearly employed here as suitable to statues which are also columns, but in a hardly less pronounced degree it appears in other statues of the time and evidently existed side by side with the clinging and flying drapery style we have already noticed. An example very like the Caryatids of the Erechtheum is a figure of a woman holding a child against her skirt, found on the Acropolis and identified with a statue of

Procne and Itys seen there by Pausanias and probably the work of Alcamenes.

A statue certainly by a famous artist of this period is a flying Victory, found, with the remains of the high pedestal on which it stood, at Olympia, where it was raised probably in 421 B.C. Here we have a signature to confirm Pausanias' statement that it is by Paeonius of Mende in Thrace. This is one of the boldest embodiments of the other manner, the blown drapery showing the body almost as though naked against the mass billowing behind. This style derives from that of figures in the Parthenon pediments. The other looks back to the early classical tradition of works like the Hestia, through such pieces as the supposed Lemnia and a lovely statue of Demeter from Cherchel in North Africa, which has likewise been guessed to be a copy after Phidias.

Paeonius and Alcamenes are the sculptors credited by Pausanias with the two pediments at Olympia. We cannot trace a connexion between those works, made well before the middle of the century, and the two statues just considered. All the other works ascribed to these artists belong to the later part of the century. If they did design the pediments it must have been as young men, and their styles must have changed radically; but that is not impossible. If we had only an early and a late work of Titian or of Giovanni Bellini we might find it very hard to see a link; and development in fifth-century Greece was quite as swift as in fifteenth- or sixteenth-century Italy. Our knowledge of Greek art is based on a considerable body of largely anonymous work, much of it certainly executed by studio hands; of traditions about old masters and old masterpieces recorded by later writers of guide-books and encyclopedias; and of copies made under the Roman empire from masterpieces of the classical age which happened then to be available and popular. On this basis we can scarcely hope to appreciate the development and interaction of individual artists, as one can in a period like the Italian Renaissance.

Painting and vase painting in the later fifth century

Phidias and Polyclitus are perhaps the greatest names in the tradition about Greek sculpture; certainly their epoch was looked back to as the high point of the art. In painting it was not so. The *grand siècle* of painting for later writers on art lies in the time of Philip and Alexander and Alexander's successors, the second half of the fourth century. Polygnotus and Mikon, in breaking with the tradition of surface-bound decoration, had begun the conquest of a new world; but that conquest was only achieved through the gradual mastery of shading and highlights, cast shadows and reflected lights, and of some form of perspective.

There were famous painters in the Periclean age, notably Panaenus, brother or nephew of Phidias and also his collaborator. Perhaps we can glimpse something of his style in the calm and lovely drawing on the white-ground oil flasks which the fashion of the day placed in tombs. Neither these, in outline and colour wash, nor contemporary red-figure, show any trace of an interest in modelling with shadow or of extending the narrow stage space of Polygnotan painting. That these problems did, however, in the later decades of the fifth century begin to occupy painters is implied in the literary tradition and confirmed by faint echoes in surviving monuments. Agatharchus of Samos is said to have decorated (under *force majeure*) a house for Alcibiades, a story which shows him active in Athens within the period of the Peloponnesian War. Vitruvius, an Augustan architect and writer on architecture, states that this painter designed a stage set for a production of Aeschylus (who died in 456 B.C., but the formula would cover a revival), and then wrote a book on it which helped the scientific philosophers Democritus and Anaxagoras to formulate theories of optical perspective. On some red-figure vases of the late fifth and early fourth century, buildings are for the first time

represented in strong and sometimes quite effective foreshortening. They show no systematic perspective, but the days
when vase painters felt themselves in the front of artistic
development were clearly past; their curious art was drifting
back to its more natural position of a decorative craft. Besides,
the sharp convexity of a pot makes it a peculiarly unsuitable
field for experiments with vanishing points. That the sudden
appearance of such representations on pots does, however,
reflect experiments towards a perspective system among wall-
painters or stage-designers seems most probable; and if there
is any truth in the story about Agatharchus it must indeed
be so. If he had had no theory, his book would not have
interested the scientists, nor indeed would he have written
about his work at all. There is evidence, as we shall see, that
before the end of the Hellenistic age artists understood the
composition of a picture on a single vanishing point; had, that
is, a perspective system like that of the Renaissance. Agatharchus seems to have taken the first step towards this idea.

At the same time Apollodorus of Athens, known as the
'shadow painter', was apparently attacking the problem of
modelling by shading; the experiment was carried further by
his pupil Zeuxis, who worked from the late fifth into the
fourth century. The most famous painters of this time were
Zeuxis and Parrhasius. They appear as rivals; and it has been
ingeniously argued from the rather obscure accounts of their
work that, while Zeuxis carried forward the new ideas of
shadow modelling, Parrhasius remained in the linear tradition.
Massive figures, rendered without shading but with a wonderfully nervous and expressive contour line, are found on some
of the latest white-ground grave vases, and have been thought
to reflect his style. Two much-damaged vessels of this kind do
show primitive shading, and it appears on an occasional red-
figure vase of this time, confirming the existence of the new
movement but hardly telling us more. The fashion for white-
ground grave vases dies out in the early fourth century.

Red-figure continues for another hundred years or so in Athens, and in various centres of southern Italy where production had begun in imitation of Attic in the second half of the fifth century and became of equal importance with it during the fourth. On some of these, and especially on some southern Italian vases in a new technique, called Gnathia – figures in added colours painted over the black – one can trace echoes of the increasing mastery during the fourth century of foreshortening, shading, and highlights.

Classical grave and votive reliefs

The pictures on the grave lekythoi often show two figures at a tomb; often, it seems, not two visitors but one survivor (sometimes bringing offerings) and on the other side the dead person, the two united by the image of the tomb in a timeless communion. Others show Charon receiving the dead into his boat, or Sleep and Death carrying off a fallen warrior; yet others (very commonly) domestic scenes with no apparent reference to death. This last type of scene predominates on the marble gravestones which become common in Athens at the time of the Peloponnesian War. Marble reliefs had been placed there on the tombs of the aristocracy during the sixth century, but the practice ceases abruptly about the time that the democracy is established, probably because a law was passed prohibiting high expenditure on the disposal of the dead – a form of economic sanction not infrequently invoked in the classical world. From the following decades we have a number of tombstones from other parts of Greece, but the great series begins with the re-establishment of the practice in Athens during the third quarter of the fifth century. The law was perhaps repealed to encourage employment for the many craftsmen who had been working on the sculptures of the Parthenon; at least the earlier are exceedingly close in style to those sculptures. These gravestones do not seem to have been in the main the work of leading artists (that Praxiteles once carved one was thought worthy of remark) but were turned out rather by craftsmen who specialized in this line. In bulk they give an impression of mass production; but the general standard is high, and the best of them are of very great beauty. The dead person is shown standing or seated, alone or attended by a slave, confronted with spouse or parent or surrounded by the family. In the pairs and groups it is often not possible to determine which is the dead person. There is seldom any sign of grief, the faces are all calm and all ideal; though this is a period in which the idea of personal portraiture begins to make some progress, it leaves no impression on this branch of art.

The archaic tombstone seems to have been an aristocratic privilege, but now they are available to all classes; and in the same way marble reliefs dedicated in sanctuaries become much more common than ever before and are shown by inscriptions to be the offerings of people from all spheres. They are devoted less often to the Olympians than to more specifically popular deities: Pan and the Nymphs, who had long received offerings, but earlier generally of a humbler and more perishable sort; local heroes; and divinities newly risen to importance, like Asclepius, or brought in from foreign parts, like Bendis (the Thracian Artemis), the establishment of whose cult in the Piraeus is celebrated at the beginning of Plato's *Republic*.

The series of Athenian tombstones was brought to an abrupt end by another law controlling funeral expenditure, enforced by Demetrius of Phalerum, who ruled Athens for the Macedonians from 317 to 307 B.C. Carved tombstones are found elsewhere during the Hellenistic age, and votive reliefs too, but the great age of both is in Athens of the later fifth and fourth centuries. This spread of the use of fine artistic monuments to a wide public seems one of the achievements of the Periclean age which did not perish in the Peloponnesian War.

Later fifth-century architecture and sculpture in the Peloponnese

Remains survive of three important temples built outside Athens during the later fifth and early fourth centuries. The temple of Apollo at Bassae (Phigaleia) has a normal Doric exterior, with an interior in Ionic varied by the introduction of the first Corinthian capital known. There were carved metopes, of which only scraps exist, and a well-preserved continuous frieze which ran round the inner room. This shows battles of Greeks with Centaurs and Amazons, in a curious style whose harshness is certainly intensified by clumsy, provincial execution, but seems to be present also in some parts of the design. In Greek art the brutality of battle is commonly softened by aesthetic means – the most savage action enclosed in a flowing and harmonious contour. At Bassae there is an angularity and roughness in the manner which seems in part a deliberate echo of the matter. The date cannot be determined with any certainty within the last thirty years of the fifth century.

The old temple of Hera at Argos was burned in 423 B.C., and some time between then and the end of the century a new one was built; but little remains of the sculpture which adorned it. A gold and ivory colossus, recorded as made for it by one Polyclitus, was perhaps not by the most famous bearer of the name but by a younger member of the same family. Another such was made in the first quarter of the fourth century by a certain Thrasymedes for the great new temple then raised in the old sanctuary at Epidaurus to Asclepius, the healer, an ancient demigod promoted at this time to the status of a major deity. A little of the sculpture from this building, much damaged but of fine quality, survives. It is of exceptional interest to us, because of building inscriptions which supplement the information we derive from those of the Erechtheum. The building took rather under five years to complete, and the architect, Theodotus, was paid throughout at the rate of a drachma a day. Between the third and the fifth year substantial sums were paid to Hectoridas for one pediment, Timotheus for the three acroteria above it, Theo— (possibly Theodotus) for the other set of three acroteria, and one whose name is entirely lost for the other gable. The system here was evidently to pay an artist to complete one section of the work, presumably designing it himself and hiring for the execution assistants like those directly employed by the state on the frieze of the Erechtheum.

Fragments of all four groups of sculpture can be identified and associated with the east and west fronts of the building, but the inscription does not make it clear which end was taken by which artists; so that, though differences of style are detectable, they cannot be associated with the given names. The eastern gable, which illustrated the sack of Troy, shows a development of the clinging-drapery style in which the almost naked-seeming body is deeply recessed in a kind of shell of hanging stuff; and this distinctive treatment recurs in some Roman copies of lost statues, notably a grave and moving Leda. Timotheus is the only one among these names which appears also in the literary tradition, and this style has, therefore, been called his, but there can be no certainty. He is recorded also as working around the middle of the century on the Mausoleum of Halicarnassus; but no connexion can be traced between the remains from that monument and those from Epidaurus.

The Corinthian order

The Corinthian capital, which we first meet at Bassae, was traditionally invented by Callimachus, an Athenian sculptor who flourished in the later fifth century and whose work, of which we have no certain traces, was notorious for over-elaboration. This was a vice of the time, and the Corinthian capital, beautiful as some specimens are, can perhaps be regarded as an example of it. The Doric capital is of extreme simplicity; the Ionic more complex, but its basic forms are large and clear compared to those of the Corinthian, with its leafy bell from which slim tendrils rise out of fluted sheaths to meet in the centre and to support the corners of the shallow abacus. It differs, too, in another respect. Some elements in the Ionic capital are of floral origin, but like most Greek florals (which we know by such names as palmette, lotus flower, lotus bud, leaf and dart, egg and tongue) their relation to any natural form is exceedingly remote. Most of these patterns are derived from designs taken over, already formalized, from Eastern models in the seventh century. The leaves of the Corinthian capital are not of this kind. They recognizably represent the serrated leaf of the acanthus, and this leaf attains a sudden popularity in the decorative art of late fifth- and early fourth-century Greece. The Corinthian capital is only one of many examples in many media, several of which became accepted into the permanent repertory of classical art. The acceptance of the new capital, however, was slow. One may think of Corinthian as one, along with Doric and Ionic, of the three orders of classical architecture; but it is the capital alone which distinguishes it from Ionic, and no temple was built with Corinthian capitals on its exterior before the Hellenistic age, and very few then. It is only under the Roman empire that it attains real popularity.

For the first century or more of its existence it is scarcely used except for the interior decoration of buildings, whose exterior is most often, like the temple at Bassae, Doric. Remains of four such buildings survive from the fourth century, only one of them a temple. The other three are circular buildings in sanctuaries, of uncertain use. In the earliest at Delphi, the Corinthian capitals crown half columns set against the interior wall. The next, at Epidaurus, had free-standing columns within, whose Corinthian capitals are the most delicate and beautiful, perhaps, that we have. The third was set up at Olympia in about 335 B.C. by Philip of Macedon, and housed gold and ivory statues of himself and his family. In this, the external colonnade was Ionic instead of Doric. At almost the same time there was erected at Athens a monument to celebrate a victory in a dramatic festival. It was not a building, since there was no access to the interior, but a hollow drum with half columns supporting an architrave and frieze. Here for the first time Corinthian capitals appear on an exterior.

Scopas and the Mausoleum

None of these buildings (except that at Bassae) are temples, but about the middle of the century another Doric temple was built which had Corinthian capitals crowning half columns round the interior. It was dedicated to Athena Alea at Tegea in the Peloponnese, and the name of the architect is recorded: Scopas. Since this artist was primarily a sculptor, one of the most famous of the fourth century, it seems safe to assume that he provided designs for the sculptures which adorned the pediments. Fragments survive, battered but with a most individual style: especially in the way the eyes are set deep in the sockets with a slight upward turn, giving an uneasy, restless effect rare in classical art, which distrusts expression. One of Scopas' famous statues was a maenad in ecstasy tearing a fawn. A much damaged statuette of Roman date reproduces such a figure, and has a daemonic quality which aligns it with the heads from Tegea. It also resembles, in the twisted violence of the stance and in the way the shift falls free from half the naked body, a fighting Amazon on a frieze slab found near the east end of the Mausoleum of Halicarnassus; and Scopas is recorded as having decorated that part of that extraordinary building.

The gold and ivory statues of Philip of Macedon's house hardly belong to the classical world of the city states, but anticipate rather the climate of the Hellenistic age. So in a way does the emotionalism of Scopas; and the Mausoleum is a product of a situation far more Hellenistic than classical. Mausolus, a native of Caria in Asia Minor, ruled it for the Persian king but was deeply Hellenized. He died in 353 B.C., and his widow (who followed him two years later, while the work was still unfinished) employed a Greek architect and four Greek sculptors to make him a temple-tomb, which became one of the wonders of the world and of which descriptions and considerable remains survive. The detail of the architecture is pure Greek, Ionic; but the Ionic colonnade stood on a high podium and supported a tall, stepped pyramid – a combination, perhaps of local and Egyptian elements in the tradition (foreign to Greece) of temple-tomb architecture. (The Carian dynasts, who borrowed so much from Greece, borrowed from Pharaonic Egypt, as the Ptolemies did after them, the practice of brother-and-sister marriage.) The building was adorned with three friezes, one probably in the normal position, the others on the podium, and with innumerable statues and figures of lions, all in marble. One splendid portrait statue, probably of Mausolus himself, survives in fair condition, and also substantial remains of one frieze, with a battle of Greeks and Amazons. According to the tradition, the four sculptors each took one side of the building, and the great differences in composition and character on different slabs of the Amazon frieze seem to confirm this. The building was looted in the Middle Ages by the Knights of St John to build their fortress at Budrun, and the site was much disturbed. The excavators a century ago did not find much of the sculpture they unearthed in what seemed a significant relation to the sides of the destroyed building; but three contiguous slabs were found lying, as though where they had fallen, at the east end, traditionally taken by Scopas, and we have seen that it is possible to link them to him stylistically. We can make no clear connexion of surviving remains with the other names. Timotheus, we saw, worked earlier at Epidaurus; Leochares and Bryaxis later for Philip and Alexander, and it is probably to one of them that should be ascribed some slabs with long-limbed, small-headed, muscle-knotted figures: a new ideal of proportion and type which comes in during the middle and second half of the fourth century and is particularly associated with the name of Lysippus. Many of the slabs, but not those connected with Scopas, make great play with arabesques of flying cloaks, a motif which had appeared already in the fifth century on the frieze of the little temple of Nike at Athens.

Praxiteles and Lysippus

The three greatest names in the tradition about fourth-century sculpture are Scopas, Lysippus, and Praxiteles, and most currents in Hellenistic art can be traced back to one of them. We have, probably, an original by Praxiteles: a marble Hermes with the child Dionysus, found in the temple of Hera at Olympia, where Pausanias saw it and ascribed it to the master. The powerful but softly modelled figure lolling against a trunk is a typical Praxitelean design; it recurs in a number of works which can be certainly identified as copied from his originals. His most famous piece, however, was not one of these but a naked Aphrodite at Cnidus; except, perhaps, for the Olympian Zeus the most renowned statue in the ancient world. The female nude was only slowly welcomed into Greek art, and the feminine ideal with it: there is a touch of masculinity about most of the goddesses and heroines of fifth-century sculpture. The copies of the Cnidia are dreary things – the art of this time depended much on delicacy of finish, so loses more in the copying than robuster manners – but we can tell from them that it was a revolutionary creation. Earlier statues stand firm, unless they are engaged in some purposeful action. Praxiteles' men often lean, and his Aphrodite is caught in a hesitant pose whose shrinking movement is carefully chosen to emphasize the broad hips and narrow shoulders, the essential geometry of the female form.

The original was in marble, and Praxiteles seems to have worked equally happily in marble or bronze. Lysippus, so far as we know, was a bronze statuary only. He came from Sicyon in the Peloponnese, where the tradition of Polyclitus was still strong; and in his athletic nudes Lysippus worked in that tradition and modified it. He systematized the changed taste of the time, working out a new ideal proportion with smaller head and longer limbs than the old. Like Polyclitus he embodied his ideal in a statue, the Apoxyomenus ('scraper' athletes used to rub oil on themselves and scrape it off with a spoon-like instrument, the strigil), and we have a copy of this. It is a dry uninspired version, but it gives us the composition and we can see the derivation from the Polyclitan tradition and also the striking newness not only in proportions but in structure and design. The pose of Polyclitan athletes is essentially restful, and the statues are most carefully composed for a harmonious effect from the main, frontal, viewpoint. The Apoxyomenus is shifting his weight between his widely placed feet in a restless momentary pose; and one arm is stretched straight out in front, the other brought across the body with the scraper, breaking the harmonious outline and insisting on the three-dimensional, space-occupying character of the statue in a way that is found in no earlier work. Lysippus worked for Philip, Alexander, and their successors. His pupils were the court-sculptors of the new age, and in their works we shall see for the first time a serious concern with composing statues to be walked round and to give a satisfactory effect from many angles.

Portraiture

Later tradition asserted that Alexander would allow no one to paint his portrait but Apelles, no one to cut it on a seal stone but Pyrgoteles, no one to cast it in bronze but Lysippus. We have sculptured portraits of him that seem to be, or to go back to, originals by many hands, and we know that the youthful one of Philip's gold and ivory group was by Leochares. All, however, have in common a very high degree of idealization; and that is true of all Greek portraiture before the Hellenistic age and much of it even then.

The Egyptians had practised realistic portraiture, but the idealizing, generalizing tendency of Greek art was hostile to it, and it is commonly excluded alike from archaic and from classical art. Only at the time of transition, when art is in ferment, do we find in vase painting and sometimes in sculpture an interest in particularized unideal types, the old, the ugly, the foreign: a kind of interest which might flower into portraiture. We have in fact a Roman head inscribed 'Themistocles' in which the hair is treated in the manner of the statesman's own time, the early classical period, yet the features are vividly realistic. The simplest and, I believe, the right explanation is that this is a true copy of a contemporary portrait, but it stands by itself and is thought by some to be a later pastiche.

Certainly Cresilas, a generation after, gave Pericles almost purely ideal features. We hear of a portraitist Demetrius of Alopece, active in Athens in the early fourth century, who was later criticized as 'fonder of likeness than of beauty', but we know nothing of his work. Many of such portraits as do begin at this time to show realistic elements come from areas of contact between Greek and Barbarian which presage the Hellenistic situation: heads of Persian satraps on coins made for them by Greek craftsmen for the payment of Greek mercenaries; the magnificent marble of the Carian Mausolus; and a beautiful bronze found at Cyrene and perhaps representing a Berber. It is in the mixed courts of Alexander's successors – Anigonids, Lagids, Seleucids, Attalids, and the adventurer-princes of remoter Bactria – that realistic personal portraiture, on coins, in bronze, marble, and no doubt in painting too, really flowers in Greek art.

Even in the Hellenistic age, Greek portraiture is limited to public figures, and one always feels that the artist aims to show *what* as well as who the sitter is : prince, poet, philosopher. The earliest philosopher of whom we have certain representations is Socrates. The first statue of him of which we hear was by Lysippus, set up probably some fifty years after his death. The copies of the head of Socrates we have go back to several originals, but they all conform to the traditional comic type of the satyr. The master's friends had said that he looked like a satyr, and it is that literary reference which is the basis of all the portraits, which are thus in their own way purely 'ideal'. The portrait of Plato by Silanion, dedicated in the Academy by a Persian admirer, from which again we have copies of the head, may have been based on the philosopher's own features, but there is certainly a strong infusion from the satyric type appropriated to the master whose *persona* he adopted throughout his life in his writings. Rather similarly, a century later the petty features of Epicurus' pupils Hermarchus and Metrodorus curiously resemble those in the splendid head of their master, whose highly individual lineaments must be taken from life but which is yet therewith emphatically 'the Thinker'.

A moving Demosthenes, known in many copies, was set up about the same time as the Epicurus, in 280 B.C. Here the tragic figure of the Last Patriot is unquestionably intended; and since the statue was made forty years after his death we cannot be sure that the convincing features are those of the man at all. Here the overtones are present not only in the face but in the whole structure of the statue. Its four-square simplicity is in what must be conscious opposition to the current fashions of court art. Without a trace of archaism in detail, it looks back to the style of Athens in her noblest age, the Athens of the Marathonomachoi.

All Greek portraits, till far down in the Hellenistic age, were full-length figures, though often only the head has been copied. The portrait-head as a sculptural form was an Italian creation, and it is only in the latest Hellenistic period, when Greece is already a province of Rome, that this idea, with that of private portraiture, becomes accepted.

Fourth-century and Hellenistic painting

We have no echo of Apelles' painted portraits of Alexander, but one painting of him is copied in a battle scene, the Alexander Mosaic from Pompeii. This is certainly a direct version of a painting of Alexander's own time or from that of his immediate successors; and it shows how far painting had progressed since the tentative steps towards space construction and modelling taken in the fifth century. We know the names of many of the artists who furthered this progress but have almost nothing to judge their work by. To the first half of the century belonged Euphranor, also a sculptor, who wrote on proportion and colour. It is conceivable that his Twelve Gods in a portico in Athens is echoed in the solemn groups of deities who look out at us, massive and still, from red-figure vases made in Athens during the middle part of the fourth century; but vase painting is near its end and no longer much of a guide or much in itself. The best of it is in the comic stage scenes on some of the pots from southern Italy.

Working in Athens a little later than Euphranor was Nicias, who coloured some of Praxiteles' marbles (this is a collaboration we find it hard to envisage) and was perhaps the first to use shading on women's skin. There was a famous Aristides (or rather apparently two) and very many others, but most important appears to have been the 'school of Sicyon'. This was founded by Eupompus and brought to high repute by his pupil Pamphilus of Amphipolis, who said that a painter could not be perfect without arithmetic and geometry, and who established panel painting as part of a liberal education in Sicyon. He had equally celebrated pupils. Melanthius and Pausias, and Apelles came to learn from him. A strong intellectual bias, the scientific study of foreshortening, shading, cast shadows, highlights, and reflected lights, seem to be implied in stories about this school; and a concern with technique which Apelles seems to have inherited.

The mosaic with the battle of Alexander and Darius is much damaged, and the technique, ideal for decorative and formal arts, is not one in which the subtleties of pictorial realism can be well conveyed. One can, however, see in it a full mastery of all those problems of representation with which fourth-century artists had been grappling, and it is a powerful and impressive work. It also shows, most strikingly, an almost total lack of interest in setting. Space is competently mastered enough to hold the massed figures, but there is no distance, the sky is a dead white, and landscape is indicated by a few conventional rocks and a dead tree. That some artists of the time, among them Apelles' great rival Protogenes, enriched their backgrounds rather more than this is implied in some anecdotes, but Greek art is still utterly dominated by man.

During the Hellenistic age this attitude seems in some degree to have changed. The actual remains are slight: some rather crude tomb decorations and some polychrome vase paintings of the third century; but the resemblances of these to the wall paintings which begin to appear in Italian houses in the middle of the first century B.C. show that those are of direct Hellenistic descent; and they have a considerable though still limited feeling for nature. We hear of at least one Hellenistic landscape-painter, Demetrius of Alexandria, resident at Rome in the second century, and he and others like him must have paved the way for the charming, dreamy, impressionistic landscapes of the Italian houses.

Similarly there are clear traces in early Pompeian decoration, and in Vitruvius' writing, of a perspective system by which an artist could compose a whole picture, in the Renaissance manner, on a single vanishing point. Of the compositions which show the clearest traces of this system many appear to be

228

based on stage-designs. We saw that it was with a stage set that Agatharchus in the fifth century began the inquiry; and it may well have been Hellenistic stage designers (we hear of several) who carried it through.

Early Hellenistic sculpture

In 300 B.C. Seleucus, once Alexander's general and now king of Syria – the whole vast eastern section of Alexander's empire from the Mediterranean coast to Afghanistan – founded a new capital city on the Orontes and named it Antiocheia (Antioch) after his son Antiochus. A colossal bronze statue was made for the new foundation by a pupil of Lysippus, Eutychides. The old cities of Greece had each acknowledged a patron deity, to whom they paid special service and under whose protection they put themselves: one of the Olympians or their compeers, or a local nymph or river god. The new cities, whose foundation is one of the features of Alexander's policy carried on by his successors, were also placed under divine protection, but not always of the old gods. For Alexandria in Egypt a new deity was created, of mixed Greek and Egyptian character: Sarapis, whose statue was made by Bryaxis. Antioch was placed by Seleucus in the charge of its own Luck or Fortune (Tyche), and it was her statue that Eutychides made. Personification of abstractions reaches far back in Greek thought and art, but the practice increases enormously in the fourth century. Lysippus had made a statue of Kairos (Opportunity); and Opportunity and Luck are fitting recipients of worship in the new age. The Tyche of Antioch became the model for innumerable personifications of the Luck of Hellenistic and Roman cities.

The most important statues of the ancient gods stood in their temples, facing the worshipper as he approached through the door. They were designed primarily for a front view, and so were most other statues, unless of figures in action, in the archaic and classical periods. There is perhaps, even down to the fifth and fourth centuries, a trace in this of a primitive concept of the statue as a being to be met face to face. The discontent with this kind of construction, visible already in the Apoxyomenus, is surely not only aesthetic but part of the breakdown of the old religious ideas, and the growth of a sophisticated view of art detached from religion, by which statues in the Hellenistic age are objects to be walked round and admired.

Eutychides' bronze, set in the open air near the river, was a colossus. We have only little souvenir versions of it in bronze and marble, but we can see that it was a programme piece of the new movement. The figure sits on a rock in a relaxed pose, one knee crossed over the other, one hand resting on the rock, the other holding a handful of corn ears laid lightly across the thigh. She leans forward; and her head, with a turreted crown, looks up and to one side. Out from under the rock swims a youth, visible to the waist, Orontes, his head looking up, away from the direction of the goddess's gaze. This seemingly casual but exceedingly cunning design is further built up and emphasized by a complex play with swathing stuffs of varied surfaces, whose folds and crumples cross each other and help to sustain the interest of the statue from many different viewpoints.

Problems of Hellenistic art

The studied casualness – on the one hand the faithful reproduction of natural poses and of surface appearance; on the other the careful creation of an all-round composition, often built on a spiral – gives us two features which remain of great importance in the development of Hellenistic sculpture. Hellenistic art, however, is much farther from a unity than that of any earlier period. These features are first particularly developed in the school of Lysippus and the art of the courts.

We have seen that the statue of Demosthenes raised at Athens in 280 B.C. shows an extreme simplicity which appears deliberately opposed to this movement; and the school of Praxiteles, which flourished in Athens, seems in general to favour a simpler, more classicizing style, which becomes exceedingly marked in some later Hellenistic work and leads ultimately to pastiche and the copy industry. The different tendencies, however, interact, and there are others, most important perhaps one which, by fair analogy, is known as Baroque, and whose seeds are possibly to be discerned in the art of Scopas.

This variety of interacting and often backward-looking styles makes dating in the Hellenistic age even more precarious than at other times; while the patronage of the courts and the consequent migrations of artists make it difficult to speak of local schools. The small, rich state of Pergamon, however, in Western Asia Minor, did give fairly continuous employment to artists over a considerable period; and one can trace there some clear lines of development.

Pergamene sculpture and the baroque; Hellenistic architecture

Pergamon, founded as an effectively independent state in about 280 B.C. by an act of treachery, and sustained for half a century by cleverly playing on the rivalries of Syria and Egypt, attained a position of influence and importance by its defeat, about 230 B.C., of the Gauls – Celtic wanderers, who had first ravaged Greece and then for many years terrorized Asia Minor. The Pergamene kings had already patronized art and literature (their Library was second only to that at Alexandria), and we have works and copies of works which were probably made for them during this period; but the first monuments we can quite definitely associate with them are over life-size figures of defeated Gauls, early and fine marble copies of bronzes probably set up at Pergamon itself soon after the victory. The best is the Dying Gaul of the Capitol.

The composition of the slumped figure is looser than that of early Hellenistic figures like the Tyche, but not less careful, and there is an instructive mixture of observation and tradition in the treatment. The rough hair and the moustache, the torque round the neck, and the arms on the ground are all studied Gallicisms; but the fine face has a basically classical-ideal structure, though expressively modified, while the nudity is pure Greek heroic tradition and bears no relation to Celtic practice.

The massive, heavy-limbed figures of these Gauls are paralleled in many other works, some associable with Pergamon, others from elsewhere, suggesting that it was a widespread taste of the time. Close to the Gauls is the Barberini Faun (Pl. 4b), an over life-size figure in Pergamene marble of a drunken satyr asleep on a rock. This was found in the seventeenth century and restored by Bernini, to whose style it has a true affinity. Remoter, but with something of the same sculptural character, is the famous Victory of Samothrace. This, perhaps the most splendid of Hellenistic statues and the finest rendering of the subject in Greek art, illustrates the difficulties of dating, since it has been in the past associated with naval victories ranging from a year or two after Alexander's death to Actium in 31 B.C. Excavation of the sanctuary in which it stood, however, on a rock above a pool, seems to have established a date of about 200 B.C., which suits its general resemblance to the Gauls: massive forms, wrenched torso, loose build-up of the all-round composition, here by means of great swags of drapery.

In the classical period mythological battles had clearly been used as analogues of contemporary victories, like those over the Persians, but the parallel was seldom if ever made explicit. A change of attitude can be seen in a dedication made on the Acropolis at Athens by a Pergamene king, which showed pairs of fighters: gods and giants, Greeks and Amazons, Athenians and Persians, Pergamenes and Gauls. Copies of some of these under life-size bronzes exist, and show a preoccupation with complex and unexpected poses and elaborate design. They are clever, but lack altogether the grandeur and feeling of the earlier big statues of Gauls dedicated at home. The kings of Pergamon saw their city, perhaps, in the role of the Modern Athens. Certainly they and other Hellenistic monarchs often patronized the old city with gifts of buildings and monuments; but also drew on it – signatures of Athenian sculptors are found at Pergamon.

The last important phase of Pergamene art is represented by the Great Altar of Zeus, set up in about 180 B.C. This celebrated not the victory over the Gauls, but a new victory over Seleucid Syria, won by Pergamon as an ally (with their rulers' unfailing eye to the main chance) of Rome. The altar stood on a lofty podium approached from one side only by a broad flight of steps. Along the other three sides, and brought round to abut on the steps, was a continuous frieze of over life-size figures representing the battle of gods and giants. A strenuous effort has most obviously been made to give new life to this ancient theme: contorted faces, swollen muscles, twisted poses, against a ground brocaded with the scales and feathers of the giants' wings and snake legs. Yet when one isolates groups and figures the strength of tradition is no less apparent – there are compositions that seem to have been lifted from the pediments of the Parthenon, but always given a twist which justifies the description of the work as 'baroque'. Where the frieze meets the steps, it is not framed off, but figures tread or kneel on them. Thus the steps belong at the same time to the world of the worshipper who mounts them and to the imaginary world of the divine contest. This is a truly new, quite unclassical, idea. Strangely, though, above this frieze stands a prim little Ionic colonnade designed, one would say, by a classical architect who had learnt nothing and forgotten nothing; and it is this contrast, it seems to me, which makes the monument unsatisfactory, rather than any vulgarity in the sculptural style.

There is some variety and experiment in Hellenistic architecture, but all within very narrow limits. Pompeian paintings, which certainly derive from Hellenistic work, suggest that there may have been some development of baroque features in the architecture of the stage and perhaps of royal pavilions and palaces; but it has left no trace in the central tradition of architecture, which had to wait for the structural revolution of Roman engineering to open a new world for it.

A smaller frieze ran, apparently, within the colonnade of the Pergamene altar. This is in quite a different style, quieter and with pictorial elements which are found in some other Hellenistic reliefs: a tree, a flying bird, and overlapping figures graded from almost full roundness to almost drawing on the stone. It tells the story of the legendary founder of the city, and seems to be the first clear example of the continuous narrative style, where scenes in which the same characters appear merge into one another in a single developing composition.

The variety of Hellenistic sculpture; the decline

Pergamon provides examples also of a very different side of Hellenistic art. We know that the kings collected old masters; and a fine over life-size marble Athena is a free version of Phidias' great gold and ivory figure from the Parthenon. Echoes of the past, free versions or pastiches of fifth- and fourth-century types, become common, seemingly in the later part of the Hellenistic age. The Aphrodite from Melos (the Venus of Milo) is an example. The half-draped figure is based on a fourth-century creation, but given a twist of the torso to suit contemporary taste for a many-view statue; and at the same time the features have been made more coldly classical, looking back to the fifth rather than the fourth century. With all this the sculptor has given the figure, if in no very high degree, a harmony and character of its own.

The naked Aphrodite popularized by Praxiteles is rendered in endless variations by Hellenistic sculptors, some based on the shrinking modesty of the Cnidia, some boldly displaying their charms. An exquisite modification is the group of the Three Graces, found as sculpture in the round, relief and painting, and returned to ever since by artists in all these media: one of the great creations of the Hellenistic age.

As a sculptural group this is designed for one view alone; and that conception – sculpture as a kind of *ajouré* relief – recurs in Hellenistic art, most notably in the Laocoön, whose baroque style links it to the Pergamene altar. The names of its Rhodian sculptors are recorded, and it has been thought possible to date them by inscriptions to the middle of the first century B.C.; but the evidence is not conclusive, and there is no other sign that the baroque style survived the second century.

Another charming and ever-popular creation of Hellenistic sculpture takes the half-draped Aphrodite type but renders her as a young girl and groups her with a boy, Cupid and Psyche kissing. There are other, younger, children in Hellenistic art too, their chubby or knobbly forms lovingly studied: the most celebrated (known only in copies) a sleek little boy struggling with a goose; the finest (an original bronze from the same shipwreck as the early classical god) a boy jockey (Pl. 7a), a scraggy, ragged urchin and a work of marvellous vitality. The phases and disfigurements of age are recorded, too; and foreign types: some wonderfully sensitive renderings of negroes. Other fields too were explored, where we find it, perhaps, harder to follow – as in the Hermaphrodite: the attempt to create a bisexual ideal; yet one such statue, the Sleeping Hermaphrodite, is a work of beauty and power. Hellenistic art has not the dedicated concentration of classical, but it has a wider range of sympathy.

During the later second and the first centuries B.C., however, while the Hellenistic kingdoms were falling to Rome, the current of originality seems to dry slowly up. The tendency to classicism and pastiche prevails over other tastes. A happy touch is sometimes found even here, as in the enchanting Spinario, a bronze of a boy taking a thorn out of his foot, where a Hellenistic body is crowned, with improbable success, by a late archaic head; but the living tradition is at an end. Under the Empire Greek artists worked either on themes of Roman inspiration – imperial propaganda monuments or private portraits – or on mechanical copies after the masterpieces of their own past.

Bibliography

General
BEAZLEY, J. D., and ASHMOLE, B., *Greek Sculpture and Painting*, Cambridge University Press, 1932
RICHTER, G. M. A., *A Handbook of Greek Art*, Phaidon Press, 1959; *Archaic Greek Art*, Oxford University Press, 1949

Architecture
DINSMOOR, W. B., *The Architecture of Ancient Greece*, Batsford, 1950
LAWRENCE, A. W., *Greek Architecture*, Pelican Books, 1957
ROBERTSON, D. S., *A Handbook of Greek and Roman Architecture*, Cambridge University Press, 1943

Sculpture
CORBETT, P. E., *The Sculpture of the Parthenon*, Penguin Books, 1959
FURTWÄNGLER, A., *Masterpieces of Greek Sculpture*, translated by E. Sellers, Heinemann, 1895
LAWRENCE, A. W., *Classical Sculpture*, Cape, 1929; *Later Greek Sculpture*, Cape, 1927
LULLIES, R., and HIRMER, M., *Greek Sculpture*, Thames & Hudson, 1957
RICHTER, G. M. A., *The Sculpture and Sculptors of the Greeks*, Yale University Press, 1950; *Kouroi: Archaic Greek Youths*, Phaidon Press, 1960; *The Archaic Gravestones of Attica*, Phaidon Press, 1961

Painting, Vase Painting, and Pottery
BEAZLEY, J. D., *The Development of Attic Black-figure*, University of California Press, 1951; *Attic Red-figure Vases in American Museums*, Harvard, 1918; *Attic White Lekythoi*, Oxford University Press, 1938; *Potter and Painter in Ancient Athens*, Oxford University Press, 1946
COOK, R. M., *Greek Painted Pottery*, Methuen, 1960

LANE, A., *Greek Pottery*, Faber, 1948

PFUHL, E., *Masterpieces of Greek Drawing and Painting*, translated by J. D. Beazley, Chatto & Windus, 1955

RICHTER, G. M. A., *Attic Red-figure Vases*, Oxford University Press, 1959; and MILNE, M. J., *Shapes and Names of Athenian Vases*, New York, 1935

ROBERTSON, M., *Greek Painting*, Skira, 1959

SWINDLER, M. H., *Ancient Painting*, Yale University Press, 1929

WHITE, J., *Perspective in Ancient Drawing and Painting*, Hellenic Society (London), 1956

Other Arts

BEAZLEY, J. D., *The Lewes House Collection of Ancient Gems*, Oxford University Press, 1920

HILL, G., *A Guide to the Principal Coins of the Greeks*, London, 1959

RICHTER, G. M. A., *The Metropolitan Museum of Art, Catalogue of Engraved Gems*, Rome, 1956

SELTMAN, C. T., *Greek Coins*, 2nd ed., Methuen, 1955

Ancient Writers on Art

JONES, H. S., *Select Passages from Ancient Writers*, Macmillan, 1895

PAUSANIAS, *Pausanias's Description of Greece*, translated with a commentary by J. G. Frazer, Macmillan, 1898

PLINY, *The Elder Pliny's Chapters on the History of Art*, translated by K. Jex-Blake, with a commentary by E. Sellers, Methuen, 1896

VITRUVIUS, *On Architecture*, edited and translated by E. Granger, Loeb Classical Library, 1931–4

E. Badian
Lecturer in Ancient History, Durham University

The meteoric career of Alexander the Great is quite properly regarded as marking a new era in history. At his accession, in 336 B.C., it was only two years since the cities of Greece had been cowed into submission by the superior power of Macedon under Philip II. They rose at once to regain their independence, but were again defeated. As a terrible warning, Alexander destroyed the ancient city of Thebes. Yet most Greeks continued to think it inconceivable that a Macedonian king should have permanent power over glorious cities like Athens: this, surely, was but an interlude – a nightmare that would be followed by an awakening. As the Athenian orator Demosthenes had said (*Philippics*, iii, 31):

This man Philip is not only not a Greek, or a man who has anything to do with us Greeks, but not even a barbarian from a country with an honourable name; no, a pestilent Macedonian fellow, from a country where one could never even buy a decent slave before.

The nightmare turned out to be reality; the classical age of the independent Greek city state was gone, never to return. No period of Western history has seen greater political changes than the century and a half that followed the accession of Alexander. The gentlemen who danced at the Congress of Vienna in 1815 would not have been more astonished to catch a glimpse of the world of the 1960's than (say) Aristotle would have been at the Mediterranean world of 190 B.C., when it was just coming under the hegemony of Rome.

Alexander, fortunate in life, was fortunate in death. King when not yet twenty, he invaded Asia two years later, and within a few years had defeated the armies of the Persian Empire – the greatest empire that Europe or the Near and Middle East had ever known. When he died, at the age of thirty-two, he had conquered a kingdom stretching from the Ionian Sea to the Punjab and from the Caucasus to the borders of Ethiopia. Had he lived, it is doubtful whether he would have known what to do with it (except conquer more). In matters of administration he had improvised, not always successfully, as he went along, while conquest had transformed him from a tribal king, the first among his Macedonian peers, and leader of a Hellenic crusade against the barbarian, to a despot surrounded with Oriental pomp and worshipped as a god by many of his subjects. This did not make him popular among his Greeks and Macedonians; nor did the fact that he was inevitably forced to lean heavily on the support of the Persian aristocracy, the traditional administrators of the empire he had won. Soon he thought old friends more dangerous than the enemy: his progress through Asia was marked by court intrigues, political trials, and the liquidation of subversive elements. His last two years saw a reign of terror among his high officers and provincial governors, and his death may have anticipated a major rebellion in Greece.

When the King died, leaving the succession unsettled, there were two fortunate circumstances: one, that there were no foreign powers left to interfere in the affairs of the Empire; the other, that the conquered nations of the East, long accustomed to monarchy, cared little about the person of the monarch. On the whole they settled down as happily under the rule of Alexander's successors as they had under his own and under that of the Persians before him. The news of his death stunned the world. An Athenian orator, refusing to believe it, exclaimed that, if it were true, the odour of putrefaction would fill the earth. Yet there were only two rebellions – both by Greeks: one by colonists in Afghanistan who wanted to go home, and one (the 'Lamian War') by Athens and other cities in mainland Greece. Both were defeated within a few months. After this, Alexander's generals were left to fight and intrigue among themselves without further distraction.

The next half century is an amazing period, dominated by the epic figures of the Successors struggling for power, with few concessions to law or morality – like Renaissance princes moving on a vastly larger stage. For a time the idea – or at least the fiction – of a united Macedonian empire was kept up. But before long the remaining members of Alexander's family were eliminated, and the rival commanders openly began to use the royal title. Finally three of these men were left: the Empire always tended to split into its natural geographical divisions. Lysimachus controlled the Eastern provinces and part of Asia Minor, Seleucus most of the Asiatic provinces, Ptolemy held Egypt and Libya and ruled the sea. Probably each of them, at one time or another, hoped to reunite the Empire under his own rule. Ptolemy died in 283 B.C. and was succeeded by one of his sons. When Lysimachus was weakened by court intrigues, Seleucus at once attacked him. At Corupedium (in central Asia Minor), in 281 B.C., the last two survivors of Alexander's generals – both over eighty and both in personal command – fought one of the greatest battles in history. Lysimachus was defeated and killed, and Seleucus was at last within sight of controlling the Empire. But on crossing to Europe he was assassinated. At once there was chaos: his son was in Mesopotamia, and was in any case not his equal in ability. Then the Gauls came. Long kept out of Greece by the Macedonian kingdom, migrating bands of Gallic warriors now took advantage of its weakness and poured into Greece, Macedonia, and Thrace. They plundered and terrorized, and they even succeeded in sacking the temple at Delphi. Finally they crossed the Dardanelles and descended on Asia Minor, looting what wealth had survived three generations of war.

Yet the Gauls helped to bring about the stabilization of the

Hellenistic world. Two men proved able to deal with them, after a fashion: Antigonus Gonatas (grandson of one of Alexander's greatest generals) in Europe, and Antiochus (son of Seleucus) in Asia. Both were acclaimed as saviours by all civilized men. Seeing their own limitations, the two men agreed to live in peace and friendship. Antiochus abandoned all claims to Europe, Antigonus all claims to Asia. In Egypt, the Ptolemies were by now quite firmly established, and no one could think of supplanting them. So, by about 270 B.C., all hope of reuniting the empire under the rule of one man was finally given up: the empire of Alexander was admitted to have split into a number of territorial kingdoms, and a new generation of rulers was content with more limited power. The next few generations saw a precarious equilibrium, roughly following the natural divisions of the old empire. The Antigonids held Macedon and controlled part of Greece; the Seleucids, who had withdrawn from India, held most of Asia from the Mediterranean to the Hindu Kush; the Ptolemies were based on Egypt and Libya, but often had control of the sea and therefore of the islands and some coastal areas (notably Coele Syria). The equilibrium thus created was never stable. In the border areas there was always a state of tension, due chiefly to Ptolemaic intrigues and aggression and to the weakness of the Seleucids, who were plagued by rebellions and succession troubles. In Asia Minor a new kingdom gradually emerged, also owing its rise chiefly to the prestige of a victory over the Gauls: the kingdom of the Attalids in Pergamum, whose capital soon rivalled Alexandria in splendour, and who, not long before 200 B.C., were wise enough to become the first Roman allies in Asia. Hardly a year passed without fighting somewhere – not unlike the state of affairs in our own age. Yet, as in the modern world, there was peace and prosperity over large areas. Above all, it was an immense improvement on the anarchy that had gone before.

The Hellenistic kingdoms thus established differed vastly in the problems they faced and in the solutions they found. The only generalization worth making is that they all relied chiefly on the Greek and Macedonian element in their populations, which meant that they stood in the Greek cultural tradition.

The Antigonids had the easiest task. Usually undisturbed in Macedonia and Thessaly (except for barbarian invasions), they made no attempt to annex the rest of Greece, beyond one or two vital fortresses; though they did challenge, and in due course overcome, the Ptolemies' control of the sea. The cities of Greece, on the whole, had to abandon their independence of classical times, since most of them were too weak to defend themselves individually. Most of Greece was organized in federations, the greatest of them the Aetolian League in the west. The Aetolians also owed their prominence to a victory over the Gauls: again we notice the importance of this common enemy in shaping the Hellenistic world. The Aetolians had defeated a band of invaders who had sacked Delphi, and they used this success to good effect. They instituted 'Salvation Games' at Delphi to commemorate it, and they called on all the Greek states to recognize the games as equal to the great sacred games of the Hellenic world.

We have several documents showing how well they succeeded. The following, for instance, is part of the rather wordy answer sent by Chios:

Inasmuch as the Aetolians have been friends and kinsmen of our people from ancient times, and now, showing their piety towards the gods and sending Cleon and Heracon and Sotion to us as sacred envoys, inform us of the Salvation Games which they are instituting to commemorate the salvation of the Greeks and the victory won over the barbarians who had marched against the sanctuary of Apollo at Delphi, which is common to all the Greeks, and against all the Greeks . . . [and so on, for over sixty words more], now therefore the People has decreed as follows: that the notification be accepted and the Salvation Games recognized . . . [it takes another sixty-five words to say this!] and that we praise the Commonwealth of the Aetolians and send them a golden wreath on account of their excellence and their piety towards the gods and their bravery against the barbarians ... [and so on for several hundred words].*

Henceforth the Aetolian League was the first power in mainland Greece. But before long a rival confederacy, the Achaean League, gained power over most of the Peloponnese. It is amusing to compare what a prominent Achaean, the historian Polybius, has to say about the Aetolians, with the eulogies by their friends:

The Aetolians, with the criminal wickedness and cupidity innate to their race, envied the Achaeans.†

And again:

The cupidity of the Aetolians, far from being satisfied within the limts of the Peloponnese, would not be satisfied with the whole of Greece.‡

For the trouble with these federations was that they were just as incapable as the classical city states had been, either of uniting or of living together on reasonable terms; and in their quarrels they were prepared to call in Macedon, and later Rome, to back them against each other. It was in this way, chiefly, that the Romans succeeded in establishing their protectorate over Greece around 200 B.C.

The two most important kingdoms, those of the Ptolemies and of the Seleucids, had, in a way, basically similar main problems; but owing to the different conditions in which the kings found themselves (and, no doubt, owing to differences of character between the founders of the dynasties) they solved them in very different ways. The kingdom of the Ptolemies was based on Egypt (though never confined to it until the days of its final decline). Ptolemy I, sent to govern that country after Alexander's death, had realized its great natural strength:

* *Sylloge Inscriptionum Graecarum*, 3rd ed., 636 f., No. 402.
† Histories, II, 45, 1.
‡ Ibid, 49, 3.

until the days of aeroplanes, it was a vast natural fortress, defended by seas, deserts, and the Nile, and abundantly supplied with food. Though he always tried to extend his power as far as he could, he made Egypt a firm base for his ambitions and was prepared to give up anything else rather than risk its loss. His successors, on the whole, followed his example. Ptolemy III, however, seized a dazzling opportunity of overrunning most of the Seleucid kingdom (which, of course, he could not hope to hold) and thereby overstrained his resources; and his successor, Ptolemy IV, had to take desperate measures – including the admission of some native units to fully privileged military service – in order to meet the Seleucid counter attack. The dynasty never fully recovered. With the accession of Ptolemy V (205 B.C.), it enters into a period of decline, saved only by the Romans, who preferred a weak Ptolemaic Egypt to any feasible alternative government there. In this way, however, it outlasted all its great competitors, ending only with the suicide of the great Cleopatra in 30 B.C.

An odd chance has made the study of Ptolemaic (and of Roman) Egypt specially interesting. Normally the historian of classical antiquity gathers most of his evidence from the remains of ancient literature, aided by a comparatively small number of documents inscribed on stone or bronze. (Fortunately, Greek cities liked this form of publication, which was admirably adapted to the needs of a small community before the invention of printing.) But Egypt was the home of the papyrus plant, from which the ancients made a kind of paper. (Our word 'paper' preserves the name.) In the dry sands of parts of Egypt, tens of thousands of these 'papers' (most of them in Greek) have survived, covering a time-span of many centuries. Naturally, nearly all are damaged, and their decipherment is one of the most highly skilled branches of ancient studies. It is also one of the most rewarding. Much of literary interest has been salvaged in this way. Recently, a newly found play by the fourth-century Athenian dramatist Menander, of whom no complete work was previously known, caused much excitement well beyond scholarly circles. Above all, however, these papyri give us a sample of the written matter that accumulated in a town or village, the contents of official files and domestic wastepaper baskets: proclamations, legal records, bills and receipts, family letters, schoolboys' homework. Here, for instance, is an extract from the law by which the government oil monopoly was organized in the minutest detail in the time of Ptolemy II:

The land sown shall be notified to the administrator of the contract and to the district finance officer and to the checking-clerk. If, after measuring it, they find that the number of acres sown does not tally, the district governor, the commune governor, the district finance officer, and the checking-clerk, each of them who is responsible, shall forfeit two talents to the royal exchequer, and to the purchasers of the contract for each bushel of sesame seed due to them two drachmas and for each bushel of cotton-seed one drachma.

Here is a man (a lentil-cook) complaining that he cannot pay his taxes owing to unfair competition:

I do my best to pay my tax every month so that you should have no complaint against me. But now people in the town have started cooking *pumpkins*. So nobody buys lentils from me any longer..... Every morning, no sooner do I start than they sit down next to my lentils and sell pumpkins and don't let me sell my lentils.

It will be gathered that many of the papyri deal with taxes. Taxes, in Egypt, were a subject of paramount importance. Egypt was practically the king's estate, run for his maximum profit. A highly organized bureaucracy ensured that, whatever happened (natural disaster, or human fraud, or error), the king should not lose a penny. Even criminals were released from jail when more hands were needed on the king's land. The king wanted to increase productivity and to get the largest possible share of it in the most convenient way. Large numbers of foreigners had flocked to the new Egypt, as traders, soldiers, technicians, and professors. It was chiefly these men who made the country so much superior to what it had been under its native Pharaohs. But the productivity of the land had to be increased to feed them. Fortunately, there was much room for this: Greek engineers planned more scientific irrigation and introduced new strains of food plants and new crops for marginal land; and the peasants were used to working hard and taking orders. (To that extent, the Ptolemaic planners had a much easier task than their successors in some modern countries.) Though the king claimed ownership of all agricultural land, he tried to use private enterprise to assist him. Foreigners (especially soldiers) were settled in colonies, as had probably been traditional; and the king's friends could receive large estates, to be held at his pleasure, as a reward for service. We know a great deal about that of Ptolemy II's finance minister, which became one of the showpieces of the new Egypt.

Yet all this did not last. After the triumphs of the third century, over-planning and excessive taxation led, in the second and first centuries, to a drift from the land, which no repression could arrest. And this set up a vicious circle: the fewer cultivators, the more repression and taxation, and the more cultivators escaped. Fortunately, owing to the weakness of the dynasty, more and more land *de facto* slipped from the control of the Crown, and much leasehold became in practice private property. We also find a new kind of lease becoming popular: the improvement lease, which gave a man long-term security on a low rent, provided he improved the land. Thus, ultimately, the planners had to take refuge in a kind of 'new economic policy', allowing a greater part to private enterprise.

The king's other problem was how to derive the maximum profit from the economy, and how to turn it into the cash that he needed. Some commodities were royal monopolies – notably oil, to which we have already referred. Only the temples were allowed to produce their own, under strict supervision. But the king kept an eye – and levied fantastic duties – on many commodities, and we know that even his finance minister had to pay his import duties. Yet the greater part of the king's income came from wheat grown on his land. This was turned into cash for him by the new institution of the tax-farmer. The latter, personally responsible for the tax yield, relieved the king of the problems of collection and the uncertainties of conversion. That he had a hard life in the economic crises of the bad days of the kingdom, is shown by the frequent references to tax-farmers as fugitives from justice.

It is not the tax-farmer, but the official (especially the petty official), who appears as an oppressor in our papyri. Egypt had only three cities (Alexandria the only one of real importance). The rest of the country was directly administered by the king, through an elaborate hierarchy of appointed officials, from the royal finance minister to the village scribe. Yet the better of the Ptolemies knew that they had to prevent serious discontent, and, in particular, they took great care to dispense justice. In a famous circular to junior civil servants, the finance minister tells them:

As you travel about, try to go from one man to another and speak words of encouragement and make them all more cheerful. And do not confine yourself to words, but if anyone has any complaints about the village secretary or mayor in some matter connected with agriculture, look into it and, as far as you can, stop the abuse.

In due course, special courts were established to judge each nationality according to its own laws. For, as we have seen, foreigners had flocked to Egypt, helping to build its new prosperity and taking advantage of it. Before long, foreign settlers were scattered through the country. Naturally, our generation is particularly interested in how successfully the problems of such a multi-racial society were solved.

On the whole, there seems to have been little racial antagonism, at least for a long time. The most important (and probably the most numerous) new ethnic element was Greek. Most of these Greeks lived in townships and villages not of 'city' status; yet they did their best to cherish Greek institutions (especially in education) and called their towns by names ending in *-polis*. But, as we shall see later, Greek exclusiveness was cultural rather than racial. Most of the immigrants, naturally, were men, and there was a great deal of intermarriage and much infiltration of native customs (especially in religion, where the training children receive from their mothers is particularly important). Though the legal systems of the various nations are carefully kept separate (not without a certain amount of cross-influence), a man's national status in law, in due course, need not have much to do with his racial or cultural inheritance. Natives were common in the lower ranks of the civil service and could rise in it; though, Greek being the official language, few of them did. But in the army natives were not allowed to serve on equal terms until Ptolemy IV found himself compelled to admit them. Henceforth, especially with the weakening of the dynasty, discontent among the natives increased. In Upper Egypt native rebellions broke out, led by the native priesthood and aristocracy. Finally the capital of that region, the historic city of Thebes 'of the Hundred Gates', was destroyed by royal forces (85 B.C.). Cleopatra tried to weld Greek and Egyptian national feeling into a united anti-Roman force; but she failed, and the Romans, on taking over the administration of the country, fossilized the social and racial structure and prevented any development towards unity.

The kings used their wealth to make Alexandria into a magnificent planned city, centred on the tomb of Alexander, whose body Ptolemy I seized by fraud and retained. They assembled a brilliant cosmopolitan court – Greek in its cultural tradition, of course. For generations their capital, with its Museum – a lavishly endowed research institute – and its unequalled Library, was the centre of Hellenistic civilization, and scholars and artists from all over the Greek world assembled there under royal patronage. Even under the Roman hegemony it retained many of the features of a great capital.

Ptolemaic Egypt was relatively small, compact, and highly organized. The Seleucid kingdom, controlling (at the start) most of the Asiatic provinces of Alexander's empire, was immense and unwieldy and could not be so tightly administered. It soon established an unfortunate tradition of succession conflicts that made the kings unable to prevent the gradual loss of their outlying provinces; and the story of the kingdom is one of constant decline, only temporarily arrested by Antiochus III around 200 B.C., until after about 160 B.C. the kingdom ceases to be really important. Yet for over a century after the death of its brilliant founder it was one of the great powers of the age – for a long time perhaps the greatest.

The Seleucids had the hardest problem of all the great dynasties. Ruling over the richest of the kingdoms, of vast area and varied population, they had no unifying principle except their own persons (soon raised to divine status) and their Macedonian troops. These men they settled as reservists in villages, and with stubborn conservatism they continued to call their empire 'the Kingdom of the Macedonians' and preserved many Macedonian customs. Greek was the official language, though the native languages survived in local use and the Seleucids made many concessions to their Oriental subjects. Even in the fourth century Greek civilization had spread widely over the countries of the Near East. The hold that it had long had on the coastal fringe of Asia Minor had been greatly expanded by thousands of mercenaries, who had flocked to the service of the king of Persia and of his governors. Then came Alexander, who, even though he had no actual policy of Hellenization, opened new worlds to the Greeks. Under him and the Seleucids, Greek soldiers, administrators, merchants, and explorers appeared all over Persia and Afghanistan and even in Pakistan. There were never very many of them; in particular, actual settlement in those distant parts was not popular. Yet even there Greek colonies existed and Greek influence can be traced. A Greek kingdom based on Afghanistan maintained itself for centuries with varying success. In the nearer East, as far as Mesopotamia, Greeks and Macedonians were numerous. The city of Seleucia-on-Tigris, successor of Babylon as capital of Mesopotamia, at one time had over half a million inhabitants, many of them of Greek and Macedonian descent.

The Seleucid kings encouraged the immigration of Greek and Macedonian settlers. For a while there was a steady influx, particularly of Greeks. But Greece and Macedon had been exhausted by wars, and before long they were unable to provide large numbers of colonists. Fortunately, the invaders had all the prestige of a victorious culture – like that of Western Europe in the last century – and Greek nationalism, though always strong, was cultural rather than racial: the Greeks were prepared to welcome converts. Soon Hellenized native cities sprang up all over the Seleucid kingdom. Educated natives, particularly in the western provinces, made every effort to assimilate themselves to the ruling class. Cities and individuals adopted Hellenized names and invented claims to Greek or at least Trojan ancestry; and local gods were equated with members of the Greek pantheon. A Jew called Joshua could become Jason, and the Jewish God became, to many, Olympian Zeus. Antiochus IV was no doubt genuinely puzzled when the majority of the Jews rejected this. In fact, the best-known instance of this Hellenization is the story told in the first two books of Maccabees. It is clear even from this biased source that before the nationalist outbreak the Hellenization of the Jewish upper class was widespread and spontaneous. It was the mistake of Antiochus IV – a mistake due to both political and psychological factors – to try to hasten it by compulsion. This mistake led to disaster both in Judaea and elsewhere. But most kings had been wise enough to encourage rather than compel.

No dynasty founded so many cities: Alexandrias, Seleucias, Antiochs, and cities immortalizing the women of the royal house; and a large number of them were merely reconstitutions of native communities. The new cities adopted the classical Greek forms of democratic administration and – above all – of worship and of education. In this way the dynasty made some progress towards achieving a national basis for the empire in its shrinking territory. They were so successful in this (at least as far as the upper class was concerned) that, when the Parthians overran Mesopotamia about 100 B.C., they carefully refrained from appearing anti-Greek.

But the Greek city not only helped to solve the Seleucids' cultural problems while, in addition, giving them all the superhuman prestige that, in Greek religion, attached to the founding of cities – it also helped to solve their chief economic problems. Like the Ptolemies, the Seleucids had to convert a vast income of agricultural produce into cash and into the non-agricultural products that they needed. The city, with its tradition of a sophisticated cash economy, and (for ancient conditions) its developed trade and industry, greatly helped in this process. It bought the king's wheat (with some persuasion, at times!) and supplied him with its taxes, its imports, and the products of its industry. In every way, therefore, the city was a godsend to the Seleucid – as, incidentally, also to the Pergamene – kings. It is not surprising that they tried to increase the number of their cities and to keep on good terms with them.

Of course, the growth of Greek cities also greatly simplified the king's *administrative* problems. The Romans, later, were to rely almost entirely on the Greek city for local administration in those areas. Cities could govern themselves, and the king could easily get what he wanted from them. Even though, as we shall see, the king lost his land when he gave it to a city, kings were very ready to do this: the revenue they got from the cities alone more than balanced the loss. And cities, moreover, were fortified and could defend themselves, at least against brigands and odd barbarians – which again saved a good deal of royal money.

Indeed, defence was the king's chief problem, at least in economic terms. Theoretically, all subjects appear to have been liable to conscription; but this was made ineffective by the nature of the kingdom itself, since each province was a mosaic of all sorts of patterns of local organization and it was difficult to call out the levy and form it into anything like a homogeneous army. Even the Persians had found this, and the Seleucids inherited the problem – particularly the shortage of heavy infantry, which was the decisive arm in Greek warfare. The king much preferred to hire mercenaries, who were much dearer, but more effective. He could afford only a small standing army: small garrisons in key centres, plus a small reserve force. The latter, when Antiochus III found himself plunged into war with the Romans, numbered only 10,000 infantry, with corresponding weakness in other arms. It is the constant temptation of non-aggressive governments to pay too little for defence and to leave it too late – and the Seleucids supply a splendid warning example. By the time Antiochus III had collected 72,000 men, the Romans were in his country and it was too late.

The Seleucids also had an expensive court to maintain. Lavish display and generosity, both public and private, were politically necessary both to gain friends and to impress one's subjects. The precedent of the Persians and of Alexander was constantly elaborated, and the masses of retainers, of expensive foods, of perfumes and gold utensils, become ever more costly as the dynasty declines. The king became a prisoner of his ceremonial, and any who tried to escape it at times (like Antiochus IV) were censured by responsible men. Yet, to an extent almost unimaginable today, the king was the centre of the system, with complete personal power. He worked from dawn till late into the night. Even Seleucus I had complained that anyone who knew the amount of mere letter writing that a king had to do would not want to keep a diadem if he found it. In addition to all this routine work, the king was responsible for all major decisions: he had advisers, whom he customarily consulted, but he had to make up his own mind on their advice. According to many Hellenistic philosophers, he was the 'living law' for his land.

Yet *vis-à-vis* the Greek cities his status was difficult and ambiguous. The divine status that was gradually bestowed upon the living Seleucids (spontaneously, it seems) gave them no legal rights in the cities. How and why was the king bound by the law of the city? The problem is worth examining, particularly as some of the kings were almost neurotically conscious of it: we find a Seleucid writing to a city that, if he has given any instructions contrary to the city laws, the citizens should ignore them.

The Greek city, in the Hellenistic kingdoms, found itself in a peculiar position. *We* are used to regarding a town as a small subdivision of a state: even the Greater London Council has no powers beyond those that Parliament has given it. But to the Greeks the city was the *polis*: the city state, the unit of international politics. The *polis* had been an independent organism long before the Successor Kings came on the scene, and the kings somehow had to come to terms with it; even the cities founded by them entered into the old tradition. Alexander, with his usual successful opportunism, had overcome the difficulty by ignoring it. Scholars are still arguing whether the Greek cities of Asia were legally part of his empire or not. It seems that Alexander himself neither knew nor cared. The legal position was never formally settled. Both the king and the cities knew who was master, and that was all that mattered. Alexander's successors seem, on the whole, to have followed this example. The position of the cities remains ambiguous. Of course, hardly any generalization will apply to the whole Hellenistic world, any more than (say) to the whole of the

Middle Ages. But on the whole, the 'city' was carefully distinguished from the 'country'. (For instance, Alexandria was officially 'near' Egypt, not 'in' Egypt.) The 'country' belonged to the king; the city owned its land. The king's writ did not run in the city, and he could not act on its behalf. There was normally no royal governor: how *could* a Greek city be subject to any authority but its own laws? The Hellenistic city conducts not only its internal affairs, but its diplomatic business, like classical Athens. It sends and receives envoys and makes treaties on routine matters. We have seen how the island of Chios acts on the Aetolian notification of sacred games:

> Inasmuch as the Aetolians have been friends and kinsmen of our people from ancient times . . . now therefore the People has decreed as follows. . .

There are many such examples. Here, for instance, is the opening of a decision by the small island of Paros on an embassy from Magnesia (in Asia Minor), which had come on similar business. It is a good example of the machinery of a Greek democracy:

> Decree of Council and Assembly. Moved by Callitheides son of Nesis. With regard to the proposal set before us by the magistrates about the decree from Magnesia, the decision being that they should present the sacred envoys sent by Magnesia about the notification of the games to the Assembly of the People, Callitheides son of Nesis moved a resolution as follows: Amendment to Decision by Council: 'Inasmuch as the citizens of Magnesia-on-Maeander who are friends of the People of Paros have sent us their decree and envoys . . .'*

And so on: Magnesia got what it wanted, in spite of some hesitation by the Council. Both communities act in full sovereignty and independence.

The kings avoid giving orders to the cities: they suggest, or request, or merely notify. This is how the Seleucid King

* *Sylloge Inscriptionum Graecarum*, II, 58 f., no. 562.

Antiochus III answers the same request by Magnesia: politely he informs the city that he has approved its request for recognition of the games; then he continues:

And we have also written to our officials, so that the cities may follow our example and give their approval.*

Notice 'the' cities (not 'our' cities): sometimes a king will say 'the cities in our alliance'; only seldom is he *really* tactless. And notice, above all, that the king cannot commit the cities: he can only ask them to commit *themselves*. In the same way, the cities seem to be free to coin money; though only the largest, on the whole, make use of this expensive privilege.

Needless to say, it was all an illusion, a polite pretence kept up on both sides – by the king to gain a city's favour and to disguise his very un-Greek status, by the city to save its self-respect and to assert its Greek heritage. In fact, the kings had many ways of controlling cities without any need for formal instruments. Very few such instruments (e.g. treaties) are known, and it is clear that they were deliberately avoided. The kings did not need the cities' military support, and they could normally ensure financial and political support when they wanted it. One way was to favour one party in the traditional party struggles of Greek cities. Royal favour would assure the preponderance of that party, which in effect became a puppet government, its basic interest identical with the king's. This technique, freely used by Philip II and Alexander, was taken over by their successors, and later by the Romans, in their dealings with Greek cities. Closely connected with the puppet government is the monarch's garrison or military force stationed near the city: it is not needed, of course, where the king is strong and the city very weak. The presence of such a force would be variously interpreted. To the king's friends, it was there (often at the request of the city government) as a

* Royal Correspondence in the Hellenistic Period, no. 31, p. 141 f., l. 25 f.

protection against external enemies and internal sedition. Its commanders, like other royal officials, might be called upon for various services and were often honoured for their friendly interest in the city's affairs. To the king's enemies, the force was an occupation army, an instrument of oppression to be expelled as soon as possible. Its withdrawal (brought about by pressure from the king's enemies) would be hailed as liberation; though what followed was usually the establishment of the rule of the opposing party, quite possibly again strengthened by a royal garrison. At the beginning of the third century, for instance, the Athenians congratulate a magistrate on his success in preserving the city 'free, democratic, and autonomous, and her laws intact' – at a time when Demetrius had a garrison in the Piraeus. They still remembered the time when an *anti*-democratic faction, headed by a philosopher, had ruled with the support of a garrison sent by another king. When Demetrius freed Corinth from a rival's garrison, the citizens begged him to leave one of his own to protect them; and thus he acquired control of the most important fortress in Greece. Nor was even the payment of tribute always avoided. At the most, the city was usually left to collect it without interference by royal officials. When the Romans first intervened in Asia Minor, they discovered a class of cities that were 'free' and had been paying tribute to various kings. It was a very useful lesson.

In fact, the courtesies of diplomatic language cover a policy of supervision and control limited only by the king's discretion. Alexander had set the tone: when it suited him, he had not scrupled to intervene by force or threat of force, both in the cities of European Greece (whose independence he had sworn to uphold) and in the cities of Asia Minor (whose liberation from oppression he had proclaimed). His successors, on the whole, had to be more tactful simply because they were weaker. This was why the majority of them showed a good deal of consideration, though some were more tactful than others: the Seleucids had the best record, while the Ptolemies and Attalids usually kept a tighter hold. But they all sought to capture Greek public opinion both by courtesy and by generosity: they made at least some concessions to the traditions of the free Greek city.

It is obvious that in a civilization extending from the Atlantic to the Punjab and from the Don to the Cataracts of the Nile there was much diversity – much regional variation due to local influences, which can be traced (where we have the information) in art, religion, and daily life. Few scholars have been able both to range widely and to delve deeply in such a field. Yet perhaps the most remarkable fact about the Hellenistic world is its fundamental uniformity. Ideas spread with a speed hardly surpassed today, and the differences between various regions can safely be said to have been much smaller than they are in the Western world today; for the language and the basic tradition were the same. A Greek intellectual – whether poet or mathematician – could feel equally at home in Syracuse and in Alexandria. The Graeco-Egyptian god Serapis and his consort Isis – and, in due course, many other Eastern deities – gained millions of hearts far from their original homes. Actors and athletes had their international associations: the Guild of Dionysiac Artists and the International Boxing Association, with their local chapters, appear as organized bodies on many documents. Upper-class Greeks (by birth or education) had friends and correspondents everywhere. We need only read the Acts of the Apostles to see how important this was in preparing favourable conditions for the spread of Christianity and, even before this, for the acceptance of the universal Roman Empire.

In spite of vast expansion and multiple changes due to varied influences, the new Greek world of the Hellenistic age remains essentially Greek: in a sense, it is the classical world writ large, and its way of life and thought is recognizably based on that worked out in sixth-century Miletus and fifth-century

Athens. Perhaps, after all, Aristotle would not have felt altogether out of place.

Bibliography

DITTENBERGER, W., (ed.) *Orientis Graeci Inscriptiones Selectae*, 2 vols., Leipzig, 1903–5, reprinted 1960; *Sylloge Inscriptionum Graecarum*, 4 vols., 3rd ed., Leipzig, 1915–24, reprinted 1960. Two standard selections of Greek inscriptions, the first is confined to, and the second including, inscriptions of the Hellenistic and Roman periods.

C. B. WELLES, *Royal Correspondence in the Hellenistic Period*, Yale University Press, 1934. A selection, with full notes and translations, of letters written by various Hellenistic kings.

The best selection of papyrus documents for the general reader is *Select Papyri*, ed. HUNT and EDGAR, 2 vols., Loeb Classical Library, 1932–4.

The *Cambridge Ancient History* will be as useful for this as for previous periods.

On Alexander the Great, U. WILCKEN, *Alexander the Great* (translated by G. C. Richards) (London, 1932) is still unsurpassed.

A. R. BURN, *Alexander the Great and the Hellenistic Empire* (London, 1947) provides a short, lively, and well-written introduction.

On the Hellenistic Age as a whole, W. W. TARN, *Hellenistic Civilization*, 3rd ed. (revised by the author and G. T. GRIFFITH, London, 1952), is the best introduction for the general reader. On the earlier part of the period, see also M. CARY, *History of the Greek World from 323 to 146 B.C.*, 2nd ed. (London, 1951). This book contains a very useful select bibliography.

M. ROSTOVTZEFF'S monumental *Social and Economic History of the Hellenistic World*, 3 vols. (Oxford, 1941), is one of the great achievements of historiography. Its wealth of learning is discreetly confined to the Notes, and the interested general reader need not hesitate to approach this work. Its lavish and carefully chosen illustrations are the best companion to any reading on the Hellenistic period.

Index

Index

Index

Index

Some other Pelican books
are described on the following pages

GREEK SCIENCE

Benjamin Farrington

After a brief discussion of the achievement in science of the pre-Hellenic peoples, Professor Farrington describes the various phases of the development of science among the Greeks. The story begins about 600 B.C. and the first couple of centuries are conspicuous for the boldness of their thought and the rapidity with which the foundations of many of the chief branches of science were laid. In the next two or three centuries the Greeks continued to accumulate information and also showed their logical powers by systematizing their knowledge into a regular encyclopedia of the sciences. In this second period, however, their creativity was less and, after it, there was a period of stagnation. This was interrupted in the second century A.D. by the appearance of the great astronomer and geographer, Ptolemy, and the great physician, Galen, with whom Professor Farrington ends his story.

'The best history of the subject available in English' – *Listener*

THE WORLD OF ODYSSEUS

M. I. Finley

Who was Homer? When were the *Iliad* and the *Odyssey* composed? When and why did the Trojan war occur? What sort of society did Odysseus, Achilles, Helen, Hector, and Priam live in? What were their beliefs about government, religion, class, and sex?

Many such questions spring to the minds of the hundreds of thousands of people who have read Homer in the Penguin Classics or elsewhere. The answers are provided in *The World of Odysseus* by a Cambridge scholar, who has used both the evidence of the texts and the latest researches in archaeology and anthropology to reconstruct a clear and absorbing picture of the Homeric age.

'It is delightfully refreshing to find a scholar like Mr M. I. Finley who has the independence to forsake the well-worn paths of Homeric criticism and to ask new questions. He has applied with great success his knowledge of institutions in many societies to the study of Greek society as Homer depicts it, and the conclusions which he draws are clear and convincing' – Sir Maurice Bowra in his Foreword

THE GREEKS OVERSEAS

John Boardman

This is the story of a nation on the move. It is a story which must, because it casts a fresh image of an extraordinary people, be studied by anyone who is curious about the sources of European culture, arts, and sciences.

In these pages we meet Greek mercenaries crudely scratching their names on statues 700 miles up the Nile; Greek goldsmiths working on the shores of the Black Sea; Greek artists employed in the palace of the Persian king and leaving 'doodles' on the walls; Greek winegrowers introducing the grape to Burgundy; Greek traders chaffering in the markets of Egypt and the Near East; and Greek colonists living at the very ends of the known world.

The Oxford Reader in Classical Archaeology has sifted all the latest evidence in this masterly book. For the first time he fully demonstrates how much the Greeks owed and gave to their neighbours as they elbowed their way into the throng of older civilizations between the eight and sixth centuries B.C.

THE IDEA OF PREHISTORY

Glyn Daniel

In this collection of published lectures, Dr Daniel describes prehistory as a study of 'the unwritten remains of the early past of man'. He studies the origins of the subject, going back to the seventeenth century and the current thunderbolt explanation of man's early flint tools (which one contemporary scientist thought to be 'generated in the sky by a fulgurous exhalation conglubed in a cloud by the circumposed humour').
The influence of the evolutionary thinking of the last century is studied, and there is a brilliant discussion of the rival theories of a cultural diffusion from one evolutionary source as against the idea of cultures evolving in parallel in different racial groups. Dr Daniel concludes that the real justification of the study of prehistory lies in the pleasure of recovering the treasures of man's prehistoric past that have been dropped on the way and lost.

'Needless to say Dr Daniel's erudition is as immense as his turn of phrase is subtle' – *Discovery*

'The lucid and logical presentation gives it a new force and vigour' – *Nature*

PREHISTORIC CRETE

R. W. Hutchinson

Crete has rightly been called the cradle of European civilization. The Bronze Age Minoans, who were Europe's first city dwellers, had a culture as rich and developed as their great contemporaries in Egypt, Syria, Anatolia, and Mesopotamia.

The thrilling discoveries already made in Crete between 1900 and 1940, as described by Evans and Pendlebury, stirred the imagination of people all over the world. But in the last twenty years archaeologists have greatly extended our knowledge of life in prehistoric Crete.

This book gives a complete account of what is known of the Minoans today – of their origins, clarified by the brilliant work of Ventris and Chadwick in deciphering the Linear B script, their social organization, their trade, their merchant navy, their religion, and their art.

For those who wish to understand the earliest stages of our civilization, the prehistory of Crete will emerge as a vital and a fascinating episode.

THE GREEKS

H. D. F. Kitto

This is a study of the character and history of an ancient civilization, and of the people who created it. Since its first publication as a Pelican, *The Greeks* has been reprinted in hard covers and translated into six other languages.

The critics have said of it:

'The best introduction I have ever read to Ancient Greece. The author's liveliness of mind and style has enabled him to make a mass of information appetizing and digestible' – Raymond Mortimer in the *Sunday Times*

'Very easy to read . . . a triumph of balance and condensation' – Harold Nicolson in the *Observer*

'Professor Kitto is a model historian—lively, accurate, and fully acquainted with the latest developments in the subject . . . never vague . . . often witty and always full of vigour' –*The Times Educational Supplement*

*For a complete list of books available
please write to Penguin Books whose address
can be found on the back of the title page*